How to Pick

the

Perfect Puppy

With Early Puppy Care and Puppy Training

LINDA WHITWAM

ISBN-13: 978-1500423469

Contents

1. Taking the Plunge

Apart from getting married or having a baby, getting a puppy is one of the most important, demanding, expensive and life-enriching decisions you will ever make.

Pick the right puppy, train and socialise him or her and you will have the perfect addition to your household. A living, loving member of the family who will love you unconditionally and who will be a joy to have around the house and to take out and about with you. What could be simpler?

Sadly, it doesn't always work out like that and many puppies end up in rescue shelters through no fault of their own. A leading figure in canine rescue says that the main reason dogs end up in shelters is "unrealistic expectations" on the part of the owner. In some other cases the dog stays with the family, but they are disappointed that he or she didn't turn out as they had hoped.

There are, however, several steps which, if followed, provide a blueprint for a happy life with your canine companion. Of course, you could always be unlucky, your dog might have a life-shortening illness – but even the chances of this can be greatly reduced by following these guidelines.

What this book will do over the next few chapters is guide you gently through the highlights and pitfalls of getting a puppy.

Not just any puppy, but the **RIGHT** puppy for you and your family or household. It will help you avoid the common mistakes that people make and guide you towards:

❖ Selecting the right breed, crossbreed or mixed breed (mongrel)

❖ Choosing the right breeder

❖ Picking the puppy with the right temperament to suit you and your family

❖ Picking a healthy puppy

- Picking the puppy with the right energy levels to suit your lifestyle

- Or, if you decide to give a young dog a second chance of happiness, the right way of going about adopting a rescue dog

- Then bringing the puppy home – the first few days

- Housetraining and crate training

- Feeding a puppy

- Basic care and training during the first few weeks and months

- And how to avert some common behaviour issues

There is one factor above all others which plays a major role in people's decision on what puppy to get – and that is the look of the dog. Most people who are looking for a pet, rather than a working dog, choose a dog based on its appearance. And that is a big mistake.

Picking a puppy based solely on how it looks can be a recipe for disaster.

That should only be a starting point. Over the next few chapters, this book will help you to make a decision not just based on emotion or cuteness, but also on which puppy will be just right for you.

Getting a new living, breathing addition to your household who will live for 10 to 15 years is no small step and should not be taken lightly. Just like babies, puppies will love you unconditionally - but there is a price to pay. In return for their loyalty and devotion, you have to fulfil your part of the bargain. Here are some of the things you have to consider:

When you first bring your new puppy home, you have to devote several hours a day to his needs, which may mean taking time off work in the beginning. When he is little, you have to patiently teach your pup not to use your house as a toilet (like this Shar-Pei pictured!), then every day throughout his life you have to feed and exercise him.

If you want him to grow into a happy, well-adjusted adult dog you can

take anywhere, you have to spend time socialising and training during his formative months. You also have to be prepared to part with hard cash for regular healthcare, and even more money in veterinary bills if he's ill.

If you are not prepared, or

unable, to devote the time and money to a new arrival – or if everyone in your household is out at work all day – then now might not be the right time for you to consider getting a puppy. Dogs are faithful pack animals; they are entirely reliant upon us, their human companions, for their welfare and happiness. It may be fairer to a puppy to wait a while until you are in a position to give the time he needs.

Some people rush into getting a pup without thinking of the long-term commitment or what type of dog would best fit in with their lives. Once the seed of an idea to get a puppy is planted in your brain, it is hard to get it out and easy to get carried away emotionally by all the images of gorgeous fluffy little pups.

Getting a puppy is a long-term commitment. Before taking the plunge, ask yourself some questions:

Have I Got Enough Time?

In the first days after leaving his or her mother and littermates, your puppy will feel very lonely and maybe even a little afraid. You and your family have to spend time with your new arrival to make him feel safe and sound.

Ideally, for the first week - or preferably two - you will be around all of the time to help your puppy settle into his new home and start bonding with him. Book time off work in the beginning if necessary, but don't just get a puppy and leave him alone in the house a few days later.

You also have to spend time housetraining and obedience training. At one time it was thought that young dogs did not need training until they were adolescents. But canine behaviourists now stress the importance of the first four to five months of a puppy's life and how these formative weeks can influence the rest of his life. Start training as soon as he has settled into his new surroundings – usually within a week or two of bringing him home.

Although young puppies should not be over-exercised, it is still a good idea to get into the habit of taking them out of the house and yard for a short walk every day once it is safe to do so after the initial vaccinations.

Dogs have a natural migration instinct. This does not mean that they want to fly south for the winter, it means that they have a natural urge to move from one habitat to another – and daily walks fulfil this need. Allowing your dog to follow this natural instinct is a major key to keeping him happy, balanced and well behaved. New surroundings allow him to sniff and explore, they stimulate his interest, help him to burn off excess energy and help stop him from becoming bored and mischievous.

Your new arrival will need feeding daily, probably twice daily as an adult and several times a day with a young puppy – and in the beginning, food and drink does not stay inside a pup for long, so the result is a lot of tedious trips for you to the garden or yard.

How Long Can I Leave Him For?

This is a question we get asked all of the time on the website and one

which causes a lot of debate among owners and prospective owners. All dogs are pack animals; their natural state is to be with others. Being alone is not normal for a dog, although many have to get used to it.

Another issue is the toilet. Dogs, especially puppies and young dogs, have far smaller bladders than humans, so leaving them unattended all day is not an option. Forget the emotional side of it, how would you like to be left for eight hours without being able to visit the bathroom?

So how many hours can you leave a dog alone for? Well, a useful guide comes from the rescue organisations. In the UK, they will not allow anybody to adopt if they are intending leaving the dog alone for more than four or five hours a day on a regular basis.

Dogs left at home alone all day become bored and, in the case of companion breeds which are highly dependent on human company for their happiness, often sad or depressed. Some of it will, of course, depend on the character and natural temperament of your dog. But a lonely dog may display signs of unhappiness by being destructive or displaying poor behaviour when you return home.

A puppy or fully-grown dog must NEVER be left shut in a crate all day. It is OK to leave a puppy or adult dog in a crate if he has been crate-trained and is happy there, but the door should never be closed for more than two or three hours during the day. A crate is a place where a puppy or adult dog should feel safe, not a prison.

Is My Home Suitable?

If you have decided to get a puppy, then choose a breed which will fit in with your living conditions. If you live in a small house or apartment, then a Great Dane would not be a good choice.

If your house is full of expensive carpets and precious ornaments, then don't pick a high energy breed which will be lively indoors and also bring dirt and water into the house when returning from all the walks he'll need. All dogs - even small ones, those with low energy levels and dogs living in apartments - need some daily time out of doors. If you live in a small flat on the 10th floor of a high rise block, then a medium or large dog, or small breed with high energy levels requiring lots of exercise, would not be a good choice.

Successful apartment living for canines involves having easy access to the outside and spending time housetraining. This may mean training the dog to use a pad or a tray as an indoor bathroom. If you can regularly take yours out at least three or four times a day to do what he needs to do, there is no need to indoor housetrain him.

If you live in a house and have a yard or garden, check that it is well fenced. When your puppy arrives, don't leave him unattended outside for long periods – he may dig, find a hole in the fence and wander off, bark his head off and annoy your neighbours, and with the price of pedigree dogs often over £1,000, or $1,500, he can also be a target for thieves. Brachycephalic (flat-faced) breeds such as the Bulldog, French Bulldog, Boston Terrier and Pug, can also overheat. Check there are no poisonous plants or chemicals he could eat or drink.

Inside, puppy-proofing your home is similar to baby-proofing. It involves moving anything breakable or chewable - including your shoes - out of reach of sharp little teeth. Make sure electrical cords and remote controls are out of the way – lift them off the floor if necessary. You may have to tie your kitchen cupboard doors together and remove any dangerous cleaning fluids or chemicals out of harm's way. Block off any off-limits areas of the house, such as upstairs or your bedroom, with a child gate or barrier - especially as he will probably be following you around the house for the first few days.

Family and Children

What about the other members of your household, do they all want the puppy as well? A pup will grow into a not-quite-as-cute adult dog which will become a part of your family for a decade or more. Are they prepared to share the workload of daily exercise and abide by the boundaries you set? For example, if you decide you don't want your puppy on the bed or furniture, will everyone stick to the rule?

Children will, of course, be delighted at the prospect of a playful little bundle of fur joining your family. If you do have children, choose one of the breeds or crossbreeds which is known to be good around youngsters. Some, particularly the companion breeds, seem to have a natural affinity or attraction to kids and babies.

Remind everyone that it's important your puppy gets enough time to sleep – which is most of the time in the beginning, so don't let enthusiastic kids constantly pester him. Sleep is very important to puppies, just as it is for babies. One of the reasons some young dogs end up in rescue centres is that the owners are unable to cope with the demands of small children AND a dog.

Remember that dogs are very hierarchical, in other words, there is a pecking order. Puppies will often regard children as being on their own level, like a playmate, and so they might chase, jump and nip at them with sharp teeth. This is not aggression; this is normal play for puppies. Be sure to supervise play time and make sure the puppy doesn't get too boisterous; train him to be gentle with the children.

Older People

If you are older or have elderly relatives living with you, dogs can be great companions, provided they are not too boisterous. A larger breed, or one with high energy levels from working stock, such as a Border Collie, may be too much for a senior citizen.

They may pull on the leash or be boisterous or destructive in the house (the dog, not the old person!) If you are older, make sure your energy levels are up to those of a young puppy. Ask yourself if you are fit enough to take your dog for at least one short walk every day.

Dogs can, however, be a real tonic for older people. My father is in his 80s, but takes his dog out walking for an hour every day – even in the rain or snow. It's good for him and it's good for the dog, helping to keep both of them fit and socialised. They get fresh air, exercise and the chance to communicate with other dogs and their humans.

Dogs are also great company at home – you're never alone when you've got a dog. Many older people get a puppy after losing a loved one (a husband, wife or previous much-loved dog). A dog gives them something to care for and love, as well as a constant companion.

Sometimes a well-behaved adult dog may be a better option as housetraining and daily obedience training are not involved. Whether old or young, a dog is not a cheap pet - especially if veterinary fees are involved - so it's a good idea to check that the finances will support this new addition to the home.

Single People

Many single adults own dogs, but if you live alone, having a puppy will require a lot of dedication from you. There will be nobody to share the tasks of daily care, exercise, grooming and training, so taking on a dog requires a huge commitment and a lot of your time if the dog is to have a decent life. If you are out of the house all day as well, it is not really fair to get a puppy, or even an adult dog. Left alone all day, they will feel isolated, bored and sad. However, if you work from home or close to home or are at home all day and you can spend considerable time with the puppy every day, then great!

Other Pets

If you already have other pets in your household, spend time to introduce them gradually to each other. If you have other dogs, supervised sessions from an early age will help the dogs to get along and chances are they will become the best of friends. Some types of dog – such as Terriers and hunting dogs -have a natural instinct to chase and so may take more time to get used to having other small animals around. Some of these dogs have a high prey instinct and may never get used to living compatibly with other non-canines.

If you adopt an older dog and have other pets, make sure they get along before you commit, as not all mature dogs are able to change the habits of a lifetime if they have instinctively chased cats, for example.

If you already have another dog, it is important to introduce the two on neutral territory, rather than in areas one pet deems as his own. You don't want one dog to feel he has to protect his territory. Walking the dogs parallel to each other before heading home for the first time is a good idea to get them used to each other.

Cats can sometimes be more of a problem; most dogs' natural instinct is to chase a cat. An attention-loving puppy may see the cat as a threat and in a minority of cases it may take a long time (if ever) to accustom them to small pets.

A lot will depend on the temperament of the individual dog and at what age he is introduced to the other animal(s) – the earlier, the better.

Your chances of success are greater if your cat is strong-willed and your dog is docile! If your cat is timid and your dog is alert, young and active, then your job will be more difficult.

Supervised sessions and patience are the answer. A pup may tease a cat, but in the end will probably learn to live with it. Make sure the cat does not attack the puppy.

Take the process slowly, if your cat is stressed and frightened he may decide to leave. Our feline friends are notorious for abandoning home because the food and facilities are better down the road. Until you know that they can get on together, don't leave them alone.

For a dog to get on with a cat, you are asking him to forget some of his natural instincts and to respond to your training. But it can be done successfully.

———————————————

2. Types of Puppies

So now you have decided that you definitely want to get a puppy, the big question is **which type of puppy?**

Getting a pup is a huge commitment and not something to be rushed into. One thing that every prospective owner should keep in the back of their mind is this: an ugly puppy has yet to be born. All puppies are incredibly appealing, some are wrinkly, others are furry – but they are all without exception CUTE.

It is for this reason that we cannot recommend too highly the following course of action:

Decide on what type of dog you want BEFORE you visit any litters. Once you see the little darlings, your heart rules your head and it is extremely difficult to walk away without agreeing to buy one - even if it's not the sort of dog you originally intended to get.

A dog is not a sparkly necklace, nor a fast car nor status symbol. It is a living, breathing creature with its own character, emotions and a lifespan of a decade or more and should not be bought on impulse. These Beagle puppies (pictured above) could well live for a dozen years or more.

According to a major figure in canine rescue, the main reason for dogs ending up in shelters is "unrealistic expectations" on the part of the owners. You may have an idealised image in your mind of snuggling up with your faithful companion, or wonderful walks through the countryside with Man's Best Friend. These images may come true, but the reality is that there is a lot of effort to be put in before you reach that stage.

Firstly, in finding the right dog and secondly, in nurturing and training him so he becomes the dog of your dreams. For example, these Beagle pups require obedience training to teach them to listen to your commands, rather than to follow their natural instinct and wandering off after a scent at the drop of a hat. This requires time, commitment and consistency.

I believe that there is a simple formula to maximise the chances of everything working out between you and your dog and the two of you having a happy life together.

Six Golden Rules

1. Do your homework before you buy a puppy. Take the time to research breeds, crossbreeds and mixed breeds before deciding on the type of dog that would best fit in with your lifestyle, finances and time commitments and energy levels.

2. Find a good breeder - one who is preferably recommended by your country's Kennel Club or the relevant breed society in your region. He or she will breed not only breed for looks and colour but, most importantly, for health and temperament. If necessary, wait until a suitable pup becomes available. DON'T be tempted by adverts on listings websites such as ebay, gumtree or nextdaypets. DON'T buy a cheap imported pup, or so called "rare colours", they don't exist. If you are buying a pedigree dog, it is either bred to breed standards or it is not. For "rare colour" read "colour not accepted by the Kennel Clubs or breed societies."

3. When your puppy arrives, take time off work or your other normal routines if necessary to be at home with him for the first week or, better still, two or more to help him settle in and overcome his fears.

4. Spend time every day obedience training your puppy for the first few months of his life – even if it is only five minutes a day - then reinforce it periodically throughout his adult life. This should include teaching him to walk nicely on the lead; especially important with large breeds, which will grow into powerful adults and the way you will control them then will be by using your voice, not brute force.

5. Socialise your dog. There is a critical window in a dog's life when he is aged between eight weeks and 18 to 20 weeks. How you treat him and what he is exposed to during this period will

have a bearing on how he reacts to everything for the rest of his life. In safe conditions, introduce him to new people, places, other dogs and small animals, loud noises, traffic and different situations. Don't limit your time with him to the home and garden, take him out and about with you.

6. Exercise your dog every single day away from the home – no matter how small he is. Every dog has a natural instinct to migrate.

The Kennel Clubs class dogs in different breed groups according to what they have originally been bred for. Here we will list each group and its characteristics, along with the most popular dogs in that group and their typical traits.

To say that all dogs of the same breed group are alike would be akin to saying that all Americans are optimistic and friendly and all Brits are polite and reserved. It is, of course, a huge generalisation. There are grumpy, unfriendly Americans and rude in-your-face Brits. However, it is also true to say that being friendly and optimistic are general American traits, as is being polite in Britain. It's the same in the canine world. Each individual dog has his or her unique character, but there are certain traits which are common within the different breeds and breeds in the same groups may also share certain similarities of temperament.

Pedigree, or purebred dogs, as they are known in North America, are bred to a **breed standard.** This is a blueprint for not only how each breed of dog should look, but also how it moves and – what a lot of people don't realise - what sort of temperament it should have. The breed standard is laid down by the main breed society in each country, and the Kennel Clubs keep the register of pedigree dogs. The dogs entered in conformation shows run under Kennel Club rules are judged against this ideal list of attributes, and breeders approved by the Kennel Clubs agree to breed puppies to the breed standards.

If you like a particular breed, you might be tempted to go for a less expensive puppy advertised by a non-approved breeder on a website or local newspaper and offered for sale without official Kennel Club registration documents. This is often false economy, as there is no guarantee that the puppy's dam and sire (parents) have been screened for any hereditary health issues which affect the breed. You also have little idea of the temperament of the parents.

Breed Groups

The breed groups are slightly different in the UK and USA and some dogs are listed in different groups.

The Miniature Schnauzer, for example, is listed in the Utility Group in the UK and in the Terrier Group by the American Kennel Club. As the owner of one, I have to agree with Americans. On our walks, Max (pictured) likes nothing better than chasing cats, squirrels, birds and anything else smaller than himself – a typical Terrier trait.

Gundogs – As the name suggests, gundogs were bred to work alongside men (and women) with guns. They all hunt by scent and can be divided into three types: the Pointers and Setters, which find the prey; the Spaniels, which flush game out of cover; and the Retrievers, which were bred to fetch game - often out of water - and deliver it to their masters.

These dogs are all medium to large in size, are generally good natured, playful and love to carry or fetch things. They have been bred to work and are usually fairly easy to train. They are also energetic, having been bred to perform a task, and often have a lot of stamina. A Spaniel or Retriever bred from working stock will require more exercise than one bred from show stock. Working dogs have the stamina to run all day, so if you like these breeds but your exercise time is limited to an hour or so a day, go for a dog from show (or conformation) stock. Pointers have high energy levels and some can have a nervous disposition.

Hounds – there are two types: scent hounds and sight hounds, and both were bred for hunting and are generally friendly. The sight hounds are the sleek speed merchants like the Greyhound, Whippet and Saluki. They are often gentle dogs, but can sometimes be aloof. They like chasing small creatures and are not always the easiest dog to train.

The scent hounds, like the Beagle, Basset Hound and Bloodhound, track prey using their incredible sense of smell. They are generally amiable and tolerant, good with families, but can wander off. All hounds are more independent and less reliant on human company than companion dogs.

Pastoral – this includes the herding dogs, such as all the Collies. Typically they are highly intelligent and sensitive dogs, sometimes protective, and require a great deal of exercise as they have been bred to do a full day's work. They can be trained to a high level and need plenty of stimulation to stop them becoming bored.

The other type of pastoral are the thick-coated dogs which were bred to guard livestock, rather than herd it. These large, strong dogs, like the Old English Sheepdog, and the striking Komondor, have strong protective instincts and are not always suitable for the first-time owner.

Terrier – these date back to ancient times and were originally bred to keep down vermin. The name comes from the Latin, Terra, meaning earth. They are feisty, having been bred to be extremely brave and tough, and to pursue fox, badger, rat and otter and other animals.

Today there are many different types of Terrier, but typical traits are that they are very alert and excitable, with strong characters. They have strong predatory instincts and chase small birds and animals. They can bark a lot and some have a tendency to be quick to snap if not socialised.

Toy – these breeds are small companion or lap dogs. Many were bred specifically to be companions, others have been placed into this category simply due to their small size. Trained well, they have sweet, friendly personalities, many can be quite vocal. They love attention and thrive on human companionship; some can be prone to separation anxiety. Toy breeds generally do not need a large amount of exercise. Some can be finicky eaters. They should be treated like dogs, not babies, as they can become spoilt, snappy and end up ruling the household.

Some, like the Miniature Pinscher and the French Bulldog, have been bred down from bigger dogs and may retain some traces of the characteristics of the larger breed.

Utility - This group consists of miscellaneous breeds of dog mainly of a non-sporting origin, including the Bulldog, Dalmatian (pictured), Akita and Poodle. The name Utility essentially means fitness for a purpose and this group consists of an extremely mixed and varied bunch, most breeds having been selectively bred to perform a specific function not included in the sporting and working categories.

Individual breed characteristics vary, according to what task the breed was originally bred to perform. This group is similar to the Non-Sporting Group in the USA, which also includes the Boston Terrier, Bichon Frise, Chow Chow and Shar-Pei.

Working - Over the centuries these dogs were selectively bred to become guards and search and rescue dogs. Arguably, the working group consists of some of the most heroic canines in the world, aiding humans in many walks of life, including the Boxer, Great Dane and St. Bernard. Generally these dogs are big, intelligent and protective and many are real specialists in their field who excel in their line of work.

As well as these breed groups, there are other groups or types of dogs with common characteristics. One such type is the **companion dog**. A canine which has been bred to be a companion to humans will generally require less exercise than working dogs, for example. They will be happy to spend time indoors close to you, and may even follow you around from room to room or nudge your hand indicating they want to be stroked.

These dogs like to be physically close to their owners and do not do well when separated from them for hours on end. They may be suitable for less physically active people or the elderly, but are generally not a good choice if you are out at work all day, when they will become lonely and depressed, leading to poor behaviour.

Time should be spent with a young companion puppy teaching him to be alone for short periods, gradually lengthening the time you are away from him. This will help to prevent separation anxiety, a common problem with companion dogs.

Another group of dogs are the brachycephalic breeds. These are short-faced dogs with wide heads. Breeding a foreshortened skull has led to some serious health problems, the most common issues being breathing, skin and eye problems, an intolerance to heat and even an elongated palate. This is where there is not room for all the soft tissue to fit inside the dog's head and which often requires surgery to help the dog breathe.

If you select a brachycephalic breed, be sure to select a puppy which breathes easily, and ask the breeder about the health records of the parents and grandparents - are they breathing effortlessly, have they undergone any corrective surgery?

The full list of brachycephalic breeds is: Affenpinscher, American Cocker Spaniel, American Pit Bull, American Staffordshire Terrier, Bichon Frise, Boston Terrier, Boxer, Brussels Griffon, Bulldog, Bull Mastiff, Cane Corso, Cavalier King Charles Spaniel, Chihuahua, Chow Chow, Dogo Argentino, Dogue de Bordeaux, English Mastiff, French Bulldog, Japanese Chin, King Charles Spaniel, Lhasa Apso, Maltese, Neapolitan Mastiff, Newfoundland, Pekingese, Presa Canario, Pug, Shar-Pei, Shih Tzu, Silky Terrier, Tibetan Spaniel, Valley

Bulldog and Yorkshire Terrier.

The incidence of health issues varies between the brachycephalic breeds, generally the shorter the muzzle, the greater the problems. Three of the most popular breeds have well documented health issues: the (English) Bulldog, the Pug and the French Bulldog, although responsible breeders are taking steps to try and improve the health of these breeds. For example, the French Bulldog has moved from Category 3 to Category 2 in the Kennel Club's Breed Watch (see next section for details of Breed Watch).

of concern listed in Breed Watch. A breed with several points of concern is statistically more likely to require more veterinary care than one with no major health issues listed. This guide to the breeds starts with the Labrador Retriever, the favourite in the UK and North America.

Labrador Retriever

Despite the rise in numbers of so-called "designer dogs", the Labrador continues to top the canine popularity list on both sides of the Atlantic, Australia and New Zealand - and by quite some margin. Classed in the Gundog Group by the Kennel Clubs, the Lab was originally bred to retrieve game and fish on shoots. But today the breed performs many different functions.

Labradors are large, adaptable dogs with easy-going and sunny personalities. They have solid temperaments and are not usually highly strung, like Terriers for example. They are generally loving, lovable and easy to train. Decide if you want a puppy from show (conformation) or working lines. Those bred from field, or working, lines are livelier, have more stamina and require more daily exercise.

Labradors have earned their place as the most popular family dog with a reputation for being good with children, as well as excelling in other areas. They are well known as Guide Dogs for the Blind, therapy and assistance dogs, and anyone who has ever seen one in action will marvel at their intelligence. The Labrador is listed as the seventh brightest in the Intelligence of Dogs list. This and their adaptable and generally easy-going personality make the Labrador a highly popular family pet.

There are three types of Labrador Retriever: yellow, black and chocolate, and opinion varies as to whether their temperaments vary slightly between the colours. The single biggest factor determining the temperament of any puppy is, however, the temperament of his or her parents. Try and see both, if possible.

Labradors need a lot of daily exercise – an hour and a half or more is ideal, split into separate walks. Dogs bred directly from working stock may need more exercise. Lack of exercise can lead to destructive behaviour or barking. Having been bred to retrieve from water, they have webbed toes and most love to swim. They also like to carry objects and chew, especially when young, so having a selection of toys and chews is a good idea. On walks, most love running after a ball or stick and fetching it back.

One of our dogs was attacked by a pack of five Labradors while trotting along a field last year and was lucky to escape with his life. This was a highly unusual incident as Labradors are not naturally predatory or aggressive, but all dogs need socialisation. It was a young, entire male Labrador which had not been properly socialised that triggered the attack and the other dogs then followed their natural pack instinct and joined the fray.

We did not blame the young dog for the attack, but his owner (who was extremely apologetic and paid all of the veterinary bills), firstly for not socialising the dog and secondly, for allowing five dogs to run free as a pack where there were lots of other dogs and people.

Labs have a double coat, a soft, downy undercoat and a harder guard coat help keep the dog warm and dry while swimming in cold waters. They shed twice a year and are not suitable for allergy sufferers. They do not need a lot of grooming, but should be brushed once a week to keep them clean and remove some of the loose hairs. They generally only need a bath if they are smelly – such as after rolling in something horrible (this was a popular pastime with our Labrador, Harvey).

According to Labs4Rescue, both sexes make good pets. In general, male Labradors are more dependent and females are somewhat more independent. For example, if you are at home working on your computer, your male Labrador will may well sleep under your feet, while your female may sleep in the next room and just come in and check on you periodically.

Labs are also extremely greedy and eat anything put in front of them – and a lot that isn't! Monitoring the dog's weight and preventing obesity is a constant challenge for owners. However, extra weight puts extra strain on the dog's joints, and this is a common problem with middle-aged and senior Labradors.

There is some anecdotal evidence that Labradors bred from backyard breeders or puppy mills can be hyper, rather than having the normal, even temperament. (Backyard breeders are people with little or no knowledge of breeding dogs and are in it mostly for the money). Pick a breeder approved by the Kennel Club to avoid this.

The Lab is in Category 2 of Breed Watch. Points of concern are: "legs too short in proportion to depth of body and to length of back, and significantly overweight." Health questions to ask the breeder about are hip and elbow dysplasia, progressive retinal atrophy (PRA) and retinal dysplasia - both affect the eyes.

In the USA ask to see OFA

(Orthopedic Foundation for Animals) certificates for hip dysplasia, and CERF (Canine Eye Registry Foundation) certificate for eyes. In the UK, it's BVA (British Veterinary Association) certificates. These are relatively inexpensive tests for breeders – in the UK around £50 to £60 (and OFA fees are often less than $50 per dog in the USA) – small price to pay considering the cost of a pedigree dog. Typical life expectancy is 10 to 12 years.

SUMMARY: Excellent, even tempered family dogs. Only commit to a Labrador Retriever if you can give him a good walk at least two or three times a day. Visit http://labs4rescue.com/faq.shtml for more information on the breed.

Cocker Spaniel

This is the second most popular breed in the UK, although less popular in North America, and is in the Gundog Group (Sporting Group in North America). The breed was originally called the 'Cocking Spaniel' as it was used to hunt Eurasian woodcock. When introduced to America, the

breed standard was changed to make the dog more suitable for hunting American woodcock (this new breed became the slightly smaller American Cocker Spaniel).

The medium-sized Cocker is gentle and sporty with a happy-go-lucky temperament. The breed is generally good with kids and makes a great family pet, provided you make the time to exercise and train him.

They are intelligent and optimistic and have a permanently wagging tail. They are also sociable dogs which don't like being left alone, being very loyal one-man dogs which form a strong bond with their owners.

If you buy a 'field' dog bred from working parents, be prepared for lots and lots of daily exercise, a working Cocker has incredible stamina and is happy to run all day – and you still won't tire him out. Don't expect to keep him on a lead; Cockers love to run around with their heads down, sniffing in the undergrowth. For every mile you walk, an active Spaniel will run several more.

His retrieving instincts may mean that from time to time he brings you gifts – even in the house, when you will be proudly presented with a shoe or a toy – with, of course, a wagging tail.

Show dogs are sturdier and heavier that those from working stock. Despite being a gundog, some Cockers are sensitive to loud bangs.

They are 18th in the Intelligence of Dogs list in the 'Excellent Working Dogs' section.

Cockers make good family dogs, provided they get enough exercise. They are intelligent, eager to learn and easy to train – although some can have a stubborn streak. In this case, patience and persistence is required when training; Cockers are sensitive critters and do not respond well to shouting or harsh treatment.

Some can be possessive, so you need to teach a Cocker games which involve him releasing his toy or other object. Due to their sensitivity, they also require early socialisation so that barking or poor behaviour does not develop.

The breed has a range of solid colours, including black, red, golden, liver (chocolate), black and tan, liver and tan, as well as bicolours, tricolours and roan (mottled). They are high maintenance on the grooming front, their long coats need daily brushing and/or cleaning and their long, furry ears are prone to infections, so they also need regular checking and cleaning. Many owners have their Cocker's coat trimmed by a groomer to prevent matting and keep the coat clean, so this is another expense to be considered. A trip to the groomer's will cost on average £20 to £30, around $30 to $50.

Cockers shed a lot and often have a doggy smell. They are not suitable for allergy sufferers and probably not a good choice for the very house-proud owner. Their coats gather dirt and lose large amounts of hair, and some Cockers (and Springers) can also display submissive urination, which means that they pee when excited or intimidated - wherever they are.

Cocker Spaniels are in Breed Watch Category 1, with no major points of concern. Health issues include ear infections and eye problems, such as progressive retinal atrophy (PRA), glaucoma and juvenile cataracts, as well as autoimmune disease and joint problems. Ask the breeder about hip and eye certificates. Life expectancy is 12 to 15 years, although the median age in a Kennel Club survey (UK) was 11 years and two months.

SUMMARY: Good family dogs. If you are looking at puppies, find out if they are from working or show lines and if you have less than an hour a day to exercise your dog, go for one from a show line. There is also some evidence concerning health and temperament issues with Cockers bred from unscrupulous breeders. Spend time to find a responsible breeder.

German Shepherd Dog

This versatile, athletic and fearless working dog has a large band of enthusiastic devotees and is quite possibly the most popular breed on the planet.

The German Shepherd Dog, as the name suggests, originated in Germany and is in the Pastoral Group in the UK and the Herding Group in the USA, having originally been bred as a herding sheepdog. This breed has done just about every possible canine job: assisting the

blind, sniffing out illegal drugs, apprehending criminals, serving in the armed forces and helping search and rescue teams, to name just some of the tasks he is capable of.

A loyal and devoted companion, the German Shepherd (which used to be called the Alsatian) is very affectionate with - and devoted to - his family. Many owners would say that this isn't a breed, but a lifestyle. This is undoubtedly an extremely rewarding dog for those who can give him the time he needs.

Energy levels vary from very high to more laid-back, but all German Shepherds need brisk walking every day and running free as often as possible. The breed is suitable for families who are prepared to put the required time in. It is also a good choice for fit outdoor enthusiasts. Puppy classes are highly recommended with this breed, in fact in our area there are puppy classes specifically for German Shepherd Dogs, where the pups and adolescent dogs learn to mix with other dogs and people and walk nicely on the lead without pulling.

The German Shepherd is a highly intelligent and physical breed which needs plenty of exercise and mental stimulation. The Shepherd loves and excels at every kind of canine activity, including agility, obedience, tracking and herding. It is third on Stanley Coren's Intelligence of Dogs list, behind the Border Collie and Poodle. Intelligence is defined as learning quickly and being able to excel at tasks, but this cleverness needs to be channelled. An intelligent dog can easily become bored.

Plenty of daily exercise and mental stimulation, such as training, games or agility, is the key to success with this breed. Early socialisation with other animals and humans is **essential**, as an under-socialised GSD can become over-protective, territorial and aggressive. Many bark a lot. It also has a strong tendency to chase and this should be channelled into games at an early age. The breed is not known for being overly-friendly with strangers, and generally makes a good guard dog.

There is a great deal of variation between the temperaments of different bloodlines of German Shepherds. When picking a puppy, find out what the parents were bred for and look at the temperament of both dam and sire; your pup will take after them. Again, there are reports of dogs with unwanted temperament traits being bred by disreputable breeders out to make money. Take time to find the right breeder and remember, the perfect German Shepherd results from a combination of the puppy you buy and the time you put in to training and socialising him; a combination of nature and nurture.

Here is a cautionary tale: an acquaintance had a lovely even-tempered GSD who used to calmly sit in the grassy lane outside their gate all day watching the world go by. We'd stroke her as we passed, and our dog would happily exchange sniffs with her. Bella passed away a few years ago and the owners got a new German Shepherd pup around a year later.

Silka has a completely different temperament to Bella. She is highly intelligent, bold and lively by nature and has not attended training or socialisation classes (neither did Jess). The owners have had to build a higher wall to keep her in the garden after she jumped out and bit the next-door neighbour; she barks constantly at people and other dogs; a post box has been built on the exterior garden wall to keep the postman safe; and she drags her owner around the village on a lead twice daily on her extremely short walks.

Silka is very loving, but she has grown into a territorial and over-protective adult. With proper training and socialisation and enough exercise, she would have been a superb dog the owners could have taken anywhere.

Most German Shepherds are fine with other family pets if introduced when young. However, some are cat chasers, and many are dominant or aggressive with strange dogs of the same sex.

They have a thick, double coat which sheds constantly - their nickname is 'German Shedder' - making them entirely unsuitable for allergy sufferers. They require regular brushing, preferably outdoors, to remove some of the loose hairs and the occasional bath.

German Shepherds are in Category 3, the points of concern are: "cow hocks, excessive turn of stifle, nervous temperament, sickle hock and weak hindquarters." Health issues include hip and elbow dysplasia, which may lead to arthritis, degenerative myelopothy (like multiple sclerosis), von Willebrand's disease (a bleeding disorder) and heart issues. Ask the breeder about hip, elbow and eye certificates. Life expectancy is 10 to 13 years.

SUMMARY: The German Shepherd is highly intelligent and extremely eager to learn and work. The breed requires an owner with a high level of commitment to training and socialisation. His many talents may be wasted if all you are looking for is a family pet.

Golden Retriever

This is a large, friendly breed in the Gundog Group which originated in the Scottish Highlands in the late 1800s. It was bred to retrieve water fowl and upland game birds during hunting and shooting parties. Their soft mouths enabled the dogs to bring back the shot game undamaged.

Goldens are cheerful, easy to train and eager to please. They are patient with children, making them the perfect family dog – provided they get the time they need. They love everyone and get along well with new people and strange dogs. They are clever, being listed at number four in the Intelligence of Dogs, and can be trained to a high level.

The breed standard describes the temperament as: "kindly, friendly and confident" and it is this equable temperament which is the trademark feature of the breed. The Golden Retriever has adapted to so many roles that there is virtually nothing he hasn't done, except be a guard dog – a task for which his friendly temperament makes him quite unsuited – although he will bark to announce new arrivals. He has been a guide dog, a drug and explosives detecting dog, a tracker and an obedience competitor. The breed has risen in popularity over the decades so that now it is often the largest entry at Championship Shows.

Goldens are energetic and loving and have an instinctive love of water and swimming. They need plenty of daily exercise – a couple of hours a day is ideal – as well as mental stimulation to prevent them from becoming destructive. A Golden who gets this is charming and a pleasure to be around. The good natured exuberance of young dogs should be channelled into exercise and activities.

They enjoy playing and fetching and are suitable as jogging or cycling companions. Like many breeds bred to carry things in their mouths, they love to chew - especially as puppies, so plenty of chews and toys is a good idea to help keep them occupied during their early months. Due to their size and energy levels, they are not suited to apartment life, being better suited to a large house and garden or yard.

The smooth, medium-haired double coat is easy to groom, and they only need a bath when smelly. This breed is regarded as an average shedder, but each individual hair is very long and you'll find them all around the house. This is definitely not a breed to be considered by allergy sufferers.

Golden Retrievers love their humans and do not do well when left alone for long periods, so they are not suitable if you are out at work all day. When they are lonely, they can become destructive. They are happiest in the midst of family life with plenty of physical and mental stimulation.

Goldens are listed in Breed Watch Category 2 with the following points of concern (the same as the Labrador Retriever): "Legs too short in proportion to depth of body and to length of back, and significantly. Some can be susceptible to cancers, as well as hip and elbow dysplasia.

They can also suffer from epilepsy, ear infections, allergies, skin infections and hypothyroidism. Buying from a good breeder with a track record for healthy breeding stock and health screening will help to avert some of these problems.

Golden Retrievers love their food, and care has to be taken not to allow them to become obese. Typical lifespan is 10 to 12 years.

SUMMARY: A wonderful family dog if you're around a lot and have the time for a couple of hours' exercise a day.

Pug

The Pug is classed in the Toy Group by all the Kennel Clubs. Over the last decade the breed has enjoyed a big surge in popularity and is now in the top six on both sides of the Atlantic. The origins of the breed are uncertain, but it is thought they may even date back to before Christ. The roots lie in Asia with the short-haired Pekingese, and some Shih Tzu along the way. Genetics suggest that the Pug's closest relatives today are two lesser known breeds, the Petit Brabancon and the Griffon Bruxellois.

The Pug's increasing popularity is due to a number of reasons. The breed is small, does not require a lot of exercise and is content with living in an apartment or small house. He is also intelligent, spirited, playful, loving and loyal - and a Pug will make you laugh. To top it all he is also generally good with children and other animals and loves being part of a family.

The Latin phrase 'multum in parvo' - a lot in a little – is an often-used description of this small, muscular breed. So what's not to like with this entertaining little dog with the big personality?

Despite being intelligent, Pugs are only listed at 57th out of 110 in the Intelligence of Dogs. This is because they can be stubborn; if they don't want to do something, you have to pleasantly but firmly persuade them to do it - they do not respond well to shouting – and this is not always easy. You have to be patient with training, make it fun, Pugs love games, as the breed can be a bit single minded if they sense they have the upper hand (or paw!) They are also not the quickest dogs to housetrain, so be prepared to be patient.

The Pug will adapt to you and your life; if you are lively and energetic, your Pug will be too; if you are a couch potato, your Pug will adopt this lifestyle. All Pugs love sleeping, but even couch potato dogs need daily walks. A Pug can be happy with 30 minutes or less of daily exercise, some get used to much more from an early age. They are usually fine with other people and dogs, provided they have been socialised.

Like all companion dogs, they love to be with their humans, and may follow you around the house, earning them the nickname 'shadow dog,' but they are not happy to be left alone for long periods.

A Pug has a short double coat which can be silver, apricot, fawn or black. They are light shedders, a weekly brush will do, but they are not suitable for allergy sufferers. You may also need to clean your Pug's facial wrinkles every week to keep them clean and prevent infections.

A Pug is one of the brachycephalic (flat faced) breeds, and many suffer from breathing problems. In some cases corrective surgery can be successful, but this is expensive. Snoring, snorting and snuffling are all fairly typical - they are also pretty windy at the other end too! They are sensitive to temperature and can have problems in too hot or too cool conditions.

Pugs are in Breed Watch Category 3. Points of concerns are: "Difficulty breathing, Excessive nasal folds, Excessively prominent eyes, Hair loss or scarring from previous dermatitis, Incomplete blink, Pinched nostrils, Significantly overweight, Signs of dermatitis in skin folds, Sore eyes due to damage or poor eyelid conformation and Unsound movement". Other health issues to ask a breeder about are hip and knee problems and a back condition known as hemivertebrae.

Check that the parents have been screened for these last problems. If a breeder says he or she doesn't need to screen because they have never had any problems, be wary. Obesity can become an issue with some Pugs. Lifespan is 12 to 14 years.

SUMMARY: If you are at home a lot and are looking for a small dog with plenty of character that does not need much exercise or grooming, then a Pug is worth considering. Make sure you buy a healthy puppy which breathes easily from an accredited breeder.

English Springer Spaniel

The English Springer Spaniel and Cocker Spaniel share a joint history and in the 1900s were born within the same litter. The smaller Cockers were used for hunting woodcock, while their larger littermates were used to flush - or 'spring' – game, startling the birds into the air to fly within the hunters' sights. In 1902 the Kennel Club recognised the English Springer as a separate breed.

The hardy Springer is the traditional rough shooting dog with great stamina capable of working all day. He's always ready to jump into water, even if it means breaking ice to do it. As with the Cocker, the English Springer is in the Gundog Group in the UK and Sporting Group in the USA. Both have webbed feet. They are also used as sniffer dogs and you may see one in action at an airport.

Like the Cocker, the handsome English Springer has a very friendly, positive outlook on life, typified by his continuously wagging tail. His cheerful extrovert nature has endeared him to the general public, and he is in great demand as an energetic companion for a family – but only one which can devote many hours to exercising this lively dog.

In physical terms, the English Springer is bigger than the Cocker Spaniel with fewer coat colourings. The accepted colours are liver and white or black and white, or either of these with tan markings. The other main difference is in energy levels, although

working Cockers also have high energy levels.

An English Springer has been bred to do a job and can run all day without getting tired. If you like the breed, but cannot devote a couple of hours a day to exercising one, take a look at a puppy from a show bloodline and check with the breeder how much exercise he will be happy with. If it still needs more time than you can give, consider a companion breed. Some owners say that English Springers can be more alert and 'needy' than Cocker Spaniels, which may have calmer dispositions, particularly those from show lines.

English Springers are lively and intelligent, ranking 13th out of 131 breeds in The Intelligence of Dogs List. If you don't want to hunt with your dog, you may decide to take part in agility, flyball, tracking or obedience. English Springers' lively, alert nature means that they like to be on the go and thrive on these activities. Their sunny dispositions also make them good therapy dogs.

These are people-orientated dogs and do not thrive when left alone. There are reports of some suffering from separation anxiety, leading to excessive barking, chewing or nervousness. They are more likely to be friendly with everybody, rather than one-person dogs. For this reason, they do not make good guard dogs, although most will bark if someone comes to the house.

They have a thick, high-maintenance coat which is weather resistant, but requires regular grooming. Like most Spaniels, the long, drooping ears are prone to infection and need regular cleaning and trimming.

With its love of the great outdoors and swimming and a long, shedding coat, this is not a breed recommended for allergy sufferers. Neither is it one for the house-proud, as Springers can get quite smelly when their coat gets wet or dirty. Like all spaniels, they can display submissive urination when excited or nervous. They do best with owners who give them constant structure when they know their place in the household.

The English Springer Spaniel is in Breed Watch Category 1 with no major points of concern. Health issues include hip dysplasia, ear infections and eye and skin problems. Ask the breeder about hip and eye certificates. Do your research and pick a responsible breeder, there are reports of dogs with unwanted temperament traits from unaccredited breeders.

SUMMARY: An energetic family companion who is happy as long as he gets enough exercise. Unless you're a hunter or enjoy several hours of outdoor activity a day, get a puppy bred from show (conformation) bloodlines.

French Bulldog

Small companion dogs have become increasingly popular over the last decade, and none more so than the French Bulldog. In the USA, the breed has become almost five times more popular over a 10-year span and it's a similar story in the UK.

Originally bred down from the larger (English) Bulldog, lace workers took this smaller version (which some say was bred with the Pug) to France in the late 1800s. The breed soon became popular, particularly among artists ... and prostitutes! It was then reintroduced to England.

This distinctive-looking dog with the bat ears has been bred as a companion dog, and is classed in the Utility Group in the UK and Non-Sporting Group in the USA. Two of the reasons for the rise in popularity are his unique looks - you'll either love 'em or hate 'em – and the fact that a Frenchie does not need a lot of exercise or grooming. To cap it all, he has an easy-going personality, doesn't bark much and loves sleeping.

Frenchies have a mischievous streak, which has earned them the unusual nickname of 'The Clown in the Philosopher's Cloak'. This sense of fun can turn to stubbornness if they are not properly trained from an early age. They can become territorial and like being the centre of attention, which can lead to behavioural problems if they are overindulged.

They are ranked 58th - one behind the Pug - out of 131 breeds tested in The Intelligence of Dogs List. However, this is not because they are stupid, far from it, but rather that the tests were based on the speed of the dog to obey commands. A Frenchie may very well understand you, but all bull-type breeds have minds of their own. They will consider your command a request rather than blindly following it and a patient approach is required when training. The good news is that they really love their food, which is a powerful training aid with Frenchies.

Training is essential if you don't want your cute little Frenchie to rule the roost. Some are notoriously difficult to housetrain; starting housetraining as soon as you bring your puppy home and being extra vigilant for the first couple of weeks should help to prevent any problems.

The French Bulldog does not need much exercise, but should be taken for at least one walk a day of up to 30 minutes, some will be happier with more exercise if they get used to it from an early age.

They are stocky and compact with a short, low-maintenance coat. The occasional brush should suffice. However, they do shed and are not suitable for allergy suffers.

There is currently a big problem with "rare" colours. These are non-Kennel Club recognised colours bred by non-accredited breeders. Some of these so-called rare colours, such as "blue," fetch large amounts of money. These breeders are only breeding for a colour, not for health or temperament and owners are discovering many problems with these "rare" Frenchies. I personally know of two which have had to be put down (euthanized) due to temperament problems. At least one of them had been imported.

If you decide to get a Frenchie, DON'T buy a rare colour and don't buy an import. Many of these dogs have been kept in concrete sheds for weeks on end and not socialised, leading to problems later in life. Buy from a breeder accredited with the Kennel Club in your country. The only colour recognised for French Bulldogs are: brindle, pied or fawn (or white in the USA). Tan, mouse and grey or grey-blue are highly undesirable.

Frenchies are very affectionate dogs and, like all companion dogs, are not at all suitable if you are out at work all day. They are, however, suitable for older people or families, when it's best to introduce them to children and other animals from a young age, as some unsocialised French Bulldogs can be snappy towards other dogs. With their fine coats and tendency to overheat, they are predominantly indoor dogs and are suitable for people living in apartments.

The black and white ones may look similar to Boston Terriers, but the two breeds are very different. A Boston is much more alert and athletic, needs more exercise and has a Terrier's tendencies, whereas the Frenchie takes much more after the Bulldog in temperament and looks. Frenchies differ from Pugs in that they are physically less stocky and they have a more mischievous streak.

The French Bulldog is a brachycephalic (flat faced) breed, needs his face wrinkles cleaning and ears checking regularly, and may be susceptible to a number of genetic illnesses – another very important reason for picking a good breeder. In a list of the most expensive dog breeds based on claims paid out by the Trupanion Pet Insurance company (USA) since 2000, the French Bulldog was listed at number five. The company said: "The French bulldog was responsible for $384,000 in claims paid out. This breed is prone to allergies, and other respiratory problems."

The health of the breed is, however, improving with selective breeding of healthy stock by responsible breeders. Frenchies have moved from Category 3 to Category 2 in the Breed Watch List. Points of concern are: "Difficulty breathing, Exaggerated roach in the top line, Excessively prominent eyes, Hair loss or scarring from previous dermatitis, Incomplete blink, Incorrect bite, Inverted tail, Lack of tail, Overly short neck, Pinched nostrils, Screw tail, Signs of dermatitis in skin folds, and Tight tail."

Other potential hereditary health issues include spine and joint problems. Ask to see health certificates before committing to a puppy. Average lifespan is 11 to 14 years. Further useful information can be found in **The French Bulldog Handbook**, available on Amazon and Apple.

SUMMARY: An amusing companion dog suitable for somebody at home a lot. The downside is that many rack up big veterinary bills, mainly due to breathing problems. Only buy a healthy pup from a Kennel Club accredited breeder - whatever the cost, it should save you money in medical bills in the long run. A possibility for allergy sufferers.

Bulldog

One of the oldest breeds, the Bulldog - also called English Bulldog and British Bulldog - has gone from being in danger of extinction in the 19th century to making the list of top 10 most popular breeds on both sides of the Atlantic. Originally bred for the bloodthirsty entertainment of bull baiting, the breed suffered a massive decline when the sport was banned in 1832. A handful of enthusiasts began to breed the aggression out of the Bulldog to create a companion dog, with considerable success.

Today's Bulldog is one of the most instantly recognisable of all the breeds with his massive head and wrinkled face. Despite a fierce exterior, he is a sheep in wolf's clothing, with a placid temperament and laid-back habits. No longer a sporting dog, he is classed in the Utility Group in the UK and Non-Sporting Group in the USA.

His nickname is Bully - or Sourmug - but nothing could be further from the truth. It's true that Bulldogs have retained their stubborn streak, but they are generally the most placid of creatures, happy to snooze the day away next to - and even on top of - their owners. An adult Bulldog may weight 40lb to 55lb, but nobody has told him he's not a lapdog. He is known for his gentle nature, loves sleeping, and enjoys snuggling up on the couch or his owner's knee.

Despite his size, the modern Bulldog is a highly popular companion dog. He is predominantly an indoor dog and is suitable for life in a house or apartment, due to the fact that he does not need much exercise. A couple of short walks a day are usually enough. Like the Frenchie, he may show bursts of energy and dash round the house having a mad five minutes of play time, but does not have stamina.

He loves to be with people – so if you are out at work all day, don't get a Bulldog. Most Bulldogs like to chew if bored, especially when young. Go for a breed which is less dependent on humans for happiness. Bullies have big hearts and respond to anyone showing them kindness, rather than being one-person dogs.

They also have a reputation for being wonderful with babies and children. Many seem to have a natural affinity and protective instinct towards youngsters. However, a Bulldog is a powerful dog who doesn't always know his own strength, and young Bullies are often boisterous, so always supervise their time spent together.

Bulldogs are also very courageous. If properly socialised, they don't look to start a fight with other dogs – and usually get on well with other pets if introduced at an early age – but they will not back down if involved in a confrontation. Don't allow a Bulldog to get into a staring match with another dog.

Bulldogs are almost at the bottom of the Intelligence of Dogs list, with only the Basenji and Afghan Hound ranked lower. The breed's dismal showing is not due to the fact that the Bulldog doesn't understand the command, it's that he will weigh it up before deciding whether he wants to obey or not. Patience and persistence are required when training, but it must be done in an encouraging manner; Bulldogs do not respond at all well to shouting or physical violence.

This is one of the brachycephalic breeds and a recent survey by a large pet insurance company revealed that Bulldogs are one of the most expensive breeds in terms of healthcare. The trademark huge, flattened skull looks very appealing, but has led to some major health issues within the breed, and breathing problems are common. Many are unable to mate naturally.

Listed in Breed Watch Category 3, these are the points of concern for the Bulldog: "Excessive amounts of loose facial skin with conformational defects of the upper and/or lower eyelids, Hair loss or scarring from previous dermatitis, Heavy overnose wrinkle (roll), Inverted tail, Lack of tail, Pinched nostrils, Significantly overweight,

Sore eyes due to damage or poor eyelid conformation, Tight tail and Unsound movement."

Although relatively undemanding dogs in terms of exercise and grooming, Bulldogs require care on an almost daily basis and are not recommended for first-time owners. Their facial wrinkles, ears and tails have to be kept clean to prevent infection, and they must not be left outdoors or exercised in hot weather as they are prone to overheating, which can be fatal.

In short, the Bulldog is the only dog for some dog lovers, and they can undoubtedly make extremely rewarding companions. Anyone thinking of getting one should first thoroughly research the breed and its sensitivities. Most importantly, choose an accredited breeder with a track record of producing healthy puppies. Don't just go for the looks, ask to see health certificates and check the pup's breathing. If he seems to be struggling for breath or wheezing, walk away - however cute he looks.

Typical lifespan is eight to 10 years, some may live slightly longer, although a UK survey revealed that the median lifespan of a Bulldog was a little over six years, taking into account those which died before reaching old age. **The Bulldog Handbook** http://amzn.to/1wRTrRS (or in the USA http://amzn.to/11BRBaC) is a good source of information on the breed and the specialist care required by owners.

SUMMARY: The Bulldog has a quiet dignity and a high pain threshold, so needs an attentive owner. One of the few larger dogs suited to apartment life as it has low exercise needs. Many potential health problems due to the extremely compressed face, so chose your breeder and then your puppy very carefully.

Beagle

The Beagle is consistently among the top five breeds in the USA and, although far lower down the list, the breed is becoming increasingly popular in the UK, according to Kennel Club statistics.

Dogs similar to the Beagle have existed for 2,400 years, with the modern breed having been developed in Britain in the 1800s. The origin of the name may lie in the French "be'geule," referring to the baying sound of the hounds when pursuing game, or possibly the diminutive size of the hound.

Belonging to the Hound Group, Beagles are scent hounds, originally bred to track hare, rabbit and other small game. Indeed, there are still packs of Beagles working today on both sides of the Atlantic, with their followers travelling on foot, rather than on horseback.

A Beagle has one of the best developed senses of smell of any breed, along with the Bloodhound and the Bassett Hound. This has led to the breed being employed as detection dogs around the world, sniffing out prohibited agricultural imports, foodstuffs and explosives. In the 1950s, two scientists began a 13-year study of canine behaviour. They tested the scenting abilities of various breeds by putting a mouse in a one-acre field and timing how long it took the dogs to find it. The Beagles found it in less than a minute.

They have a cheerful, gentle disposition and are even tempered. The breed is relatively healthy, listed in Breed Watch Category 1 with no major points of concern. One factor any prospective owner should be aware of is that the Beagle is a hardy, active dog which needs lots of daily exercise if he is not to become bored or destructive, particularly during the early years when he has higher energy levels. Many Beagles slow down as they grow older.

If you like the Beagle, but cannot give up a couple of hours a day to exercise him, you might want to take a look at a Puggle, a cross between a Beagle and a Pug. They have many features of the Beagle, but are slightly, less excitable and need less exercise. They also do well in cities, whereas a Beagle is happiest running off the lead in countryside.

By nature the Beagle is friendly and tolerant and, as an athletic working pack animal, is happiest with people and/or other dogs and plenty of exercise. Behaviour problems can develop if he spends too much time alone, when barking or trying to escape can become a problem. The main reason for Beagles being given up for rescue is their baying or barking.

Training and plenty of exercise is the best way of preventing yours becoming a problem barker. Beagles are intelligent but independently-minded, which is why they are ranked at 73 in the Intelligence of Dogs list, in the 'Lowest Degree of Working/Obedience Intelligence' section.

A typical scent hound, the Beagle is highly active and has a strong instinct for following a trail. He is happiest outside with his nose to the ground following a scent. This means that he is likely to forget you and wander off on his own if not supervised. He loves to run off the lead, but you need to make sure he is trained to return and keep a sharp eye on him. The Kennel Club says of the Beagle's natural desire to follow a trail: "This instinct is mimicked in his everyday behaviour in the park: the man with the lead in his hand and no dog in sight owns a Beagle."

The breed is relatively easy to train, although some dogs can be stubborn, and do best with an owner who combines kindness with firmness and clear leadership. They can be difficult to housetrain, and the correct use of a crate may help. Beagles generally get along well with children, provided they have been properly socialised around them and trained how to behave with them – the children as well as the dog. Youngsters should not tease a Beagle while he is eating or sleeping, and Beagles should be taught not to nip children when playing (they have a habit of 'mouthing' things when playing.)

The Beagle has a short, coat which is easy to keep clean, so doesn't need baths unless he has rolled in something horrible. Their short hair does shed, so they are not suitable for allergy sufferers. The most common coat is tricolour with a saddle, or patch of black, on the back, although any hound colour is acceptable. The drooping ears should be checked and cleaned regularly to prevent infections occurring.

There are two sizes of Beagle in the USA, one is 13" at the withers (shoulder) and the other is 14". In the UK, dogs can be anything from 13" to 16" tall. As with all breeds, males tend to be larger than females.

A relatively healthy breed, the Beagle is in Category 1 of the Kennel Club's Breed Watch, with "no points of concern". Health issues known to affect some Beagles include disk disease, epilepsy, dwarfism, hip dysplasia and immune disorders. There are no 100% health guarantees with any animal, but the best way of avoiding future health problems is to buy from an accredited breeder. Typical lifespan is 12 to 15 years.

SUMMARY: Easy going, gentle breed which needs regular exercise. May not be suitable for a household with cats or other small non-canine animals. With human leadership they make excellent pets, although they have tendency to wander off after a scent.

Border Terrier

The Border Terrier is extremely popular in the UK, although less so in the USA. Originally bred to hunt foxes and rats, the Border has shared ancestors with other Terriers, including Dandie Dinmonts, Patterdales and Bedlingtons.

He was bred to have legs long enough to keep up with horses and other foxhounds, and a body small enough to crawl into the burrows of foxes and chase them out. Although much older, the breed was officially recognised by The Kennel Club in 1920, and by the

AKC in 1930.

The Border is a true Terrier, with their typical characteristics, and classed as such by all Kennel Clubs. The word 'Terrier' comes from the French *terre*, meaning earth, and also burrow. Most are lively and alert, and will chase small animals and birds at the drop of a hat. And as with all Terriers, the Border is full of character.

Border Terriers were bred to have the courage and stamina to work all day in all weathers. They were often left to find their own food and so have a strong hunting instinct which remains today. They also have a powerful drive to dig and bark and have retained their high energy levels for a small dog. These traits can make the breed a challenge for some owners, while others find them to be wonderful companions who play hard and are extremely loyal and affectionate.

Temperaments and energy levels will vary according to bloodlines. If you want a less active Border Terrier, spend time choosing an accredited breeder who is not breeding from active working lines, and look at the temperament of the parents - or at least the mother, if the sire is not present. Is she feisty and noisy or more laid-back? Your pup will inherit his temperament from his parents.

Border Terriers need a lot of exercise for a small dog, a minimum of an hour a day is recommended, with a lot of this time spent running off the lead. But before you can do this, you have to train your dog to come back, as his hunting instinct will take him at breakneck speed out of your sight within minutes. The breed excels in hunting and hunting trails as well as agility and obedience contests.

One of the reasons for his popularity is that the Border tends to be more tolerant of children and other dogs than other Terriers, some of which can have a tendency to bark or snap.

Borders are intelligent and eager to please their owners. During training, they respond well to praise. They are ranked 30th in the Intelligence of Dogs, appearing in the 'Above Average Working Dogs' section. They learn quickly and respond well to obedience training, but must be kept engaged and well-exercised, as they are active dogs. If allowed to run free in the garden or yard, they need to be well fenced in, as their love of digging and jumping makes them expert escape artists.

This breed loves to be engaged; a dog left alone for long periods may well become destructive or resort to excessive barking. However, given the exercise and attention they need, Border Terriers make wonderful, loving companions who are happy and full of fun. Like all Terriers, they make excellent watchdogs and will bark if somebody comes to the door.

But only take one on if you have the time and energy to deal with their lively personalities.

The hardy Border Terrier has an all-weather double coat. A short, dense undercoat is covered with a hard and wiry outer coat. This can be red, blue and tan, grizzle and tan or wheaten (pale yellow or fawn). Some have a small patch of white on the chest. They are regarded as low shedders and require only weekly brushing, but should be hand stripped a couple of times a year. Although not hypoallergenic, the low shedding wiry coat may make the breed suitable for some allergy sufferers; read the chapter on **Puppies for Allergy Sufferers** to find out how to tell if a specific Border Terrier pup might be suitable.

Listed in Breed Watch Category 1, the Border is a relatively healthy dog. Health issues include joint problems, heart murmur (which affects many small breed dogs), and eye problems. Ask to see hip and eye screening certificates.

SUMMARY: Hardy, lively Terrier with bags of energy and character who will chase small animals and may bark a lot. Needs daily exercise.

Boxer

The Boxer traces his roots back over hundreds of years through the Molossus, or Mastiff, a large working dog. In more recent times, the breed was developed in Germany in the late 19th century, where his direct ancestor was the Brabant Bullenbeisser (bull biter). The Boxer is also a cousin of the Bulldog, a smaller type of Mastiff.

They were bred to hunt and then hold on to the prey with their powerful jaws, and later also used as guard dogs. The name reputedly comes from the breed's tendency to play by standing on its hind legs and 'boxing' with its front paws.

Today's Boxer is a large dog which still retains his impressive, athletic appearance. Don't get a Boxer if you want a quiet life, Boxers approach life full-on. They are boisterous, lively, and full of fun. Some owners would even say that a young Boxer can act a little crazy – he will certainly make you laugh with his antics. They can be extremely rewarding dogs, but must only be considered by owners who can give them the time and exercise they need to be content.

Exuberance, boundless energy and a desire to please sum up this versatile breed, especially when young. Many slow down as they age but, like the Bulldog, the Boxer does not reach maturity until about three years old. They tend to be very good with children, being patient and playful as well as protective, making them a popular choice for families.

These are active, strong dogs which require plenty of exercise to avoid their nemesis – boredom - which can result in destructive chewing, digging or licking. I know of one family who left their young Boxer alone for long periods while they went out to work and the dog ended up chewing its way through several kitchen cabinets.

Boxers are intelligent, but are listed only at 48th - in the 'Average Working/Obedience' Intelligence' section - of the Intelligence of Dogs list. This is because they can be headstrong and require a firm and patient hand when training. Some owners disagree with this rating and have found that with reward-based training methods, Boxers have far above-average intelligence and working ability. It's important to make the time to train a young Boxer, so that his charming and playful boisterousness does not develop into uncontrolled energy as a big adult dog. Puppy classes are an excellent way of training and socialising at the same time, and this should be backed up with further socialisation sessions, especially when young.

The Kennel Club recommends more than two hours a day exercise for the breed, which loves a physical and mental challenge. A Boxer is a good choice if you are fit and spend a lot of time outdoors; they were bred as working dogs with plenty of muscle and stamina. They are canine athletes and many excel in agility, obedience and other sports. Because of their strength and courage, they are used for military, police and search-and-rescue work, and some are specifically trained as guard dogs.

The Boxer makes a good watchdog and will bark when somebody comes to the house. How they act to strangers varies and will largely depend on how they have been socialised. The breed is not aggressive

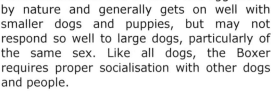

by nature and generally gets on well with smaller dogs and puppies, but may not respond so well to large dogs, particularly of the same sex. Like all dogs, the Boxer requires proper socialisation with other dogs and people.

These are companion dogs and do not do well when left alone for long periods; they are known for being extremely loyal and loving to their humans and often get on well with other dogs in the household. They have a sleek and short low-maintenance coat, which sheds but requires little grooming. The coat may be fawn or brindle, with or without white markings. In the USA, many have their ears cropped and tails docked. They are not a suitable breed for allergy sufferers.

Despite being a working dog, the Boxer is not suited to outdoor living. This is due to his short, fine coat and the fact that he is a brachycephalic (flat faced) breed, none of which tolerate extremes of temperature. If you are house-proud, a Boxer may not be the breed for you, they drool, snuffle, snore and are gassy!

They are listed in Breed Watch Category 1, no particular points of concern. But if you are buying a puppy, check his or her breathing – does it sound relaxed or laboured? Health issues include cancers, aortic stenosis (a heart problem), hypothyroidism, hip dysplasia and epilepsy. Ask a breeder about hip dysplasia and hypothyroidism. They are also prone to environmental and food allergies. Average lifespan is 10 to 12 years.

SUMMARY: A big, boisterous, lovable dog which needs plenty of physical and mental stimulation and a firm hand when training. Buy from healthy stock, many have shortened lives due to health problems.

Miniature Schnauzer

The Miniature Schnauzer is the most popular of the three Schnauzer breeds. The Schnauzer originated in Southern Germany in the 14th or 15th century when farmers and traders travelled around selling their skills and produce at markets. They needed a medium-sized, versatile dog, strong enough to guard the cart, but small enough to easily fit into it. These practical men also wanted a good ratter to keep down the vermin back at home.

They probably crossed the black German Poodle and the grey Wolfspitz with more than a pinch of Wire-Haired Pinscher. This 'prototype' most closely resembled today's Standard Schnauzer, and the Miniature Schnauzer was bred down from this, probably with Affenpinschers, and first exhibited as a separate breed in 1899.

In the USA, they are classed as Terriers, while they are in the Utility Group in the UK. Having owned a Mini for 10 years, I think they definitely have Terrier-like tendencies, especially when it comes to chasing small animals and birds. They also love to get their heads down and wander off after a scent. Many will live happily with cats and other small animals, but usually need to be introduced at an early age.

These stylish dogs are generally perky, playful, extrovert and very affectionate. Some owners would even say they have a sense of humour. They are adaptable and at home both in town and country. They need a medium amount of exercise – the exact amount will vary depending on what they have got used to - however, at least 30 to 45 minutes a day is recommended. When he was younger, ours was happy to go hiking all day. However, if you are looking for a jogging partner, the Standard Schnauzer is a better choice.

This is a handsome breed with a square, boxy shape and unique beard. Physically, these dogs combine elegance with a certain ruggedness and a jaunty gait. They are minimal shedders with a double coat, the outer coat trapping the dander, and this is a breed which allergy sufferers can consider. However, allergies are very individual things and you have to spend time with the specific puppy you are considering. The coat needs hand stripping or trimming every eight weeks, which is another expense to consider, and ears require regular cleaning as the small hairy ear canals are prone to infection.

Accepted coat colours are pepper and salt, black, and black and silver. White Minis are becoming increasingly popular, but are not accepted by the Kennel Clubs. There is no such thing as a 'teacup' Schnauzer, this is a marketing term used by breeders of undersized Schnauzers, and health problems have been reported with some 'teacups'.

Minis make good watchdogs and, although they may be quiet as puppies, they get more vociferous as they grow in confidence. Adults will usually bark when somebody knocks at the door, and most will then greet the intruder like a long lost friend. They are not by nature laid-back dogs, so don't expect them to be happy to snooze in a corner all day. They want to be involved and demand your attention. If you have a garden, you'll have to fence them in to stop them running off in pursuit of small animals and birds, or simply to say hello to passers-by.

Mini Schnauzers want to be with humans, they love being part of the family and form strong bonds with their owners. They definitely don't like being left alone and can suffer from separation anxiety if not trained to be apart from their humans for short periods from an early age. They often do well with another Schnauzer or dog in the household.

Early training and socialisation is important. Get them used to other dogs and people, traffic, loud noises and other new experiences. Some Minis are frightened of loud bangs, but socialisation can help. They are often easily distracted by people, other dogs or interesting smells, so training should be kept short and fun. They are, however, intelligent and have a great desire to please their owners, so they generally soon pick up new commands and housetraining. They are listed as the 12th most intelligent dog in the Intelligence of Dogs list.

Minis thrive on their owners' attention and may even follow them around the house. They like to sleep on the bed or at least in the same room, when allowed. They make excellent companions, but given too much attention and a free rein, can develop 'Little Emperor' or 'Small Dog Syndrome' and become stubborn, attention-seeking and even snappy.

It's sometimes easy to forget that they are canines and not humans, and difficult not to form strong emotional bonds with these affectionate little dogs that become members of the family. But it's important to keep training going throughout their lifetime to remind them every now and again that you are in charge. Properly trained and socialised, they make delightful companions.

They are listed in Breed Watch Category 1 with no major points of concern. Diets should be low in fat and sugars to avoid potential problems and health issues to ask a breeder about are cataracts, diabetes, Cushing's disease, bladder stones and pancreatitis. Skin issues caused by environmental allergies are not uncommon in Minis, including ours. These can usually be managed with tablets and food supplements. Ask the breeder if the parents have any history of allergies. For more information visit www.max-the-schnauzer.com or read **The Schnauzer Handbook** http://amzn.to/1uNQGjx for detailed information on the breed.

SUMMARY: Stylish and playful breed with a perky personality. Some are more Terrier-like than others, check the temperament of the parents. Also ask breeders if there is a history of skin problems or allergies. A possibility for allergy sufferers.

Shih Tzu

The exact origins of this breed are unknown, but they stretch back some 3,000 years. The Shih Tzu is thought to have originated in Tibet and developed in China as a result of crossing the Lhasa Apso and Pekingese. The Shih Tzu was the house pet for most of the Ming Dynasty and they were so prized that the Chinese refused to sell or give away any of the dogs for many years.

The first were imported into Europe (England and Norway) in 1930, and classified as "Apsos" by the Kennel Club. The European breed standard was written in England in 1935 by the Shih Tzu Club. The breed was introduced to the United States after World War II, when returning soldiers brought the dogs back from Europe. The American Kennel Club recognised the Shih Tzu in 1969 and classed it in the Toy Group; it is in the Utility Group in the UK. The name comes from the Chinese for "lion dog."

As with most breeds, the temperament of the individual Shih Tzu varies from one to the next. However, the breed's typical character is loyal, affectionate, extravert and alert. The Shih Tzu was bred solely as a companion dog for occupiers of the palaces and he is sweet natured and generally friendly and trusting with all people, including strangers.

In contrast, the similar-looking Lhasa Apso was bred to alert monks to intruders inside Buddhist temples, and can be wary of strangers until he gets to know them. Shih Tzu tend to be a bit more playful and affectionate than the Lhasa, which may be bolder. Both breeds are confident and cheerful.

The Shih Tzu loves to carry himself in a haughty manner with his head and tail held high, and looks resplendent when just groomed. Their nickname in 1930s England was 'the chrysanthemum dog', and the breed standard calls for a chrysanthemum face, meaning that the hair should grow in all difference directions. The coat of the Shih Tzu may come in many different colours, but all have long, fine hair.

Although there is no such thing as a non-shedding dog, the breed is a minimal shedder and is suitable for consideration by allergy sufferers (as is the Lhasa). He has a beautiful coat, but the downside is that it needs daily grooming to prevent matting, so you will have to allow time for this. You'll also have to factor in the expense of a trip to the groomer's every few weeks. Some owners favour the sheared look as it is easier to keep clean and tangle-free. The Shih Tzu's facial wrinkles and ears also need to be cleaned regularly by the owner.

On the positive side, this is a breed which, despite being sturdy, requires little exercise as it is not particularly active, being more of a lap dog. He's happy as long as he's with you and a couple of short walks a day are enough, The Kennel Club describes the exercise requirement as "up to an hour a day," making Shih Tzu suitable for the elderly or for people who live in apartments.

The Shih Tzu is listed 70th, two places below the Lhasa, in The Intelligence of Dogs list. The breed is in the 'Lowest Degree of Working/Obedience Intelligence' category. Some are not the easiest of dogs to train, they can have a stubborn streak. It is worth putting the time in early on to teach the Shih Tzu basic commands and manners around the house.

They are notoriously difficult to housetrain, so vigilance is needed early on to ensure that this does not become an issue. Some dogs eat faeces (coprophagia) and for some inexplicable reason, Shi Tzu can be particularly prone to doing this. Clean up poo(p) regularly and keep cat litter trays out of reach.

The Shih Tzu is in Breed Watch Category 1, no major points of concern. But like all brachycephalic (flat faced) breeds - including the Lhasa Apso - Shih Tzu can easily overheat, some may have difficulty breathing and anaesthetic can present a risk. Choose a puppy that appears to breathe normally and a veterinarian who is familiar with brachycephalic breeds. For walks, use a harness rather than a collar, as this can exert pressure on the narrow windpipe.

Other health issues include allergies, hip dysplasia and eye problems (ask to see the breeder's health screening certificates for these two issues), congenital liver shunt, teeth and gum problems, and disk disease.

If you are looking for a puppy, be aware that there is no such breed as an 'imperial' or 'teacup' Shih Tzu. These are terms used by unrecognised breeders to describe oversized or undersized pups they have bred and should be avoided. Choose an accredited breeder. The Shih Tzu is long lived, from 10 to 16 years. A UK Kennel Club survey puts the average life span at 13 years and 2 months.

SUMMARY: Characterful companion dog who likes to be with people and has low exercise requirements. The breed can be difficult to housetrain. He's a sweet companion dog in households where the owner - not the dog - is pack leader. A possibility for allergy sufferers.

Lhasa Apso

The Lhasa Apso has a fascinating history. It was bred as an indoor watch dog to alert monks in Buddhist monasteries to any intruders who entered. The breed's keen hearing and sharp bark warned the monks, like a modern day burglar alarm, if an intruder got past the exterior guards, which were often Mastiffs. Lhasa Apso means 'long-haired dog from Lhasa', the capital of Tibet.

Incredibly, the Lhasa Apso originated over 4,000 years ago as a small breed of mountain wolf. They were domesticated and actively bred as long ago as 800 BC, which makes it one of the 14 oldest dog breeds in the world. Despite most people thinking of the Lhasa as a cuddly lap dog, recent research has shown it to be one of the breeds most closely related to the ancestral wolf.

Some of the breed's physical characteristics - such as the head and body structure, dense double coat which flows over the eyes, and muscled body - have evolved as a result of the breed's native land and climate. High altitudes, a dry windy climate, dusty terrain, short hot summer and long bitterly cold winter of the Himalayas have all led to the dog we see today.

Tibetans believed that the bodies of Lhasas could be entered by souls of deceased lamas (holy men, not woolly camelids) while they awaited rebirth into a new body and so they were never sold, only ever given as a gift. In the early 1900s, a few were brought to England by soldiers returning from the Indian subcontinent, they then were called the Lhasa Terrier. Today the Lhasa is classed in the Utility Group in the UK and the Non-Sporting Group in the USA (unlike the Shih Tzu, which is classed in the Toy Group in the USA).

Referred to in Tibet as the Bearded Lion Dog, this is also how the dog sees himself. It is said that when a Lhasa Apso looks in the mirror, he sees a lion, as the adult Lhasa is one of the hardiest, toughest and strongest-willed of all the small breeds. He was bred to do a job, to guard the monastery, rather than as a companion (as the Shih Tzu was) and still retains some of these inherited characteristics.

Some have a heightened sense of hearing and other senses, and many like jumping up on to the furniture to get a good look-out position – especially if they are awaiting your return. This breed is not suitable for people out of the home a lot. Lhasas thrive on being with their owners and families; many develop separation anxiety if left alone too long. If you get one, start by leaving your puppy for short periods and then gradually add a few minutes to the length of time you are absent.

Like the Shih Tzu, the Lhasa carries himself in an imperial manner, but unlike the Shih Tzu, Lhasas can be wary of strangers and even aggressive towards them if not properly trained. They require socialisation with other dogs and people, not only as puppies, but throughout their lives.

Listed 68th, two places above the Shih Tzu, in The Intelligence of Dogs list, the breed is in the 'Lowest Degree of Working/Obedience Intelligence' category. Despite having an independent streak, Lhasas do like to please their owners and generally enjoy training sessions –

provided they are not too long. They require patience when housebreaking, as they can sometimes taken months to get the hang of it. Early vigilance is the key.

So what's the attraction - apart from their incredibly appealing looks? Well, there are many. They are fiercely loyal to their owners and, as long as they know who is boss and are properly socialised, they make wonderful, entertaining companions with relatively few health problems. They are spirited and affectionate and with training, very obedient with their owners.

However, like all small dogs, they can develop "Little Emperor Syndrome" if allowed to rule the household, and this manifests itself in barking and even snapping. Treat this hardy little chap like a dog, not a child and you will be rewarded with a loyal and affectionate companion.

The breed has a dense, double coat, which flows straight and long over the entire body, including the head and eyes, to the floor. This is a breed for consideration by allergy sufferers. Any colour of coat is acceptable in the show ring, where this handsome dog excels, but gold, cream and honey are the most popular. The coat may also be dark-

grizzle, slate, smoke and multi-colours of brown, white and black.

Puppy coats often change colour as the dog grows. Daily grooming is required to prevent knots and tangles, which is why many owners who do not show their Lhasas have their hair cut short. The cost of a trip to the groomers should be factored in when buying a Lhasa.

This breed does not need much exercise, although will happily walk for miles over any terrain. He has a jaunty gait and carries his head high in a regal fashion, all set off by his beautiful plumed tail.

The Lhasa Apso is in Breed Watch Category 1, no major points of concern. But like all brachycephalic (flat faced) breeds, some can experience breathing problems and all overheat easily. Anaesthesia can also pose a risk, so choose a free-breathing puppy and then a vet familiar with brachycephalic breeds. A Lhasa has a thick coat and should be monitored in hot weather. Generally, this breed is regarded as one of the healthiest, although some suffer from sebaceous adenitis, a hereditary skin disease. Eye conditions can be another issue, ask to see the breeder's eye screening certificates.

Lhasas are long lived, some have even reached 20 years old. A Kennel Club survey put the median lifespan at 14 years 4 months, while data from a UK vet clinic put it at 13 years exactly.

SUMMARY: A hardy, loyal companion with a strong character. Suitable for apartment life and for consideration by allergy sufferers. Some can be difficult to housetrain.

Cavalier King Charles Spaniel

The Cavalier King Charles is the only Spaniel not classed in the Gundog Group. Instead it is listed in the Toy Group by the major Kennel Clubs. It is one of the most popular breeds in the UK and is now in the top 20 in the US.

The Cavvie's ancestors are the small Spaniels seen in so many famous paintings dating back to the 16th, 17th and 18th centuries. In the 1500s Toy Spaniels were quite common as ladies' pets, and King Charles II (1630-1685) was so fond of his little Spaniels that he decreed they should be accepted in any public place - even the Houses of Parliament - and this still stands today.

It was during the late 1700s that the King Charles Cavalier Spaniel changed radically when it was interbred with flat-nosed (brachycephalic) breeds. It is said that all modern Cavaliers can trace their ancestry back to six dogs and, sadly, the breed is affected by a number of inherited defects. Cavaliers were one of the breeds featured on the 2008 BBC programme **Pedigree Dogs Exposed**.

This highlighted the breed's suffering caused by a distressing neurological condition called syringomyelia, resulting from having a large brain in a small skull and thought to affect up to half of all CKCs. The other major issue affecting almost all Cavvies is an inherited heart condition called mitral valve disease - the number one killer of the breed. Do not consider buying a Cavvie puppy unless you see the breeder's health screening certificates for these problems. The breed is in Breed Watch Category 1.

The Cavvie is smaller than other Spaniels and in character is a cross between a lap dog and a sporting dog. He is first and foremost a companion and is entirely dependent on humans for his happiness, so don't consider one if you are out at work all day; he won't be happy. On the other hand, he needs more exercise than other dogs in the Toy group. The Kennel Club recommends up to an hour a day.

Cavvies are fairly adaptable, some love to take part in organised activities, while others are more sedate, they tend to take after their owners in this respect. As long as they are regularly exercised every day, they can be suitable for apartment life. They do, however, have a natural instinct to chase small animals and birds. And early socialisation is important to prevent them from becoming too timid.

The CKC is an affectionate, undemanding and easy to train family dog which does well with children. Care should be taken with young children and puppies, as the pups are very small and delicate. Temperaments vary within the breed, some will bark at visitors, many won't. They are generally friendly with everyone, their tails wag constantly and they are very affectionate, loving to snuggle up in your lap – if you'll let them. They are lower down the Intelligence of Dogs list than most other Spaniels, number 44 in the 'Average Working/Obedience Intelligence' section. They are, however, generally easy to train and quick to housetrain.

Their coat is long and silky with plenty of feathering, and comes in colours with marvellous names: Blenheim (rich chestnut), Black and Tan, Ruby and Tricolour. It requires regular grooming and ear cleaning to prevent infections. The breed is regarded as high shedding and is not at all suitable for allergy sufferers. Regular trips to the grooming salon for a trim and clean-up will have to be factored in when considering this gentle, handsome breed. Lifespan for a healthy Cavvie is over 12 years.

SUMMARY: The Cavvie is a sweet, well-mannered dog with lower exercise requirements than other Spaniels, although they still need a couple of walks a day. Choose your puppy carefully, with health being the main consideration.

Dachshund

Strictly speaking, this is not one breed, but six! There are two sizes (Standard and Miniature) and three coat types (Long-Haired, Smooth-Haired and Wire-Haired). The name means 'badger dog' in German and all are classed in the Hound Group by the Kennel Clubs. Some breed experts argue that with their love of digging and feisty personality, Dachshunds - particularly the Wire-Haired - have characteristics more akin to the Terrier Group.

In the UK, the Miniature Smooth-Haired Dachshund is the most popular of all the six types. The Wire-Haired is the least popular coat in the US, despite being the most common in Germany and the most recent to appear in breed standards.

Some historians believe the early roots of the Dachshund can be traced as far back as Ancient Egypt, following discovery of engravings featuring short-legged hunting dogs. The earliest specific references appear in 18th century books when they were originally called a 'Dachs Kriecher' (badger crawler) or 'Dachs Krieger' (badger warrior). The original German dogs were bigger, weighing 30lb to 40lb, and were either straight-legged or crook-legged - modern Dachshunds are descended from the crooked-legged type.

With his long body, short legs and paddle-like paws for digging, the standard Dachshund was bred to scent, chase and flush out badgers and other burrow-dwelling animals. His distinctive shape has also led to the nickname of Wiener or Sausage Dog - my neighbour has even called her Dachshund 'Sizzles,' after the sound of sausages frying! The Miniature Dachshund was developed to hunt smaller prey, such as rabbits, and in the American West they have also been used in hunting prairie dogs. Today they are bred as family pets and for showing, although some participate in earthdog trials in North America.

Like all hounds, the Dachshund has a keen sense of smell and he'll be off after a small animal or bird as quick as he can. Make sure he is on the lead near traffic as, like a Terrier, he'll dash off after anything moving, regardless of whether cars are in the way or not. Dachshunds are lively and playful; little dogs with a lot of character. The Americans call them "spunky", the Brits have a rather more reserved description: "courageous and determined." They love games and chase balls with great determination.

A Dachshund is bold and pretty sure of himself, resulting in many being stubborn and a challenge to train. American writer E. B. White wrote: "I would rather train a striped zebra to balance an Indian club than induce a dachshund to heed my slightest command. When I address Fred I never have to raise either my voice or my hopes. He even disobeys me when I instruct him in something he wants to do."

Boldness and independent minds are part of these dogs' character and appeal. The AKC states: "The Dachshund is clever, lively, and courageous to the point of rashness, persevering in above and below ground work, with all the senses well-developed. Any display of shyness is a serious fault."

Dachshunds are at number 49 in the Intelligence of Dogs list, in the 'Average Working/Obedience Intelligence' section. Although they don't need a great deal of exercise (up to 30 minutes a day), they can easily become bored, so a good owner ensures their 'Doxie' has plenty of entertainment and enough walks to keep him stimulated. Despite their size, Dachshunds have a relatively loud, deep bark, which they use frequently, making them excellent watchdogs - but sometimes a tad annoying for the neighbours.

They are loyal companions which can become very attached to one person. Early socialisation helps to prevent them becoming jealous and snappy with other people or dogs. For them to get on with a young child, a cat or other animal, it is a good idea to introduce them while the Dachshund is still a puppy. Unsocialised dogs may be tempted to nip a toddler. They often do well with other dogs, especially other Dachshunds and many owners have more than one. Left alone for long periods, Dachshunds can also suffer from separation anxiety and may whine or chew.

Although the Wire-Haired sheds less than the other varieties, none of the six breeds are hypoallergenic and therefore are not suitable for allergy sufferers. Grooming requirements are fairly minimal for the Smooth-Haired, while the Long-Haired needs more regular brushing. The Wire-Haired is a low shedder, but needs hand stripping or clipping every few weeks.

All Standard Dachshunds are in Breed Watch Category 1, while Miniatures are in Category 2 with the point of concern listed as "body weight/condition." If you are looking to get a puppy, the stand-out feature should be the short legs, not an extra-long back, which can cause health problems. One in four Dachshunds suffer from spinal problems, particularly intervertebral disk disease (IVDD). The problem will be made worse by obesity (not uncommon with Dachshunds), jumping on to furniture, rough handling and intense exercise. Lifespan is 12 to 15 years.

SUMMARY: In very general terms, the Wire-Haired tend to be the most energetic, mischievous and obstinate, probably due to the fact that they are thought to have some Terrier ancestry. Long-Haired Dachshunds tend to be the quietest and sweetest-natured – this may be attributable to their Spaniel ancestors – and the Smooth-Haired is most likely to be a one-person dog and less friendly with strangers. Miniature Dachshunds are often more active than Standards and other breeds are more suitable with very small children.

Poodle

The Poodle is not a single breed either, but three breeds: the Standard, Miniature and Toy Poodle. No round-up of dog breeds would be complete without discussing the Poodle, which has become extremely popular not only as a pedigree (purebred) dog in its own right, but has also been mated with other breeds to create many highly popular crossbreeds in recent years (much to the displeasure of pedigree Poodle breeders).

The Poodle has been the stud of choice due to his unique coat with its non-shedding (technically, low-shedding) properties.

The Poodle is a water dog which originated in Germany, where its name – Pudelhund – meant 'splash in water dog'. The Standard Poodle is considered the original and was a gundog used mainly for hunting duck and sometimes upland birds. Large Poodles have featured in paintings dating back to the 15th century.

Although developed in Germany, the breed was standardised in France, where its popularity led to it becoming the national breed. There is some evidence that the smaller types developed only a short time after the large Poodle. The Toy Poodle, the smallest of the three, was known in England as early as the 18th century. All three types are classed in the Utility Group in the UK. In the US, the Standard and Miniature (which is actually medium-sized) are in the Non-Sporting Group, while the Toy is unsurprisingly classed in the Toy Group.

Apart from his striking appearance, the Poodle has two other outstanding features: his coat and his intelligence. Yes, the Poodle has beauty AND brains! After the Border Collie, the Poodle is the most intelligent canine on the planet, according to the Intelligence of Dogs List.

One of the biggest misconceptions is that Poodles, with their often elaborate hairstyles, are somehow 'soppy' dogs. Nothing could be further from the truth – these clever, handsome dogs are full of character, as any owner will testify.

Poodles have been used as working dogs in the military since at least the 17th century, and in 1942 the Poodle was one of 32 breeds officially classified as war dogs by the Army. Due to their intelligence, they need plenty of challenges in the form of both physical and mental stimulation. You don't want a bored Poodle on your hands. Many Standards in particular are boisterous, lively dogs which need a lot of exercise and challenge. They excel at agility and obedience classes, being both athletic and highly intelligent.

All Poodles – even small ones - like to run, play and swim, and exercise is a necessity for their happiness. With a Standard this may be one to two hours a day. Miniature and Toy Poodles require less, it will vary from one individual dog to the next. All Poodles are among the easiest to train of all the breeds.

They pick up obedience, housetraining and tricks easily – and indeed, most love being the centre of attention and showing off their skills. Make sure to spend the time housetraining, some males have a tendency to mark their territory - and that can be indoors if not educated otherwise.

All three types are attentive to their owners and some are 'intuitive', picking up on their owner's moods. Because of this, some Poodles do not respond well to stress, tension, and loud noises. When choosing a puppy, go for one whose parents have calm temperaments, as some bloodlines can produce highly strung offspring.

They are also not dogs you can leave all day as they thrive on interaction with their owners and may suffer from separation anxiety if left alone too long. The Standard will get on with children if introduced

properly and the youngsters are not allowed to taunt him. Miniatures and Toys may have less patience with young children, with their accompanying antics and high noise levels. All Poodles should be properly socialised with other dogs and people, the smaller ones can become snappy and selfish if allowed to rule the roost, so puppy classes are recommended.

The Poodle's coat is the reason he has become so popular as one half of crosses such as the Labradoodle, Goldendoodle and Cockapoo. All three types of Poodle have a single layer coat of dense, curly fur almost like fleece. They shed hardly at all, are regarded as hypoallergenic and are suitable for consideration by allergy sufferers. The coat is beautiful when cared for and can be trimmed into a variety of exotic styles, or simply trimmed short for easy care.

The Poodle's is a coat of many colours. Solids include white, cream, black, brown, silver, grey, silver beige, apricot and red. Non-solid colours, such as parti (white and another colour), are NOT accepted by the Kennel Clubs, so if you buy one of these colours, the dog will not be Kennel Club registered or produced by an accredited breeder.

All Poodles are extremely high maintenance when it comes to grooming, requiring daily care to prevent the coat from becoming tangled and matted. The insides of ears should be cleaned and plucked regularly, as ear infections are common. They also need a visit to the groomer's every few weeks for a trim, which will add up to several hundred pounds - or dollars - a year.

Poodles are regarded as relatively healthy breeds. They are in Breed Watch Category 1, with no major points of concern. Health issues include Addison's disease (a hormonal problem), bloat, thyroid and skin problems, epilepsy and hip dysplasia.

SUMMARY: This highly intelligent and sensitive dog is highly rewarding if you can give him the time and stimulation he needs. Many Poodles prefer a quiet household which is not too stressful for them, so a different breed would be a better choice if you have a busy household full of noisy children. The breed is hypoallergenic.

Chihuahua

The Chihuahua's claim to fame is that he is the smallest of all the dog breeds - but he compensates by having a big personality. He is also the oldest recognised breed in the Americas. Unsurprisingly, these diminutive dogs are classed in the Toy Group by all the Kennel Clubs.

There are two types: the Long-Coated Chihuahua - the most popular type in the UK - and the Smooth-Coated Chihuahua (called Long-Haired and Short-Haired in the USA). They are classed as two breeds in the UK, despite being very similar apart from coat, and two types of the same breed in the USA.

The history of the Chihuahua has fuelled much debate. It is thought that the breed was already present at the time of the Toltec civilisation in ninth century Mexico and that it is a descendent of the Techichi, a slightly larger and sturdier dog. What is known is that the Chihuahua takes its name from the Mexican state of the same name.

In the US, the breed first became popular in bordering states such as Texas, New Mexico and Arizona before spreading across the rest of the continent. The Chihuahua is one of the oldest registered breeds in the US. A Chihuahua called Midget was the first to be officially registered by the American Kennel Club in 1904, just 20 years after the formation of the AKC.

When picking a puppy it is extremely important to make your decision based on a number of factors: the breeder's track record, health certificates and the temperament of the parents. This is especially true of Chihuahuas, where their temperament varies enormously, with the biggest single factor being the temperament of the parents. Often these dogs are lively and bold, but some may be timid, while others are more sedate.

Chihuahuas are complex characters. They are generally entertaining, extremely loyal to their owners and eager to give and receive affection from them. They make great companion dogs as they form such a strong bond with their owners and require little exercise – up to 30 minutes a day is enough - making them suitable for the elderly. They get exercise running round the house and garden, but all dogs have a need to 'migrate' and this is satisfied with a daily walk away from the home enjoying new experiences and places to sniff.

They are also very fond of snuggling up and sleeping under the covers with you, if you allow them to. All Chihuahuas shed, although not very much, but nevertheless they are not regarded as suitable for allergy sufferers. A Chihuahua can appear to be a calm even-tempered dog until somebody new knocks on your door, and if you have more than one they will bark in unison. One of the downsides of some Chihuahuas is that they are very noisy, barking at the slightest thing. Early socialisation is the key.

The main factor, other than parentage, governing your Chihuahua's character is how you socialise and train him. A well-socialised and trained Chi is a delight to live with. From puppyhood get them used to different people, dogs, noises and experiences to help them become less suspicious.

Teach them to respect their place in the household, and, above all, treat them like a dog, not a baby. They are strong willed and can be difficult to train, listed at number 67 in the Intelligence of Dogs, just scraping into the 'Fair Working/Obedience Intelligence' section.

The best way to train a Chihuahua is to get him engaged by persuading him that what you are doing is fun. Praise and food are powerful training tools, this breed does not respond well to shouting.

Training is essential if you don't want your little Chi to develop 'Small Dog Syndrome,' where he becomes manipulative and rules the roost, resulting in him being a pain in the you-know-what to live with. Aggression from a dog is not comical and should not be tolerated, no matter how small the dog.

Interestingly, Chihuahuas seem to prefer other Chihuahuas to other dog breeds, towards whom they can be aggressive if not socialised as a pup. They can have very delicate legs and some may be unpredictable around youngsters, so this breed is not recommended if you have small children. They also don't tolerate cold very well, or being left along for long periods, as they have been bred as companion dogs. In short, don't baby your Chi. Properly treated and knowing his place in the household, he will be an affectionate companion.

There are no such things as teacup, miniature or micro Chihuahuas. These are names invented by breeders who create under-sized examples of the breed. Chihuahuas are small enough already. Inexperienced breeders meddling about with genetics by making size the only consideration only leads to health and temperament problems. Buy a Chihuahua within the breed standard guidelines (4lb to 6lb in the UK, 2lb to 6lb in the USA) from a breeder recommended by the Kennel Club in your country.

Another thing to look out for is the shape of the dog's head, only the apple shape is accepted by the Kennel Clubs. If you want to show your dog, it should have a well-rounded domed head like an apple. The deer head is more elongated with a longer, narrower snout (more like a deer) and does not conform to the breed standard, resulting in disqualification from any show run under Kennel Club rules. A deer head Chihuahua typically has a longer body and legs than the apple head, but not always.

Chihuahuas are in Breed Watch Category 1, no major point of concern. Health issues include neurological issues such as seizures, hydrocephalus and low blood sugar. Choose a vet proficient with tiny Toy breeds.

SUMMARY: Teach him his place in the household and you will have a loving and loyal companion which requires little exercise. Above all, treat a Chihuahua like a dog, not a baby. Because of their size and delicate nature, they are not recommended for homes with small children.

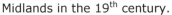

Staffordshire Bull Terrier

Like the Bulldog and the Boxer, the origins of the Staffordshire Bull Terrier lie with the big Mastiffs way back in the mists of time. The breed today is a mixture of Bulldog and Terrier, created in the English Midlands in the 19th century.

The Bulldog was used for bull baiting and during these bloodthirsty bouts, these athletic, fearless dogs would hold on to the bull with their powerful jaws, often being tossed off and injured.

In 1832 the sport was finally banned, and after that working men began crossing the courageous Bulldog with smaller, tenacious Terriers to create a dog to fight in dog pits – a less expensive and often clandestine sport which also took place in the US.

This dog was originally known as the Bull and Terrier. It had the powerful jaws and bravery of the Bulldog, but its Terrier heritage made the dog smaller, faster and more agile. A group of enthusiasts sought to adapt the Bull and Terrier to create an animal more suited to the show ring and family home. It became known as the Staffordshire Bull Terrier and was officially recognised in the UK in 1935, and in America in 1975. Today the 'Staffie' is classed in the Terrier Group.

The Staffordshire Bull Terrier is, perhaps, one of the most maligned breeds. There has been a tendency in recent years for some young men to keep these former fighting dogs – and dogs crossed with Staffies - as macho status symbols, encouraging them to be aggressive. This has led to some bad publicity for this much-loved breed. Like all powerful breeds, the Staffie needs proper handling. Yet with the right training and socialisation, he makes an excellent family companion.

RSPCA chief vet Mark Evans has said: "Staffies have had a terrible press, but this is not of their own making—in fact they're wonderful dogs. If people think that Staffies have problems, they're looking at the wrong end of the dog lead! When well cared for and properly trained they can make brilliant companions. Our experience suggests that problems occur when bad owners exploit the Staffie's desire to please by training them to show aggression."

The original Staffordshire Bull Terriers were trained to be highly aggressive with other dogs, but placid enough with people to allow them to be handled. A much toned-down version sums up the natural instincts of the breed today: wonderful with adults and children, but can show aggression towards other dogs if not properly socialised. Some will chase cats and never get along with other animals in the house, while others socialise well if introduced at an early age. If you have other pets, you need to make sure the Staffie will get on with them before committing yourself to the puppy.

The Staffie is a muscular, athletic dog, with males often being somewhat bigger than females. Energy levels vary from one dog to the next depending on what they get used to, but an hour a day is recommended for most. The breed has stamina and if you're a fitness or outdoors enthusiast, a Staffie will happily get used to more. Exercise is important to keep his muscles toned and to prevent obesity, which the breed is prone to.

They are not recommended for apartment living due to their exercise requirements and if you have a garden or yard, make sure you have a high fence around it – this dog can jump and dig as well as run, which is why most love agility and obedience competitions. The breed has plenty of character and enthusiasm for life, loves to be stroked and is surprisingly sensitive for such a tough looking canine. Expect to be nuzzled, licked and nudged by your Staffie.

At home he is gentle, affectionate and adaptable. Like the Bulldog, the Staffie loves his family, especially children, and has even been nicknamed the 'Nanny Dog' because of his devotion to them. Inside the home he loves nothing better than assuming the role of couch potato on your couch - where else? – surrounded by his family. As with all dogs, time spent with young children should be supervised.

He has been bred to be a companion dog and thrives on being with people, he dislikes being left alone for extended periods. Left to his own devices he may well chew and his powerful jaws can inflict some serious damage on your prize possessions. All Staffies chew, especially when young, so buy a selection of durable toys he can work his way through.

The Staffie is not mentioned in The intelligence of Dogs although his cousin, the American Staffordshire Terrier, just makes it into the top half of the list in the 'Above Average Working Dogs' section. Like all Bully breeds, the Staffie can be an independent thinker and have a stubborn streak, so he needs to learn his position in the household – and that should be below you. Obedience training and socialisation with other dogs and people should be an absolute priority. Don't let him off the lead until he has learned to behave around other dogs. Training should be reward-based - never punishment-based - and a firm but patient approach is the best method.

The Staffordshire Bull Terrier has a low-maintenance short, smooth coat which requires a weekly brush and sheds a little, so is not suitable for allergy sufferers. Colours can be red, fawn, white, black or blue or any one of these with white, as well as brindle or brindle with white. Staffies should not be kept outdoors, they are a brachycephalic breed and do not tolerate heat or cold.

Classed in Breed Watch Category 2, the points of concern are: "Difficulty breathing, Misplaced lower canine teeth." Ask the breeder about screening certificates for hereditary cataracts and L2HGA, a metabolic disorder. A UK Kennel Club survey puts the median lifespan at 12.75 years, while UK vet clinic data puts it at 10.

SUMMARY: This breed does not deserve its bad Press. With a responsible owner, socialisation with other dogs and training, this is a very loving and affectionate family dog which is good with children. Generally healthy and low maintenance.

Whippet

The Whippet was bred to hunt by sight, coursing game over open land at high speed and the breed is descended from the Greyhound. References to this sleek hound go all the way back thousands of years to Ancient Egypt when the pharaohs bred a small sight hound to keep in their palaces. In medieval England a small type of greyhound became popular for ratting, but the first use of the word 'Whippet' to describe a type of dog was not until 1610.

The history of the breed involves an element of cruelty. The original Whippets were English Greyhounds that were too small for stag hunting in the forests. These dogs were often returned to their peasant breeders, who were not allowed to hunt, so the dogs were maimed - usually by cutting a leg tendon or removing the toes of one paw. However, the owners kept and bred these dogs, producing a smaller version of a Greyhound that was ideal for hunting rats, hares and rabbits. When the hunting laws changed, these small Greyhounds became very popular for coursing and dog racing and were known as 'snap dogs' for their tendency to snap up prey.

In the 1800s Whippet racing was a major sport, especially among coal miners and other working men in northern England and Wales, resulting in the nickname of 'the poor man's racehorse.' Whippet racing is still practised in the UK and USA - although these days the hare is electric - and the breed loves events such as agility, flyball and lure coursing. Despite being developed in Britain, the Whippet was recognised by the American Kennel Club first in 1888, followed by the (UK) Kennel Club three years later. The breed has since won Best in Show at both Crufts and Westminster.

The Whippet is a sight hound, it sees prey and runs... and runs... and runs! Pound for pound this dog is the fastest canine on the planet, reaching speeds of up to 35mph and weighing as little as 15lb – although American Whippets tend to be larger than their British cousins. If you are considering getting a Whippet, know that this dog is hard wired for speed and should be allowed to run free every day in order to be truly content. A Whippet in full flight is a joy to behold, when the true instinct of the dog is there for all to see. This natural athlete has it all: speed, poise, balance, style, elegance and a tremendous turn of speed over short distances.

Provided they get enough daily exercise, they are normally calm at home, being perfectly happy to snooze most of the rest of the day away. The Whippet is a charming dog, he can be summed up in three words: neat, sweet and fleet. Because early Whippets were bred to run with other dogs without fighting, they have an even temperament and usually do well with other canines. Being pack hounds they thrive in households with other dogs. They still have an extremely strong instinct to chase small animals, including cats, so if you already have a cat, a Whippet might not be a suitable choice.

These favourites of the working classes also endured cramped conditions with their humans and learned to live alongside them in a gentle and unobtrusive manner. They still like to be close to their humans and may follow their owner around the house or snuggle up on the couch. Being athletic and without much padding on their bones, they love a soft surface and can easily jump up on to furniture - or even kitchen worktops if there's food about - so train them not to jump up when they are young.

Generally the Whippet has more energy than a Greyhound and wants to be closer to his owners. He is amusing and playful in a gentle way, particularly when young. He should be trained and socialised, not only to get him used to other animals, but some Whippets can be highly strung (or over-sensitive) if not exposed to loud noises, traffic, new people and places early in their lives. He does not usually like rowdy households and can become frightened or stressed by too much noise. Indoors he is calm - although he might have an occasional mad five minutes, especially as a pup or adolescent. He is eager to please and with kindness and patience, should be relatively easy to train and housebreak.

Like other hounds, the Whippet has an independent mind, a minority can even be aloof. The Whippet is at number 51 with the Wire Fox Terrier in the 'Average Working/Obedience Intelligence' section of the Intelligence of Dogs list. The AKC says: "Amiable, friendly, gentle, but capable of great intensity during sporting pursuits." However well you train a Whippet, you may not be able to stop him racing after prey, such as squirrels or rabbits. Unless you are looking for a watch dog, the

Whippet has another advantage over some breeds: many almost never bark. Some bark when they are excited, others may be vocal when demanding something from you. Whippets love company and one left alone too much may also bark and whine

The breed has a short coat and, unusually, any colour is acceptable. The fine coat requires only minimal grooming, as Whippets are generally very clean animals, but they should not be left outside as they feel the cold easily. They are light shedders and so generally not suitable for allergy sufferers.

The Whippet is a healthy breed, listed in Category 1 of Breed Watch. However, he may occasionally nick and tear his thin skin while racing around. The Whippet has a large heart, some have an arrhythmia and many breeders also screen for eye and hearing disorders. Like other sight hounds, they are intolerant of barbiturate anaesthetics.

SUMMARY: A quiet, gentle addition to the household. Some can be sensitive to loud noises, etc, and others may be aloof. They need to run free to be truly happy.

Yorkshire Terrier

The Yorkshire Terrier comes from Yorkshire in northern England. The breed was developed by weavers in the 1850s to catch rats in the textile mills and his ancestors were various Terrier breeds, including some from Scotland, as well as a dog similar to the Skye Terrier and possibly even the Maltese.

A dog named Huddersfield Ben born in 1865 became the top show and stud dog and is considered to be the father of the modern Yorkshire Terrier.

The breed was first recognised in the UK in 1870 and 15 years later in America. Today this handsome and perky canine is one of the most popular breeds in North America, being consistently in the top 10.

Despite being classed in the Toy group, this feisty little canine is a true Terrier. Weighing just four to seven pounds, the Yorkie is one of the smallest breeds, but makes up for his lack of size with an assertive personality. The AKC describes the desired temperament as: "Brave, determined, investigative and energetic," and adds: "The dog's high head carriage and confident manner should give the appearance of vigor and self-importance."

The Yorkie is full of himself, his natural tendency is to chase anything small - and often to confront dogs much bigger than himself. Socialisation with other animals and dogs in puppyhood is extremely important. If not, Yorkies can bark or show aggression towards other dogs, causing them to pick fights which they have no chance of winning and can end badly. They can also be hostile towards strangers if not socialised with other people.

They are undoubtedly attention seekers and very affectionate with their owners. Whether a Yorkie turns out to be a delightful little companion or a snappy little aggressor depends very much on his owner. Treat him like a dog, not like a baby. An over-pampered Yorkshire Terrier is a pain in the ass; yappy, possessive, protective of his owner and grumpy with everybody else.

On the other hand, a properly trained Yorkie is a joy, he is loving, spirited, fun and well-rounded. Temperaments vary from one bloodline to the next, with some being more highly strung than others. Discuss this with a breeder and choose a puppy from more laid-back parents.

Yorkies are the most intelligent of all Terriers according to Stanley Coren's Intelligence of Dogs. They are at number 27, just one position below the 'Excellent Working Dogs' section. Although easy to train with treats and encouragement, the Yorkshire can be difficult to housetrain.

The secret to keeping him happy and well rounded - apart from training and socialisation - is to be around a lot of the time, a lonely Yorkshire becomes very grumpy, and give him enough daily exercise.

Despite being very small, he is still a canine and all have a natural need to migrate, or spend time outside the home. Up to 30 minutes a day is enough, making him eminently suitable for apartment living or as a companion for the elderly. The breed is tiny and delicate, and for this reason is not recommended for households with small children.

The Yorkie's stand out feature is his beautiful trademark coat. His silky hair must be glossy, fine and straight and is high maintenance. Traditionally the coat is grown very long and parted down the middle of the back, with some owners showing off their little companion with a topknot or ribbon.

To maintain the coat in optimum show condition requires regular expert grooming, so some owners have the coat regularly trimmed for easier care. Even if you are not showing your dog, daily grooming is required to keep the coat in tiptop condition and prevent matting. The good news is that the breed is regarded as hypoallergenic and therefore a suitable consideration for allergy sufferers, although anyone with allergies should spend time with the specific puppy before committing.

Puppies are born black and tan, showing an intermingling of black hair in the tan until they are matured, when the only acceptable colour is blue and tan. The blue is a dark steel blue, not silver blue and not mingled with fawn, bronze or black hairs. Prospective owners should be aware that these are the ONLY acceptable colours.

Some unaccredited breeders are charging high prices for "rare colours" - be aware **there is no such thing** and these dogs do not conform to breed standards. Similarly, there is no such thing as "teacup" Yorkshire Terriers. Undersized Yorkies weighing three pounds or less generally have a shorter life span, as they are especially prone to a range of health problems, including chronic diarrhoea and vomiting, they are even more sensitive to anaesthetic and more easily injured.

The Yorkie, although very sensitive to heat and cold, is fairly healthy, listed in Breed Watch Category 1 with no major points of concern. Generally the breed has delicate limbs and digestive system and does not always tolerate anaesthesia well, so choose a vet familiar with Toy breeds.

Unusually, the breed does not always lose its milk teeth when it should, so have your vet check the dog's mouth when visiting for regular checkups or vaccinations. Other health disorders include hypoglycaemia (low blood sugars), liver shunt, hip and eye disorders – ask to see the breeder's health certificates for this last issue. A healthy Yorkie is long-lived with a lifespan of over 12 years.

SUMMARY: A sparky little companion akin to a Terrier. Suitable for the elderly and a possibility for allergy sufferers, but not recommended for families with small children. Pick one from a bloodline with a history of even temperaments.

West Highland White Terrier

Scottish white terriers were recorded during the 16th century reign of King James VI of Scotland (1567-1625), who ordered a dozen terriers to be brought from Argyll, western Scotland, and presented as a gift to France. Sandy and brindle dogs were thought to be hardier than those

of other colours; white dogs were seen as weak. At various times, the Westie has been considered a white offshoot of both the Scottish Terrier (which is black) and the sandy coloured Cairn Terrier.

In 1588 a Spanish Armada ship carrying white Spanish dogs was wrecked off the Isle of Skye. Descendants of the survivors were kept separate from other breeds by Clan Donald. Other Skye families, including Clan MacLeod, preserved both white and sandy coloured dogs, It was recorded that at least two Clan chiefs kept white terriers, including "The Wicked Man," Norman MacLeod (1705-1772), 22nd Chief of Clan MacLeod.

The little-known Poltalloch Terriers and Pittenweem Terriers are thought to be the Westie's ancestors. Edward Donald Malcolm (1837-1930), 16th Laird of Poltalloch, is the man who is credited with developing the modern Westie. He hunted game and the story goes that after a reddish-brown Terrier was mistaken for a fox and shot, he decided to develop a white Terrier which became known as the 'Poltalloch Terrier'. The first generation of Poltallochs had sandy coloured coats and the trademark pricked ears. The name West Highland White Terrier first appeared in 1908.

Today the Westie is one of the most popular Terriers on both sides of the Atlantic, but particularly in the UK. He is classed in the Terrier Group and has a strong prey instinct, but is often easier to train and handle than some Terriers. The American Kennel Club says the breed is: "known for its friendly, strong-willed personality and a remarkably bright white coat. Said to be "all terrier," this breed possesses a large amount of spunk, determination and devotion stuffed into a compact little body. The confident Westie excels in a variety of AKC events, from conformation to agility to obedience."

The Kennel Club (UK) says: "The West Highland White has a cheerful, outgoing personality. He makes an ideal companion and playmate for youngsters as he is full of fun and virtually tireless. He is always ready for a walk come snow or shine, and is small enough to pick up and take anywhere. The right size for house or flat, he really is an all-purpose pet."

The Westie is ranked 47th in the Intelligence of dogs, in the Average Working/Obedience Intelligence section. The Westie does, however, respond well to training as he's motivated by food, and indeed is a better dog with a confident owner. A lack of leadership can lead to issues such as biting and possessiveness over food and even furniture. A Westie with an owner who shows firm, consistent leadership is a much happier dog and one less likely to develop 'Small Dog Syndrome'.

The temperament of this game little dog can vary; some are very child-friendly, while others prefer more solitude. But generally, the Westie has a cheerful personality and loves people, making an affectionate addition to any household. Like all Terriers, he is tenacious rather than laid-back. Typically the breed is independent, assured and self-confident. The AKC says that the Westie should be "possessed with no small amount of self-esteem" and generally this dog will NOT tolerate rough handling, such as a youngster tugging at its fur, tail or ears. This faithful companion generally travels well.

Like all Terriers, Westies make good watch dogs and will bark when someone knocks at the door, only too happy to greet them with a wagging tail or roll on their back for their tummy to be tickled by someone new.

They also live more happily alongside other dogs compared with some other Terrier breeds and are less aggressive towards strange dogs – although they may boss some dogs around! For a small dog, a Westie needs a fair amount of exercise - the Kennel Club recommends up to an hour a day. An under-exercised Westie can find plenty of mischief - including digging, barking and over-possessiveness.

A Westie's paws are slightly turned out to give the dog a better grip over rocky surfaces. In young puppies, the nose and paw pads are pink and slowly turn black. The white coat combines a soft dense undercoat with a rough outer coat. Daily brushing and regular clipping or stripping of the coat is necessary, and unless you can do this yourself, you'll have to pay for trips to the groomers every couple of months or so. The Westie is considered a hypoallergenic dog and so may be suitable for some allergy sufferers.

The breed is in Category 2 of Breed Watch, with points of concern listed as "Misplaced lower canine teeth and skin irritation". In fact, skin issues with Westies are well documented. Atopic dermatitis – which is hereditary - is the number one health issue reported by owners, affecting one in four dogs, followed by luxating patella, bowel disease and Legg-Calvé-Perthes Disease (a hip condition).

The American breed club puts the lifespan at 12 to 16 years, another survey says 11.4 years, while data from UK vet clinics shows an average lifespan of 10.5 to 15 years.

SUMMARY: An affectionate and lively dog for the right owner who is prepared to spend time training. Choose a puppy with even-tempered parents with no history of skin problems.

Border Collie

The herding sheepdog, or shepherd's dog, has probably been around in Britain since Neolithic times, which ended 4,000 years ago. During this period Man began to farm and he domesticated sheep, goats and dogs. The term 'shepherd's dog' was used to describe any canine which worked with sheep.

By the 18th century, this type of dog had become a necessity in Scotland, as sheep played an increasingly important role in the country's economy. The breed's name comes from its likely place of origin along the Anglo-Scottish border. Mention of the 'Collie' or 'Colley' first appeared in the late 19th century, although the word is older, thought to come from the old Celtic word for useful.

In Australia, New Zealand and parts of the US where there are still huge flocks of sheep, specialised types of sheepdogs have developed and are still used - heelers, barkers and dogs capable of going over the backs of closely packed sheep or driving them long distances. But in Britain and in parts of the US, the Border Collie has emerged as the dominant herding dog.

Many of the best Border Collies today can be traced back to a dog called Old Hemp (1893-1903), who sired over 200 puppies. He was bred by Adam Telfer, a Northumberland farmer who was not only a shepherd, but a breeder and great sheepdog trainer. Old Hemp isn't number one in the International Sheep Dog Society stud book as he was added after the book began.

The Border Collie is in the Pastoral Group in the UK and Herding Group in the USA. According to the Intelligence of Dogs List, this breed is the brainiest on the planet; numero uno. No other canine can match him for the speed at which he learns commands and then carries them out, as anyone who has seen a shepherd training a young Border Collie will testify. It's not unusual for a dog to learn a new command in a few minutes with only a few repetitions.

This hardy dog was bred for hill conditions and is outstanding when it comes to working sheep. Unlike specialists of the past, the Border Collie is able to perform a variety of tasks, and the defining traits of the breed are the silent use of the concentrated stare, or 'eye,' to control the sheep, the crouching creep and the wide-circling outrun to gather the flock.

The Border Collie's good looks and ferocious intelligence has led to it becoming very popular. Unfortunately, the dog has become a victim of its own success and many hundreds have ended up in rescue centres after the owners are unable to cope with their obsessive behaviour when under-exercised or under-stimulated.

This is not a dog that can ever be happy sitting at home all day, and if he doesn't get the daily hours of exercise he needs, then poor or destructive behaviour can result. This breed should only be considered by farmers, owners who live a predominantly outdoor life, or those who are prepared for several hours of outdoor exercise on a regular basis – hiking, biking, jogging or canine activity contests. This dog is a workaholic, has a low boredom threshold and extremely high energy levels.

While the Border Collie is undoubtedly loyal and loving and bonds quickly with the right owner, he requires continual stimulation - mentally, emotionally and physically - much more than the average dog. In fact, many Border Collie experts say that the breed does NOT make a great family pet.

If Collies don't have a job, they will find one. They may give you the 'eye,' watching you constantly, as if you were a sheep, and then rush in front of you if they think something is going to happen. They may chase and nip anything that moves to keep themselves busy - this may include passing traffic, other animals, you, and small children in particular. A bored Collie often exhibits obsessive behaviour, such as chasing lights, shadows or running water, or barking excessively at an object, animal or person.

A Border Collie has been bred to work all day ... and then the day after and the day after that. A long walk at weekend isn't going to satisfy him. This breed needs as much exercise as he can get, ideally several hours a day. He loves to fetch balls or sticks and absolutely excels at any canine activity ever invented. Their greatest desire is to please you with their actions and they like to go everywhere with you – even if this means sitting in the car or truck sometimes. A second active dog helps to keep the Border Collie amused and exercised - but then you have double the cost and responsibility.

Some can be highly sensitive – to emotions, noise etc - and all should be well socialised with other dogs when young to prevent them becoming too timid. The breed is affectionate with those it knows and trusts, but can be wary of strangers.

The Border Collie is physically hardy - many farmers keep them outside in kennels - and has a dense, weather-resistant double coat which sheds a lot, making them unsuitable for allergy sufferers. There are two types of coat: long and smooth, which is shorter. Many Border Collies are black and white, but a number of colours are permitted by the Kennel Clubs. The bred is hardy and healthy, being in Breed Watch Category 1, no major points of concern. Hip dysplasia, Collie eye anomaly (CEA) and epilepsy are the main hereditary diseases.

SUMMARY: An exceptional working dog for a farmer or active outdoorsy owner. However, this instinctive canine can be extremely challenging without enough exercise and entertainment. If you haven't got a few hours a day to exercise this dog, consider a less demanding breed.

Doberman Pinscher

We have a German tax collector to thank for this breed. The Doberman Pinscher, which is simply called the Dobermann in the UK, is unique as it is the result of specific breedings to produce anticipated characteristics in a protection dog. In other words, the purpose for this dog was determined before the breed existed. The Dobermann is the only breed known to have been developed for this purpose.

Herr Karl Friedrich Louis Dobermann was born in 1834 in Thuringia, Germany. He ran the local dog pound and worked as a tax collector by day and a police officer at night. He wanted a protection dog that was strong, agile, intelligent, loyal and fearless; such a dog did not exist in Germany at that time.

In 1880, Herr Dobermann began his breeding programme with Thuringian Shepherds (ancestors of the German Shepherd Dog), early Rottweilers and German Shepherds. He visited dog shows and breeding kennels to find the characteristics he wanted.

German Pinschers, Black and Tan Terriers, Weimaraners, Greyhounds and German Shorthaired Pointers are all thought to have contributed to his early breed stock. Years of trial and error went by before the breed capable of reproducing itself now known as the Doberman Pinscher emerged.

After Dobermann's death in 1894, the Germans named the breed Dobermann-pinscher in his honour, but 50 years later dropped the 'pinscher' on the grounds that this German word for Terrier was no longer appropriate. The British did the same a few years later. During World War II, the United States Marine Corps adopted the Doberman Pinscher as its official War Dog, although the Corps also used other breeds in the role.

Dobermanns were originally known for being ferocious and aggressive. As a personal protection dog they had to be big, bold and intimidating, but obedient enough to do so only on command. These traits served the dog well in its role as a personal protection dog or police dog, but were not ideal for a companion. In fact over the decades, the breed's aggression has been much toned down by modern breeders.

Today's Dobermanns are far more even tempered and good natured, some are even therapy dogs. They are very loyal, highly intelligent and easy to train, making them much more desirable as a house dog. They are ranked at number five in the Intelligent of Dogs List, being one of the brightest of all the dog breeds. A typical Dobermann is also energetic, bold, watchful and obedient.

A Doberman has a keen sense of hearing and is extremely alert, making him an excellent watch dog and guard dog - the very sight of him barking is enough to deter most intruders. In the US, the ears and tail are often cropped, although this is illegal in Europe. With his powerful physique, sleek coat and clean lines, the Dobermann is striking - one reason why he is one of the most popular breeds in the USA. Less so in the UK, possibly due in some part to the fact that houses and gardens are smaller, the breed is growing in popularity.

The Kennel Club says: "The Dobermann has a very adaptable outlook to life and fits into a family well, playing with and guarding children. He enjoys riding in a car, and will take over the most comfortable chair in the house without even a second thought. He makes an excellent obedience dog."

With so many good traits, what's the downside of a Dobermann? Well, the main point is that these are extremely muscular and energetic dogs, particularly when young, and need a great deal of exercise – over two hours a day is recommended.

They excel at mental and physical challenges, such as tracking, agility, Schutzhund and advanced obedience, and are a good choice if you are looking for a fitness partner when you hike, jog or cycle.

Dobermans are big chewers, especially when puppies or when not getting enough exercise. My friend's dog Jingo has chewed the sofa, carpet, wall, skirting boards and numerous shoes and gloves (in fact he completely ate the gloves), the only thing he hasn't chewed is the window sill. Crate training can be useful until a young dog learns not to chew.

They do not tolerate cold and are not suited to life outdoors, as they thrive on contact with humans - although they are not as needy as some breeds. They need a firm hand when training to learn that the human is the leader and they are the follower. Respect and protect are the bywords.

Early socialisation with other dogs, people and children is essential, as under-socialised Dobermanns can be aggressive. From puppyhood they should be taught to walk calmly on a lead and not pull. These are extremely powerful dogs and you don't want to get into a strength contest or battle of wills with a fully-grown Dobermann.

The low-maintenance coat is short and smooth, but sheds a little and so the breed is not one for allergy sufferers. Almost all Dobermanns are black and tan, but can also be brown, blue or fawn with rust-red markings.

In Breed Watch Category 1, there are no major points of concern and average lifespan is 10 to 11 years. However, there are a number of health issues which can shorten a dog's life. Dilated cardiomyopathy (DCM or enlarged heart) can lead to sudden death and is a major problem within the breed.

According to UFAW (Universities Federation for Animal Welfare), some 58% of all Dobermanns in Europe are affected. Breeding stock can be screened for the DCM gene with a blood test.

SUMMARY: A striking companion for energetic owners. Dominancy levels vary within litters, choose a pup which is not too dominant, as he will be less wilful and easier to train. Ensure the parents have been screened for DCM.

German Shorthaired Pointer

The German Shorthaired Pointer is a handsome and athletic dog which, as the name suggests, was developed in Germany as a versatile hunting dog. It is classed in the Gundog Group in the UK and Sporting Group in the USA.

Not a great deal is known about the exact origins of this highly intelligent and trainable breed, which is becoming increasingly popular with hunt and canine activity enthusiasts in both the UK and North America.

It is thought that the GSP was developed in Germany in the late 1800s to be an all-purpose hunting dog capable of carrying out a number of different tasks in the field, while being relatively easy to train.

According to the AKC, its ancestors were probably a breed known as the German Bird Dog, related to the old Spanish Pointer introduced to Germany in the 17th century. It is also likely that various German hound and tracking dogs, as well as the English Pointer and the Arkwright Pointer, also contributed to the development of the breed. As the first studbook was not created until 1870, it is impossible to identify all of the dog's ancestors. The breed was officially recognised by the AKC in 1930.

The GSP was bred to point, retrieve, track wounded game, hunt both large and small game - fur and feather - and to work in deep cover as well as in water. He was also intended to be a family companion, and is good with both adults and children. By temperament the typical GSP is highly active – as are most dogs bred to work – and requires at least two hours of exercise off the lead every day. He is ideally suited to sportsmen and women or active, ourdoorsy owners who want a dog they can take anywhere and who can give the dog the exercise he needs to be happy.

The selective breeding to produce the German Shorthaired Pointer has resulted in a highly intelligent dog, listed at number seventeen in the 'Excellent Working Dogs' section of the Intelligence of Dogs. However, this intelligence, combined with the breed's independent-mindedness, can lead to problems if the dog is not properly trained.

Many GSPs will ignore commands if they don't feel like obeying at that particular moment. They are scent hounds and easily distracted, setting off after an interesting scent or sight at the drop of a hat if not trained.

GSPs tend to be eager to please and training should start early with short, entertaining sessions. Even though some may appear physically mature at six months, their brain may not be engaged until they reach two years old, and you may find yourself with a child housed in the body of an adult dog.

Pups and adolescents tend to be very bouncy and completely unaware of everything else, so guard your young children and prize ornaments if you don't want them to get knocked over in the excitement.

A German Shorthaired Pointer thrives on structure and leadership, and is easily biddable with the right owner who is prepared to put in the time at the beginning. Training teaches the dog not only obedience, but gives him the confidence to carry out the commands. Well-trained GSPs excel in so many fields, not only hunting, but also field trials, obedience and agility events, search and rescue, bomb and drug detection, and even as therapy dogs. This is a dog which thoroughly enjoys to work.

The other stand-out feature of this striking breed is its unwavering loyalty to, and affection for, its humans. GSPs are very centred on their owners, and sometimes even referred to as 'Velcro' dogs, as they can be very clingy. They are not suitable to be left alone for hours on end every day, and neither should they be kept outside in a kennel. They need to be living as companions within the family home.

When lonely, they can lose confidence and become nervous or destructive or bark a lot. Although these are even tempered and good natured dogs, they can sometimes be mischievous – and will certainly make you laugh from time to time.

GSPs are not generally aggressive with other dogs or people. They can be reserved with strangers and make good watch dogs. They should, however, be socialised with other dogs when young, as some can show aggression towards strange dogs. They have an instinct to hunt, so if you have a cat, introduce them while the dog is still a pup.

Physically, the GSP is sleek and elegant yet powerful and muscular, appearing to possess every physical attribute a dog could ever wish for. The UK Kennel Club says: "Noble, steady dog showing power, endurance and speed, giving the immediate impression of an alert and energetic dog whose movements are well co-ordinated."

The breed is clean to keep and has a short, easy to maintain coat which sheds a little, making it unsuitable for allergy sufferers. The coat can be liver, liver and white, solid black or black and white; it may be spotted or ticked or both. Like all breeds with floppy ears, the GSP is prone to infections and regular ear cleaning should be a part of normal grooming. In the UK and Europe the tail is left natural unless working, in the USA the tail is docked to around half length.

This is a generally healthy breed which stays fit well into old age. It is listed in Breed Watch Category 1 with no major points of concern and has a typical lifespan of 12 to 14 years. A UK survey put the median age at 12 years, with one dog living 17 years. Health issues include hip dysplasia – ask to see screening certificates – heart, eye and skin disorders.

SUMMARY: A handsome and athletic working dog suitable for active owners and those with an interest in canine activities.

Jack Russell Terrier

The Jack Russell Terrier is the only breed in this list not recognised by the Kennel Clubs. KC and AKC recognition for the Jack Russell has been opposed by the breed's societies – which has resulted in the breeding and recognition of the not dissimilar Parson Russell Terrier.

The reason is outlined by the Jack Russell Club of America: "Jack Russell Terriers are a type, or strain, of working terrier; they are not pure bred in the sense that they have a broad genetic make-up, a broad standard, and do not breed true to type. This is a result of having been bred strictly for hunting since their beginning in the early 1800s, and their preservation as a working breed since.

"The broad standard, varied genetic background based on years of restricted inbreeding and wide out crossing, and great variety of size and type, are the major characteristics that make this strain of terrier known as a Jack Russell such a unique, versatile working terrier."

The Jack Russell Terrier was developed by the Reverend John Russell (known as Jack), from Devon, England, in the mid-to-late 1800s. He enjoyed hunting foxes, a popular pastime with Victorian clergymen, and was a keen breeder of foxhunting dogs. He bought a small white and tan female called Trump from a milkman and started a breeding programme to develop a Terrier with enough stamina for the hunt as well as the courage and body shape suitable to pursue foxes that had gone to ground. It is thought that the JRT and the Fox Terrier share common ancestors.

If you sliced a Jack Russell in two (heaven forbid!), you would find the word 'Terrier' stamped though him, like a stick of seaside rock. He has the high energy levels of a Fox Terrier, the hardiness and working stamina of a Border Terrier, and is as cocky and tenacious as a Yorkshire Terrier. He has a very strong prey drive and great determination and intensity.

A Jack Russell Terrier approaches life full on and is not for the faint hearted. If you want a quiet life, then don't get a Jack Russell. On the other hand, if you ride horses and want a dog to run alongside, or enjoy walking in the countryside every day, then this lively Terrier with the big personality could be just the dog for you. Some time ago we looked after a Jack Russell called Butch at the same time as Gus, a German Shepherd, for several weeks. The dogs got on pretty well together, despite them both being males and elderly, but there was no doubt who the boss was – and it wasn't Gus.

The Jack Russell is feisty and quite vociferous, they love to bark at new people and things, although are often friendly towards strangers. When he's not barking, two of his other favourite hobbies are digging and chewing, especially when as a pup and adolescent.

Their temperament has not changed much over the last 160 years or so. This is why the Jack Russell Terrier breed societies didn't want their dog recognised by the Kennel Clubs. They don't want the breed to have to conform to an exacting physical appearance, like pedigree dogs, where the look of the dog is all-important. In contrast, the JRT has been bred specifically to do a job, and that is the most important aspect of this little Terrier.

The Jack Russell Terrier Club of Great Britain (JRTCGB) says: "The terrier must present a lively, active and alert appearance. It should impress with its fearless and happy disposition. It should be remembered that the Jack Russell is a working terrier and should retain these instincts. Nervousness, cowardice and over-aggression should be discouraged, and it should always appear confident.

"A sturdy, tough terrier, very much on its toes all the time, measuring between 10″ and 15″ at the withers. The body length must be in proportion to the height, and it should present a compact, balanced image, always being in solid, hard condition."

The dog's appearance may vary. He can have a smooth coat, a rough coat or a combination of the two. The height of the breed varies considerably from around eight inches high at the withers (shoulders) to about 12 inches high (taller in the USA). Over half the body should be covered in white with black, brown and/or tan markings or, typically, patches.

The Jack Russell Terrier and the Parson Russell Terrier are similar and share a common origin, but they have several marked differences — the most notable being the range of acceptable heights. Parson Russells generally have longer legs, a bigger body and longer head, and they are taller, ranging from 12 to 14 inches in height.

Jack Russells are clever, active dogs which like to spend time (but not live) outside. Pound for pound, the breed's energy levels are extremely high, and they are not generally suitable for apartment life or as a companion for the elderly - although older dogs are less active. Nor are they hypoallergenic; their coat is low maintenance, but they still shed hair. Sadly too many JRTs finish up in rescue centres, as prospective owners fall for their cute looks, not realising that this is a physically active and demanding dog that requires time-consuming obedience training, socialisation and a daily hour of exercise to be content, preferably running free. The breed loves farms and large gardens and will generally show the typical Terrier trait of chasing cats, squirrels and other small creatures unless they have been introduced to them at a young age.

An indicator to the fearless and active nature of these dogs can be gained from the fact that show dogs can be accepted with scars. JRTCGB states: "Old scars or injuries, the result of work or accident, should not be allowed to prejudice the terrier's chance in the show ring unless they interfere with its movement or with its utility for work or stud."

Jack Russells are relatively easy to train, they love learning tricks and do well in canine competitions. Socialisation and obedience training from puppyhood is important to prevent them showing aggression to other animals and people and barking at the drop of a hat. Puppy classes are an excellent way to start training with a JRT. In short, they are super, feisty little dogs, but only for the right home where owners have the time and desire to train, exercise, play with and supervise this fun little bundle of energy. JRTs definitely don't like being left for long periods and can become destructive or noisy when lonely.

The breed has a reputation for being healthy with a long lifespan of 13 to 16 years. Some bloodlines have shown problems with cataracts, deafness and patellar luxation; ask the breeder if the parents or grandparents have any history of these issues.

Although the breed is not registered with the Kennel Club, you can find responsible breeders through The Jack Russell Terrier Club of Great Britain at www.jrtcgb.co.uk or the Jack Russell Terrier Club of America at www.therealjackrussell.com. The breed clubs also maintain a register of Jack Russell Terriers.

The image below shows a smooth coated Jack Russell Terrier (left) and a Parson Russell Terrier.

4. Crossbreed or Mixed Breed?

If you get a purebred dog, you have a good idea of how the dog will turn out physically, what it was originally bred for and what its natural instincts will be. But not everybody wants a pedigree dog.

Pedigree breeders select their dams and sires based on a number of attributes, but over the years inherent faults have sometimes been inadvertently passed on through the bloodlines along with all the good points. For example, some Dalmatians are deaf, some Labradors have hip problems and Dachshunds may suffer from back problems.

Because specific dogs within the breed were selected for mating, the gene pool of a pedigree is likely to be narrower than that of a mixed breed or mongrel. It is said that all Cavalier King Charles Spaniels can trace their ancestry back to six dogs.

Some people believe that a crossbreed (also called a hybrid) or mongrel will be naturally healthier than a pedigree dog, which may have inheritable weaknesses. However, it is worth bearing in mind that two unhealthy crossbreeds or mongrels will not necessarily produce healthy puppies, so picking a good breeder and looking at the health and temperament of the parents (the puppy's, not the breeder's!) applies just as much, if not even more so with a crossbreed.

COCKAPOO

There is much discussion on something called hybrid vigour, which is one reason why some people choose to get a crossbreed dog. This is the tendency of a cross-bred individual to show qualities superior to those of both parents.

Hybrid Vigour

According to scientists, hybrid vigour (heterosis) is: "The increased vigour displayed by the offspring from a cross between genetically different parents.

"Hybrids from crosses between different crop varieties (F1 hybrids) are often stronger and produce better yields than the original varieties. Mules, the offspring of mares crossed with donkeys, have greater strength and resistance to disease and a longer lifespan than either parent."

Hybrid vigour applies to plants and animals.

Cockapoos, Labradoodles, Goldendoodles, Schnoodles, all the Poos and Doodles and other so-called 'designer dogs' are causing a big debate. The hybrid vigour theory as it applies to the canine world is that a crossbred puppy may be stronger and healthier than a purebred, as he or she is less likely to inherit the genetic faults of either purebred parent.

For example, one parent dog could be blind with PRA, the other suffering from Von Willebrands disease and the offspring would be carriers, but perfectly healthy as long as they don't share the diseases in common. A Labrador with hip dysplasia mated to a Poodle with luxating patellas will almost certainly produce normal offspring, but – and this is a big but - **hybrid vigour declines in successive generations.**

So, taking the above example, a first generation puppy (F1) with a pedigree Labrador and pedigree Poodle for parents will almost certainly be healthy, but a second generation puppy (F2), such as a puppy with two Labradoodle parents, will naturally carry a much higher chance of suffering from or carrying the gene for PRA or hip dysplasia. Of course, responsible breeders of crossbreed puppies should also be taking this into account, just as good pedigree breeders do, when selecting their breeding pairs.

Because crossbreed and mongrels are not pedigree dogs, you cannot get Kennel Clubs or AKC registration papers with your dog. But despite this, you should always find out about your dog's parents and ancestry – because provided you care for him well, his genes will be the major factor in deciding how healthy he will be. Also, some crossbreed societies keep registration details of puppies from recognised breeders.

F Numbers

If you are considering a crossbreed dog, then you need to understand just what you are getting – and the breeders' terminology involves F numbers, which have nothing at all to do with Formula 1 racing or camera lenses! F stands for filial; it comes from the Latin *filius* (son) and means "relating to a son or daughter."

A first generation **(F1)** crossbreed is one where both parents are pedigree dogs. The next generations are worked out by always adding one number up from the lowest number parent.

An **F2** could be the offspring of two F1 dogs or the product of an F1 dog crossed with an F2 or F3 or F4.

An **F3** is the offspring of one F2 parent where the other was F2 or higher, for example: an F2 crossed with an F3 or F2 or F4.

Then it gets even more complicated in some cases with F1B, F2B, F3B, and so on crosses. The B stands for Backcross. This occurs when a litter has been produced as a result of a backcross to one of the parent breeds – often a Poodle to produce a more consistent coat - so this could be a Goldendoodle bred with a Poodle. It is not common practice for breeders to backcross to the non-shedding breed, in this case a Golden Retriever. So a typical F1B might be one quarter Golden Retriever (or Labrador in the case of Labradoodles or Cocker Spaniel in the case of Cockapoos) and three-quarters Poodle.

Sticking with Goldendoodles, a second generation backcross pup (F2B) is the result of an F1 Goldendoodle bred to a Goldendoodle backcross (F1B). Although three generations in the making, F2Bs are technically second generation dogs.

All clear?? Well, we're moving on anyway! With Labradoodles (and several other crosses) there is also such a thing as a **multigeneration or multigen** Labradoodle, which is the result of successive Labradoodle to Labradoodle breeding, rather than breeding purebred Labradors and Poodles. However, in practice, backcrosses and Poodles are also used in the early generations. This is why some older lines of multigeneration Labradoodles have a lot of Poodle in their genetic make-up.

Poodles are less expensive and, as they have a wool coat, increase the likelihood of the puppies having a low-shed or non-shedding coat. They also introduce some popular new colours such as red and parti (white and another colour). Hybrid vigour may be lost, but the advantage of multigens is that good breeders can reproduce a more consistent size, appearance and coat type by breeding multigen to multigen.

NOTE: All Australian Labradoodles are multigeneration, but not all multigenerations are Australian Labradoodles.

The main point to remember with the Poodle crossbreeds is that none of them is guaranteed to be non-shedding or hypoallergenic. You need to spend time with the individual dog before you can be 100% sure.

AUSTRALIAN LABRADOODLE

Today there are literally dozens and dozens of crossbreeds, far too many to mention here. You may be going for a particular cross because you like the look of the dog, if so then check out the health records and temperaments of the parents as well as just how the dogs look.

If you are selecting a crossbreed because you have allergies, it is also worth considering a hypoallergenic pedigree breed, and even then you have to spend time with the individual dog. Some responsible hybrid breeders will not sell to families or individuals who are selecting their puppies purely because they have allergies. Allergies are so individual that there is no guarantee from one person to the next and one puppy to the next – and they don't want to risk their puppies going to unsuitable homes.

This is what the website VetStreet has to say: "Opening your heart and home to a crossbreed is like opening a beautifully wrapped package on your birthday: you can never be sure what's inside.

"It's often assumed that a crossbreed will combine the best of two or more breeds, but genetics doesn't always work that way. The way genes express themselves is not always subject to a breeder's control, even less so when two different breeds are crossed.

"That's something to keep in mind before you lay down lots of money for a dog that you have been assured will be hypoallergenic or healthier than a purebred."

Six Key Tips When Selecting A Crossbreed

If you decide to get a pedigree dog, you can be pretty sure of several factors:

- ❖ Which Kennel Club group the breed is in

- ❖ What the breed was originally developed for

- ❖ The natural instincts of this breed, e.g. whether it is likely to chase cats and other small animals, whether the dog has a high work ethic and how the breed in general responds to training

- ❖ The typical temperament of the breed

- ❖ How big your puppy will grow

- ❖ What coat type it will have

- ❖ What health issues the breed is susceptible to

If you get a crossbreed, there are many more uncertainties at to how your puppy will turn out. Even puppies within the same litter will grow to different sizes, often have different coat types, and some even have a coat which changes after a few months. While all puppies are a mix of both parents, some will take on more characteristics from the father (or sire), while others will have more in common with the mother (dam). When the father and mother are from different breeds, this enormously increases the possible variations of how your pup will look and act as an adult dog.

All the dogs pictured on the previous page are Schnoodles yet, as you can see, they vary tremendously in size, colour, coat and probably temperament too. None, one, some or all may be hypoallergenic, but there is no guarantee. The Kennel Clubs say that crossbreeds don't 'breed true', meaning that the puppies don't display a consistent set of characteristics.

Some breeders of hybrids breed multigeneration dogs, such as the Australian Labradoodle, which is Australian Labradoodle bred with an Australian Labradoodle. The advantage of this is that they produce a more consistent puppy; the disadvantage is that any hybrid vigour is lost.

Here are our Top Tips to help you make the right decision when selecting a crossbreed to help steer you towards a healthy puppy with the attributes you are looking for:

1. If hybrid vigour is one reason you are choosing a crossbred dog over a purebred dog, pick a first generation (F1) cross. Hybrid vigour decreases with each successive generation.

2. Research both of the parent breeds. For example, if you are interested in Goldendoodles, read about Poodles and Labradoodles, your puppy will be a combination of these breeds.

3. Go on the internet and look up the breed societies or associations for the crossbreed you are interested in - virtually all hybrids have them. The societies lay down a code of ethics for breeders and many also state how the dog should look and what sort of temperament it should ideally have.

4. Select an approved or recommended breeder. This is especially important with crossbreeds, which are not regulated by the Kennel Clubs. Anybody can take two dogs off the street, allow them to mate and call their puppies "designer dogs". With puppies fetching hundreds and even thousands of pounds or dollars, a lot of unscrupulous people have been tempted into the "designer dog" breeding game. The crossbreed societies have lists of breeders who conform to their standards.

5. Once you have chosen your breeder, read **Chapter 7.** on how to select the temperament of the puppy. For example, you

might be interested in a Puggle, a cross between a Pug, which is affectionate and loving, and a Beagle, which is more independent-minded. Do the PAT test to see if the pup is more likely to take after the Pug or the Beagle.

6. Research the health problems of the parent breeds. Ask the breeder if he or she screens the breeding pair for these disorders and ask to see the certificates. Three of the most common hereditary ailments are eye and hip or elbow conditions, all of which can be screened for.

Now we'll take a look at some of the most popular crossbreed dogs.

Cockapoo

The Cockapoo, Cockerpoo, Cock-A-Poo or Spoodle is a cross between a Cocker Spaniel (English or American) and any size of Poodle. This is probably the number one crossbreed in the UK and extremely popular in North America. The Cockapoo is one of the oldest so-called "designer crossbreeds" having originated in the US from the early 1960s or even late 1950s.

This crossbreed's popularity is largely due to the fact that not only are they extremely cute, but they are known for having the friendly, outgoing and non-aggressive temperament of the Cocker, coupled with characteristics from the Poodle's non-shedding coat. That's not to say that Cockapoos don't shed – most do, but nowhere near as much as a Spaniel and most types have low dander coats.

According to the Cockapoo Club of Great Britain: "The coat type of the Cockapoo will vary as characteristics are inherited from both the Poodle and the Cocker Spaniel. There may even be some variety within a litter.

"The three possible coat types are a tight curly coat, a loose wavy/ringlet coat and a straighter coat. An experienced breeder will be able to advise you what the likely coat type of a puppy will be from their Cocker Spaniel/Poodle mix that they breed, and when the puppies are just a few weeks old it is possible to see the coat type starting to develop.

"The texture of the Cockapoo coat usually consists of dense, soft or silky fur, unlike the coarser fur found on many dogs, and all three coat types of the F1 Cockapoo will be low-shedding/dander with low-allergen qualities."

NOTE: These are generally low shedding dogs, not non-shedding dogs. A Cockapoo may be suitable for some allergy sufferers, but it is by no means guaranteed.

The Cockapoo Club adds: "The Cockapoo bred back to a Poodle, the F1b, is more likely to have a tight curly coat as there is more of the Poodle in the gene pool. Similarly, the Cockapoo bred back to a Cocker Spaniel may have a straighter coat. The curlier coat types are generally less likely to shed any hair."

Cockapoos can be groomed to look like a Poodle or a Spaniel; you can also keep them in a puppy clip with the body coat trimmed to a short, fluffy length, with the hair on the legs left a little fuller and the tail left long and plume-like. Some owners learn to use clippers themselves, but most rely on trips to a professional dog groomers every couple of months – another cost to consider.

In between, Cockapoos are high maintenance on the grooming front. They need daily or near-daily brushing to prevent matting, as well as regular baths to keep them clean. Neglecting grooming can soon lead to a matted mess that can lead to painful skin infections.

Like all Spaniels, a Cockapoo's ears should be kept clean and dry and regularly checked for any sign of infection. If you notice a nasty smell, redness or swelling, the ear has become infected and it's time to visit your vet. Also, Cockapoos commonly develop reddish-brown tear stains beneath their eyes, so regular washing of the face and careful wiping beneath the eyes should also be part of your regular grooming regime.

The colour varies a great deal, it can be: black, tan, beige, or buff, red - including auburn and apricot – light to dark brown, sable, cream, white, silver, brindle, roan or merle (mottled). Cockapoos can be one solid colour or have complex markings; they can be white with patches of any colour or have spots or freckles of colour, called ticking.

The well-trained and socialised Cockapoo has a sweet temperament, is friendly with people and is generally happy-go-lucky. He is also quite robust. However, be prepared for lots of exercise, many have high energy levels – higher than some people realise. This should not be a surprise to anyone, since both Spaniels and the original Poodles were bred as working dogs.

Make sure to ask the breeder whether the Cockapoo puppy you are looking at has been bred from working or show (conformation) lines. If you are looking for a more placid Cockapoo with lower energy levels, go for one bred from show stock and check out the parents - are they hyper or placid? Your pup will take after the parents. It is very difficult to tire out a Cockapoo bred from working lines. Cockapoos are, however, normally very biddable and easy to train.

Cockapoos, just like pedigree dogs, can suffer from health issues. One of the main ones is eye disorders, including progressive retinal atrophy (PRA). The Cockapoo clubs on both sides of the Atlantic strongly recommend testing breeding stock for this – ask to see CERF (USA) or CCGB certificates in the UK. Other issues include luxating patella, hip dysplasia and von Willebrands disease. Cockapoos are generally long lived, with 12 to 15 years being the norm.

If a breeder tells you the tests aren't necessary because (s)he's never had any problems in his or her lines, that the dogs have been "vet checked," or gives any other excuse for skimping on the genetic testing of their dogs, walk away. The Cockapoo's popularity has led to puppy farms and backyard breeders springing up with the main aim of making money from the craze – without paying too much attention to the long-term health and temperament of the puppies they produce, or the welfare of their breeding dogs.

VetStreet says: "Cockapoos who are carefully bred and lovingly raised should be happy, affectionate dogs that love families, children, other dogs, and even cats. Without the benefit of health and temperament testing, however, they can be a mess of genetic and behavioral problems."

There are, however, Cockapoo clubs in North America and the UK which are working towards developing the Cockapoo by breeding successive generations and establishing it as a recognised breed. The Cockapoo Club of GB promotes "Open and Ethical Breeding to Protect the Cockapoo of Tomorrow, Today."

These societies have registers for Cockapoos produced by approved breeders who agree to work to a Code of Ethics and have his or her dog's health tested. The first point of call for anyone interested in getting a Cockapoo should be one of these breed societies to find their list of approved breeders. Some useful links are: www.cockapooclubgb.co.uk, www.cockapooclub.com, and www.americancockapooclub.com.

SUMMARY: Friendly, affectionate, trainable and intelligent medium-sized dogs who like to be around people. They are often good with cats, children and other dogs and animals. Some have high energy levels and all need a lot of grooming. They are usually friendly with strangers, so they don't make good watchdogs. Many are low shedding.

Labradoodle

Since Wally Conron first crossed a Standard Poodle with a Labrador in 1988 and coined the phrase 'Labradoodle', this honest, sociable and fun-loving canine has made his home at the centre of families across the globe. Originating in Australia, the Labradoodle has become extremely popular elsewhere, particularly in the USA, Canada and the UK.

Wally worked as breeding manager for the Royal Guide Dog Association of Australia in Melbourne in the 1980s. He received a request from Pat Blum, a visually-impaired woman in Hawaii who had never applied for a guide dog before because of her husband's allergy to dogs, and who wrote to Wally in the hope that he might be able to help. He had the novel idea of breeding a Labrador with a Standard Poodle with the goal of combining the low-shedding coat of the Poodle with the gentleness and trainability of the Labrador and ultimately produce a service/guide dog suitable for people with allergies to fur and dander.

The first three pups were Sultan, Sheik and Simon. Coat and saliva samples were flown to Pat in Hawaii, where it was discovered that her husband was allergic to two of the three but had no reaction to Sultan, who went on to live a happy life as Pat's guide dog in Hawaii.

The media hype and the fact that all Labradoodles have been promoted by some breeders as being perfectly suitable for all allergy sufferers has led to some criticism of the crossbreed, as well as a rash of puppy farms being set up by people looking to make a quick profit – but none of this is the fault of the dog.

To set the record straight, as the Kennel Clubs will tell anyone who asks, **there is no such thing as a totally non-shedding dog.** There are, however, certain breeds – and crossbreeds - which may be more suitable for allergy sufferers. Some MAY be suitable, but by no means all. If you suffer from allergies you need to spend time with the specific puppy.

Labradoodles come in three different sizes with three different coat types and many different colours. Miniatures weight 15 to 30lb, Mediums are 30 to 45lb, while Standards seems to be getting bigger every year and can weigh anything from 45 to more than 100lb.

A Labradoodle may be a first generation crossbreed, a second, third or fourth generation or a multigeneration, also called multigen. In extremely general terms, an F1 (first generation) Labradoodle has a scruffy look, while multigens and Australian Labradoodles look more like teddy bears. When you have decided what type of Labradoodle you'd like, you then have to decide what F number of dog you want - or whether to go for a multigen.

Whether Australian or simply Labradoodle, one reason why these dogs are so popular is their temperament, combining the placidity and steadfastness of the Labrador with the intelligence of the Poodle.

By nature Labradoodles are sociable, friendly, affectionate and non-aggressive with other dogs. They love to be with people and at the heart of family life and are therefore not suitable pets to be left alone all day. They are also intelligent, playful and highly trainable, but need plenty of mental and physical stimulation.

Standards are big dogs and can be boisterous and mischievous. Miniatures are becoming more popular, but still average around 18" in height. They want nothing more than to please their people and thrive on interaction. They enjoy a challenge, love games and are easily bored.

Most Labradoodles love water - and mud – so if you are particularly house proud, a smaller, less active breed might be a better choice. Labradoodles love to run, swim and fetch. Their energy levels vary greatly, so it's a good idea to try and see the parents, as puppies will generally take after them in this respect. They will bark if someone comes to the door, but are watch dogs rather than guard dogs, as they are likely to welcome any intruder with a wagging tail.

As with all dogs they should be treated with respect and given firm, fair training and handling from a very early age, or they will try to outsmart you. They often live happily with other dogs, cats and other animals, and usually do well with children. They do not like being left alone for long periods.

A Labradoodle can have one of three coats, and each type has variations. There are a large number of coat colours, including apricot/gold, red, black, silver, blue, caramel, chocolate, cafe, parchment and lavender. The three main coat types are:

Hair coat: also known as a flat or slick coat, although it may be straight or wavy, usually seen in F1 and other early generation

Labradoodles. It is harsher in texture that wool or fleece and this coat normally sheds, so is not suitable for allergy sufferers.

Fleece coat: This is the coat that most people associate with an Australian Labradoodle and is also the one that requires most maintenance, requiring regular grooming to prevent matting. It should have no body odour and little to no shedding, although it is typical to find the occasional fur ball around the house. A fleece coat is acceptable for some people with allergies.

Wool coat: This is very dense and similar in texture to lambs' wool. It can be kept long, but that requires more grooming in this style. Kept short it is easy to maintain, has little or no doggie smell and minimal shedding. This coat is most like that of the Poodle and may be suitable for some allergy sufferers.

Health issues which can affect Labradoodles are similar to those affecting Labradors and Poodles. They include eye problems such as PRA (Progressive Retinal Atrophy) and hereditary cataracts, hip and elbow dysplasia, as well as Addison's disease in Australian Labradoodles.

Lifespan is anywhere from 10 to 15 years.

Useful contacts: UK - www.labradoodletrust.com, www.labradoodle.org.uk; USA - http://alaa-labradoodles.com, www.australianlabradoodleclub.us, http://labradoodle-dogs.net

---

Goldendoodle

The Goldendoodle is a cross between a Golden Retriever and a Poodle, usually a Standard or Miniature. They come in three sizes: Miniature (weighing 15 to 30lb), Medium (30 to 45lb) and Standard (45 to more than 100lb). On colour, they can be white, cream, apricot, gold, red, sometimes grey and black (phantom), black or a light sandy brown.

In the 1990s, breeders in both North America and Australia began crossing Golden Retrievers with Standard Poodles with the aim of developing guide dogs suitable for visually impaired individuals with allergies, similar to what Wally Conron had done with the Labradoodle years earlier. Although not all Goldendoodles exhibit the non-shedding coat type of the Poodle, many have a low to non-shedding coat.

Often the Goldendoodle moults less than a Golden Retriever (which sheds a lot), but the degree varies from one dog to the next and grooming requirements vary with coat types. The coat length when left unclipped grows to about four to eight inches long.

As with Labradoodles, some breeders claim that the Goldendoodle is hypoallergenic, but this is simply not true as the variations within a crossbreed are greater than that within pedigree dogs and even puppies within the same litter may have different coats. Although it is true to say that some Goldendoodles are suitable for some allergy sufferers.

There are three main coat types: **straight**, which is flat and more like a Golden Retriever coat, **wavy** is a mixture of a Poodle's curls and a Golden Retriever's straighter fur, and **curly**, which is more like the Poodle coat.

The amount of grooming depends on the coat type – and if yours is low-shedding, you will have to factor in the cost of regular trims at the groomers every two or three months. In between, a Goldendoodle should be brushed at least every other day. As with many long-eared dogs, ear infections can be a problem. The ears should be kept dry and clean, especially after a bath or swimming; redness, a bad smell and head shaking are all signs of a potential infection, which needs dealing with promptly by a veterinarian.

The appearance of the Goldendoodle runs anywhere from shaggy Retriever to curly Poodle, but usually falls somewhere in between.

This crossbreed has become hugely popular in North America, where many owners describe it as a wonderful family pet which is sociable, intelligent, affectionate and easy to train. It often combines the outstanding temperament of the Golden Retriever - with its friendliness, affection and even-temperedness - with the intelligence and intuition of the Poodle.

Goldendoodles are usually very affectionate with people and other pets. They are human-oriented dogs, and tend to develop a strong bond with their owners and companions. They often have an uncanny ability to communicate with people. Most are calm and easy going, but they are active dogs that do require a fair amount of daily exercise. Generally they could be described as having moderate energy levels, although this varies from one individual to the next – check out the parents, - what are they like? Larger ones are often more active.

The Goldendoodle's Poodle and Labrador Retriever ancestors were hunters and water dogs. Some like to swim, but not all. They need a good walk or active playtime each day, and they are athletic enough to participate in such dog sports as agility, flyball, obedience and rally. They can also be excellent therapy dogs. They tend to be great family pets and are known to be especially good with children, being inclined to be careful around infants or toddlers, and can be great playmates for older children.

GANA (Goldendoodle Association of North America) has laid down a basis upon which the breed standard will be created for the Goldendoodle:

- ❖ A balanced mix of physical characteristics of the Golden Retriever and the Poodle
- ❖ A consistently friendly, social temperament similar to that of the Golden Retriever
- ❖ Consists of Poodle and Golden Retriever only - no other breed infusion is accepted
- ❖ No tail docking or body altering other than the removal of dew claws - dew claw removal is optional.

Many Goldendoodles are first generation (F1) crosses, and as such may be expected to benefit from hybrid vigour. However, Goldendoodles

generally can be susceptible to the health problems of Golden Retrievers, Standard Poodles, or Miniature Poodles. These include eye and heart problems, hip dysplasia and Addison's disease. Ask the breeder to see both of the puppy's parents' certificates for eye and joint issues.

Like the Labradoodle, lifespan can vary from 10 to 15 years.

Contacts:
http://www.goldendoodleassociation.com, http://goldendoodles.com

---

Puggle

A Puggle is a cross between two dogs which have seen a big rise in popularity recently – the Pug and the Beagle. And their offspring is rapidly becoming one of the most popular hybrid dogs of all time. This is slightly surprising as the breeders of Puggles, unlike the breeders of many other crossbreeds, make no claims to their dogs being hypoallergenic.

No, the appeal of the Puggle lies primarily in his personality, coupled with his other attributes of being a fairly small dog with moderate exercise and low grooming requirements.

As with many so-called "designer dogs", it all started in the USA. Wisconsin breeder Wallace Havens bred the first Puggle in the 1980s. He invented the name and was the first to register the breed with the American Canine Hybrid Club. By 2000, Puggles were being sold commercially.

At first glance, these two breeds might seem like an odd mix. Pugs are affectionate little homebodies. They are one of the brachycephalic (flat-faced) breeds and their short noses can make them less exercise-tolerant than other breeds the same size. This is an affectionate, stubborn, playful companion dog which loves nothing better than sitting on his owner's lap.

Beagles are great family dogs that can walk all day, but they are often ruled by their nose and can be escape artists and hard to lure back if they wander off. They also have a tendency to howl if they are bored or unhappy. The Beagle is altogether more independent minded and nowhere near as reliant upon humans for his happiness.

Indeed, the Beagle has a tendency to roam, and there is a saying if you want to find a Beagle owner in a park, it's the man with a lead looking for his dog! Beagles are scent hounds bred to track game and have an incredible sense of smell. They are sometimes called a nose on four legs, which is why they often wander off on the trail of an interesting scent.

Pugs and Beagles are both short-coated, small, cute and popular - and that's where the similarity ends! Bred skilfully you have the best of both worlds: a robust, healthy little dog with a playful spirit, a sense of humour and a desire to please. At best the Puggle can be a hardy little dog with the adventurous yet quieter spirit of a Beagle and the clever antics of a Pug. But you could end up with a puppy which has inherited the other traits: stubborn, exercise-intolerant, hard to train, uncooperative, not very attached to you and who will wander off at every opportunity.

Some unscrupulous people are making a lot of money out of breeding Puggles for profit, with no great interest in improving this crossbreed. Make sure you pick your breeder carefully, don't just fall for the first cute Puggle pup you clap eyes on – one thing all Puggle pups have in common is that they are ALL cute!

The importance of selecting the right breeder and then the right puppy cannot be stressed enough with Puggles. It's essential for you to visit the breeder's home, watch the puppies and look at the temperament of, ideally, both parents. If that's not possible, then spend some time with the mother to see if she has an affectionate temperament or if she is stand-offish. Look at the Pug parent, how flat is the nose? Does (s)he appear to be having difficulty breathing, is he or she snuffling or snorting a lot? If so, avoid a pup from this parent, go for a Puggle with a longer nose more like a Beagle.

And before you visit the breeder, read **Chapter 7. Picking the Individual Puppy** for some invaluable advice on choosing the right temperament to fit in with you and your family or household. With good breeding, the Pug's love of humans and home should balance the Beagle's independent ways and offset the little hound's tendency to be an escape artist and a roamer.

Puggles can be barkers if they take after the Beagle side, and this wants nipping in the bud when young. They usually get along with other dogs, but not always with cats, as the Beagle's chase instinct may predominate. Both Pugs and Beagles can have a stubborn streak, especially when it comes to training. Patience and treats are the answer – but not too many. Both the Beagle and the Pug are notorious for being willing to eat until they pop, as well as for their ability to steal food from under your nose. Generally all Puggles love their food, so monitoring their daily intake is essential if they are not to become obese.

Crossbreed puppies like the Puggle can look very different from each other, even within the same litter – and from their parents. The Puggle's size, colour, coat type, temperament, energy levels and health risks will vary depending on what traits of the two breeds an individual puppy has inherited from his parents. Puggles range in weight from 15 to 30lb, but one thing to bear in mind is that they often turn out to be larger than people expect.

Generally this crossbreed is chunky, with a short-haired, smooth coat. This is often fawn or black and tan. They have some of the Pug's facial wrinkling as well as the curly tail and relatively short legs. Standing 10 to 15 inches high at the withers (shoulders), they are more akin to the Beagle in size and have the breed's trademark drooping ears.

Puggles have a short coat which is easy to take care of; a weekly brush is usually enough, unless they have been running through or rolling in mud (or something worse, which is not uncommon). The hairs are short, but Puggles are generally fairly consistent shedders.

They require moderate exercise; again, this will vary according to what traits they have inherited and how much exercise they get used to when young. They need at least one daily walk away from the home, preferably more, to satisfy their need to migrate. Given this, they are suitable for apartment life.

Puggles are fairly long lived, with 12 to 14 years being typical, but they can inherit health problems from the Pug or the Beagle. These are cherry eye, epilepsy and hip dysplasia, and some suffer from food and environmental allergies.

If you are considering a Puggle, choose one with a longer nose more like the Beagle. Puggles with flatter faces like the Pug can have breathing problems. One common (non-life threatening) respiratory ailment that Puggles sometimes suffer from is reverse sneezing.

Schnoodle

A Schnoodle is a cross between a Schnauzer and a Poodle. There are three types of Poodle: Standard, Miniature and Toy, and three types of Schnauzer: Giant, Standard and Miniature.

A Schnoodle can be any combination of these, resulting in four types of Schnoodle: Giant, Standard, Miniature and Toy. The most common are the Miniatures - which usually weigh between 10lb and 16lb - however, Giant Schnoodles are also popular.

A Toy Schnoodle is 10 inches or under at the shoulders and under 10lb in weight. This is a cross between a Toy Poodle and a small Miniature Schnauzer. A Giant is a cross between a Standard Poodle and a Giant Schnauzer. A fully grown one will weigh as much as 65 to 80lb and stand 24 to 27 inches high at the shoulders.

Some breeders think the Poodle takes the chunkiness out of the Schnauzer, while the Schnauzer takes the pointed head away from the Poodle. Although there are no written breed characteristics, the Schnoodle should be well-proportioned and athletic with a keen, bold, and lively expression.

Schnoodles are generally F1, or first generation, crosses. In other words, one parent was a Schnauzer and the other was a Poodle. One of the reasons for the Schnoodle's popularity is that both his parents are regarded as hypoallergenic breeds and therefore there's a good chance that the Schnoodle could also be hypoallergenic – although you have to spend time with the puppy to be sure you have no reaction.

The Schnoodle could have a single coat of dense, curly fur like the Poodle, a double coat with a wiry outer coat like the Schnauzer, or a combination of the two. The coat can come in many colours: black, white, grey, apricot, chocolate, black with white markings, wheaten, sable, parti (white with patches of colour) or phantom (black and tan like the Doberman).

Although there is a variety of colours, the Schnoodle coat is almost always curly or at least wavy. As the puppy matures it may develop the rough, wirier hair of the Schnauzer, the softer hair of the Poodle or something in between. Some develop coarser Schnauzer-like hair in places - most notably on the back - with softer Poodle hair on other parts of the body.

One thing that will be almost guaranteed is that the resulting puppy will be low shedding, although you might find the odd fur ball around the house. This is good news to all house-proud owners, but bear in mind that a Schnoodle has to be clipped every eight to 10 weeks and this can cost anything from around £25, or $40, upwards per trim.

There is no defined cut for this crossbreed. Most of them get a general groom - with, perhaps, a #7 shear - with rounded semi-long hair left on the face. Some have a more Terrier-like look with a squarer trim around the face. Owners should check inside their Schnoodle's ears regularly for signs of infection, which both Schnauzers and Poodles are prone to. The area inside the ears is a potential breeding ground for bacteria, and you should ensure it does not become matted with fur, red, hot or smelly. The fur inside the ears should be plucked regularly. If you don't do it, ask your groomer to do it every visit.

Schnoodles' ears are left naturally uncropped. They may have a long ear flap that lays closer to their head and hangs down – like a Poodle - or a shorter ear that stands upright at the base and folds over midway toward the front - like the uncropped ears of a Schnauzer.

The Schnoodle temperament mixes the intellect of the Poodle with the companionship and devotion of the Schnauzer. If treated well when young, Schnoodles make loving, loyal and amusing companions. Being eager to please, they are relatively easy to train. Training should be done in short bursts and efforts should be made to keep it interesting, as it may not be easy to keep their concentration for a long period.

They love playing and distractions. Smaller Schnoodles may be happy as lapdogs; large ones are friskier with higher energy levels and require more time and attention. One of the reasons some Schnoodles end up in rescue shelters is that they have higher energy levels and exercise requirements than their owners realised – particularly large Schnoodles – this can lead to destructive behaviour or excessive barking. Giant Schnoodles are happiest with a couple of hours exercise or more a day.

Schnoodles love to run and jump and require a fair amount of exercise for their size, as well as mental stimulation. They are generally good at canine competitions, being athletic and eager to please. Many love to swim and most love snow.

Schnauzers are affectionate, playful, intelligent and strong-willed, while Poodles are very clever, active and intuitive, and excel in obedience training. Giant Schnauzers can be protective and Miniature Schnauzers can be demanding. Schnoodles may inherit any combination of these attributes, but they are generally very people-orientated dogs which thrive on interaction with their humans. They do not enjoy being left alone for hours on end and can suffer from separation anxiety.

By nature neither of the parent breeds is aggressive with other dogs, and provided a Schnoodle is socialised with other dogs when young – and this is particularly important with Giants – they do well with other canines. Schnoodles are now being used as therapy dogs in hospitals, schools and nursing homes.

The potential Schnoodle health problems are those associated with Poodles and Schnauzers, and include eye issues, (if one of the parents is a Mini Schnauzer, ask to see eye screening certificates), urinary stones, Addison's disease and Cushing's disease. Having said that, Schnoodles are relatively healthy dogs, with the small ones living anywhere from 12 to 16 or 17 years; larger generally dogs have a shorter lifespan.

Maltipoo

The Maltipoo is a cross between a Toy or Miniature Poodle and a Maltese, a small breed in the Kennel Club's Toy group which is thought to have originated in ancient times on the Mediterranean island of Malta.

The Maltese has had a few different names during its long history; it was known as the ancient dog of Malta, the Roman ladies' dog, the Maltese lion dog and even as "Cokie" in the USA in the 1960s for some inexplicable reason. Its origins have also become blurred in the mists of time, with evidence of the breed being  descended either from a Spitz-type dog in Switzerland or the Tibetan Terrier, or a mixture of both.

The Maltese was bred as a companion, although it is a lively little dog for its size, and remains active well into old age. As Poodles are also alert and lively dogs, the Maltipoo is normally jaunty and, like the Maltese, keeps going for years.

These are affectionate dogs which very much love their humans, so are not suitable for leaving at home alone all day as they can suffer from separation anxiety – even to the extent of harming themselves in extreme cases. They are playful dogs which have a sense of fun and love to chase after a ball. Be aware that this little crossbreed does not tolerate very hot or very cold conditions, so exercise should be limited on hot days and a coat may be needed for winter.

Maltipoos are ideally suited to a person who is around all day and who has time to take them out for a daily walk. They can live in an apartment, but are happier in a house with an enclosed garden. If you live in a flat, you might consider a breed or crossbreed with lower natural energy levels. The Maltipoo should get at least 30 minutes of exercise a day – although some of this could be playing in the home or garden.

By temperament, many Maltipoos are what the Brits call feisty and the Americans call spunky. Early socialisation and training is a must to get them used to other dogs and people, although they often do well with other canines. Once trained with positive techniques and rewards, the Maltipoo will love to show off his or her tricks. The critical age for socialisation is up to 18 or 20 weeks; take the dog everywhere with you. After that the window closes rapidly, which doesn't mean an older dog can't be socialised, it is just more of a challenge as they are less receptive to new things than when young– just like us humans! You CAN teach an old dog new tricks, it just takes longer.

As with all small dogs, the Maltipoo should be treated like a dog, not like a baby. They are happier and more relaxed when assured of their place in the home's pecking order – and that should be below their owners. This crossbreed may not be a good choice if you have very small children, due to its size, delicacy and also the fact that some can be a little intolerant of toddlers. If this is the case, time should be spent training the dog and all time spent with little children should be supervised.

Sadly, research in Australia has shown that the Maltese is the number one dog in rescue shelters there, and the reason is constant barking. Again, early socialisation and plenty of exercise and play is the key. The Maltipoo is undoubtedly cute and cuddly, but don't make the mistake of thinking that he doesn't need exercise or stimulation, because he does. By the way, he barks but will probably welcome strangers with a wagging tail, so he's an excellent watch dog, but no guard dog.

The Maltipoo varies in size from around eight to 14 inches at the withers (shoulders), weighing from five to 20lb. The coat may vary widely from dead straight to wavy or curly and in texture it might be silky like the Maltese or more frizzy or woolly. There are many different colours although, as the Maltese is always white, the most common colours are anything from white to black and every shade in between.

Don't be surprised if your Maltipoo puppy's coat turns much lighter or darker as (s)he grows, this is normal. Regular brushing and trips to the grooming parlour are required with this crossbreed, and cleaning inside the ears to prevent infection should be a part of your grooming regime.

The Maltese and all Poodles are regarded as hypoallergenic breeds, so there is a good chance a Maltese puppy will be low shedding. That does not mean this hybrid is suitable for all allergy sufferers – only time spent with the individual puppy will determine if there is an allergic reaction.

Health problems include Legg-Calve-Perthes disease, luxating patella, PRA (Progressive Retinal Atrophy) and White Shaker Syndrome. Skin problems and allergies can also be an issue with Maltipoos. However, if he remains healthy, this crossbreed stays relatively puppy-like for many years and a typical lifespan is anywhere from 10 to 15 years.

5. Puppies for Allergy Sufferers

Tens of millions of people across the world have allergies. According to the Asthma and Allergy Foundation of America, there are an estimated 50 million sufferers in the USA alone. And one in five of these - 10 million people - are pet allergy sufferers.

Most people think that pet allergies are caused by fur, but that's not true. What they are actually allergic to are proteins – or allergens. These are secreted by the animal's oil glands and then shed with dander, which is dead skin cells. These proteins are also found in dog saliva and urine. So, it is the dander, saliva or urine of a dog which humans normally react to.

Hypoallergenic

It is, however, possible for pet allergy sufferers to enjoy living with a dog without spending all of their time sneezing, wheezing, itching or breaking out in rashes. Millions of people are proving the case - including our family. There are some breeds and crossbreeds which are definitely more suitable for consideration by allergy sufferers. These types of dog are called **'hypoallergenic'**, but what does this mean exactly?

Generally, hypoallergenic dogs are those which do not shed a lot of hair. The official definition of the word hypoallergenic is:

"Having a DECREASED tendency to provoke an allergic reaction."

In other words there is NO CAST IRON GUARANTEE that an allergy sufferer won't have a reaction to a certain type of dog or even an individual dog. But if you do choose a hypoallergenic dog, the chances are greatly reduced. Any dog can cause an allergic reaction, although a low-shedding, hypoallergenic breed such as a Poodle is a much better choice than other shedding breeds, crossbreeds or mixed breeds.

Some breeds of dog, such as Schnauzers, are double coated and the outer coat traps the inner coat and the dander, thereby reducing allergens. Many Australian Labradoodle crossbreeds, for example, have been selectively bred to have a certain type of coat which hardly sheds at all and is often - but by no means always - suitable for people with allergies.

From personal experience and numerous comments on our website, it is fair to say that many people who normally suffer from allergies are perfectly fine with hypoallergenic dogs. My partner is allergic to horses, cats and usually dogs, but has no reaction whatsoever to our Miniature Schnauzer, Max. (The good news for dog lovers is that there are more people allergic to cats). However, the other side of the coin is that recue centres are littered with dogs from owners who thought they would not be allergic to their pet – only to get the poor puppy home and find that they couldn't stop sneezing.

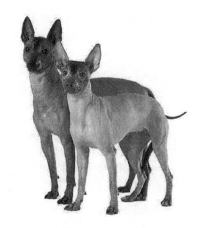

But – and this is a very big **BUT** - it is not simply enough to choose a breed or crossbreed which is hypoallergenic – that is only the first step. Let's clear up a couple of points right away:

- ❖ **No dog is totally non-shedding**
- ❖ **No dog is totally hypoallergenic**

Here are two more very important points:

1. People's pet allergies vary greatly
2. Pet allergy sufferers may react differently to different breeds **as well as individual dogs within that breed.** A sufferer may be fine with one puppy yet have a reaction to another in the same litter.

All dogs - even so-called 'hairless' dogs, like the Xoloitzcuintle, or Mexican Hairless dogs pictured here - have hair, dander (dead skin cells, like dandruff), saliva and urine. Therefore all dogs *can* cause allergic reactions. But not all dogs do. Some hypoallergenic dog breeds do not affect pet allergy sufferers as much because of the type or amount of hair that they shed.

Choosing a Puppy

If you have decided to go for a low-shedding, hypoallergenic puppy, then that is just the first step. Your next step is to find a reputable breeder. If you are looking at a pedigree (purebred) dog, a good way of doing this is to check with the Kennel Club in your country by going on to its website and clicking on the breed that you are interested in to find a list of approved or assured breeders. Bear in mind that top breeders often have a waiting list for their pups.

If you are thinking of getting a crossbreed like the Schnoodle (a cross between a Poodle and a Schnauzer), go to Google and type in the name of the crossbreed, followed by the words "breed society." Although crossbreeds are not registered with the Kennel Clubs, there are organisations which strive to improve the crossbreeds and they have codes of ethics. They also usually have a list of breeders who have agreed to conform to the society's ideals and animal welfare standards. This is no guarantee of a healthy, hypoallergenic pup, but it is a good starting place, you then have to follow it up with lots of questions – see the section on **Breeders** for what questions to ask.

Mixed breeds are not suitable for people with allergies, as you generally have no idea of the parentage of the dog and it is highly unlikely that all of the pup's ancestors were from the so-called 'non-shedding' breeds. And even if they were, it is still no guarantee. Better to stick with a breed or a crossbreed where you can ask lots of questions of the puppy, its parents and their history.

Once you have found your breeder, DO NOT send money without spending time with a puppy. Indeed, many responsible breeders will not allow this, as they want to be sure their pups are going to good, forever homes and don't want the distressing prospect of having to re-home their puppy because of the owner's allergies. It is upsetting for the family and a disaster for the puppy.

Buying a dog from a breeder with a good reputation is a two-way process. If the breeder isn't asking you any questions – other than how you are going to pay - walk away.

First of all ask if you can visit their adult dogs. Make sure there are no cats around, which could also trigger allergies, and if possible spend

time with both parents of any pup you are considering - especially if it's a crossbreed. Within some crossbreeds, like the Labradoodle, some puppies do not shed initially but start to lose hair later as their coat develops. Choose an experienced breeder with a good track record of breeding low-shedding pups, he or she will have a good idea of how the puppy's coat will develop as the dog grows older.

Four Golden Tips for Allergy Sufferers

❖ **Spend some time alone with the specific pup you are considering** to determine if you have a reaction – and this may be up to two days later. Handle the dog, rub your hands on your face, and lick your hands after you have handled the dog in order to absorb as much potential allergen as you can on your short visit. Allow the pup to lick you – as you may be allergic to his saliva.

101

- ❖ **Go back and visit the pup at least once or twice more** before you make that life-changing commitment to buy.

- ❖ **Take an old towel or piece of cloth and rub the puppy with it**. Take this home with you and handle it to see if you get a delayed reaction.

- ❖ **Check with the breeder to see if you can return the pup** within a certain time period if you have a reaction to him back at home. But remember that you cannot expect the breeder to take the dog back if the allergies only occur once he has reached adulthood.

Everyone with pet allergies can tolerate a certain amount of allergens (things they are allergic to). If that person is just below his or her tolerance, any additional allergen will push them over the edge, triggering a reaction. So if you reduce the general allergen load in the home, you'll be much more successful when you bring your puppy home.

Top Ten Tips for Reducing Pet Allergens

1. Get a HEPA air cleaner in the bedroom and/or main living room. HEPA stands for High Efficiency Particle Air - a type of air filter that removes 99.97% of all particles.

2. Use a HEPA vacuum cleaner. Neither the HEPA air nor vacuum cleaner is cheap, but if you suffer allergies and really want to share your life and home with a dog, they are worth considering. Both will dramatically improve the quality of the air you breathe in your home.

3. Regardless of what vacuum you use, clean and dust your home regularly.

4. Keep the dog out of your bedroom. We spend around a third of our lives here and keeping animals out can greatly reduce allergic reactions.

5. Do not allow your dog on the couch, bed or any other furniture. Keep him out of the car, or if this is not possible, use car seat covers or a blanket on the seat.

6. Brush your pet regularly - always outdoors - and regularly clean his bedding. Avoid using normal washing powder, as it may trigger a reaction in dogs with sensitive skin.

7. Keep your dog's skin healthy by regularly feeding a good multivitamin and a fatty acid supplement, such as fish oil.

8. Consider using an allergy-reducing spray such as Allerpet, which helps to cleanse the dog's fur of dander, saliva and sebaceous gland secretions. There are also products to reduce allergens from carpets, curtains and furniture.

9. Avoid contact with other dogs and always wash your hands after you have handled any dog, including your own.

10. Consult your doctor and discuss possible immunotherapy or medication. There are medical advances being made in the treatment of allergies and a range of tablets, sprays and even injections are currently available.

Experts aren't sure whether bathing your dog has any effect on allergy symptoms. Some studies have shown that baths reduce the amount of airborne dander, while others haven't found a difference.

You can certainly try bathing your dog regularly and see what happens; just make sure that it's not the allergy sufferer doing the bathing. Bear in mind that bathing a dog too frequently strips his skin and fur of its natural oils, and always use a medicated shampoo, such as Malaseb, as human shampoos can trigger canine skin problems.

Of course, the only sure-fire way to GUARANTEE no allergic reaction is not to have a dog. But if you have allergies and are determined to go ahead and share your home with Man's Best Friend, then the safest route is to select a 'non-shedding' dog. The UK and American Kennel Clubs do not make any claims about hypoallergenic dogs or breeds, but they both publish details of **"breeds that generally do well with people with allergies."** We are not recommending one over another, simply supplying you with the information to make an informed decision.

List of Hypoallergenic Pedigree Dogs

Here is a list of hypoallergenic dogs from both the American Kennel Club (AKC) and The Kennel Club (UK). These are all purebred dogs. While the Kennel Clubs do not guarantee that you will not have an allergic reaction to a particular dog, certain hypoallergenic and non-shedding dog breeds are generally thought to be better for allergy sufferers.

American Kennel Club List

The American Kennel Club's list of "breeds that generally do well with people with allergies" is:

Bedlington Terrier (pictured)
Bichon Frise
Chinese Crested
Irish Water Spaniel
Kerry Blue Terrier
Maltese
Poodle (Toy, Miniature and Standard)
Portuguese Water Dog
Schnauzer (Giant, Standard and Miniature)
Soft Coated Wheaten Terrier
Xoloitzcuintli (FSS Breed)

Kennel Club (UK) List

The KC has this to say about hypoallergenic and non-shedding dog breeds: *"For those owners who wish to obtain a dog which SUPPOSEDLY does not shed its coat, one of these listed breeds may be a suitable choice:"*

Gundog Group
Lagotto Romagnolo
Irish Water Spaniel
Spanish Water Dog (right)

Working Group
Bouvier des Flandres
Giant Schnauzer
Portuguese Water Dog
Russian Black Terrier

Pastoral Group
Hungarian Puli
Komondor

Toy Group
Bichon Frise
Bolognese
Chinese Crested
Coton de Tulear
Havanese
Maltese
Yorkshire Terrier

Utility Group
Lhasa Apso (right)
Intermediate Mexican Hairless

Miniature Mexican Hairless
Standard Mexican Hairless
Miniature Schnauzer
Standard Poodle
Toy Poodle
Miniature Poodle
Shih Tzu
Tibetan Terrier

Terrier Group
Bedlington Terrier
Dandie Dinmont Terrier
Glen of Imaal Terrier
Sealyham Terrier
Soft Coated Wheaten Terrier

Crossbreeds

The Doodle and Poo crossbreeds have become extremely popular over the last few years. All of these are crossed somewhere along the line with a Poodle. Many of these crossbreeds are marketed as suitable for allergy sufferers. Buyer beware, in reality many of them are not. As already discussed, it depends on the individual person's reaction to the individual puppy.

Some people don't want a purebred puppy, they'd rather have a crossbreed, which is the product of crossing two breeds of dog, for example a Cocker Spaniel and a Poodle to create a Cockapoo (left).

You cannot register a crossbreed with the Kennel Club or get pedigree papers. But despite this, you should always find out about your dog's parents and ancestry – because provided you care for him well, his genes will be the major factor in deciding how healthy he will be.

Just because you get a cross does not mean that the pup will have no health problems. Check what problems the parent breeds are susceptible to and whether health checks have been carried out on the parents and/or pups. Some Poodles, for example, have an inherited disposition to eye, hip or epilepsy problems. Ask to see health certificates.

Although you will not be able to enter your Doodle or Poo in a conformation class run under Kennel Club rules, there are plenty other shows and activities to enjoy with a crossbreed. Agility shows and flyball are becoming increasingly popular, as well as local dog shows. Some are also used as therapy or assistance dogs.

If a crossbreed is for you, then you need to understand the complicated subject of F numbers - or at least have a vague idea what breeders are talking about. F stands for filial when describing cross bred dogs and it comes from the Latin *filius* (son) and means "relating to a son or daughter."

An **F1** Doodle or Poo is a first generation cross. So, with Labradoodles for example, one parent was a Labrador and the other was a Poodle. An F1 Labradoodle is more likely to shed hair than higher generation Labradoodles, as half of its genes are coming from the Labrador, which moults. According to an unofficial Doodle database involving 237 dogs, over half of the F1 Labradoodles shed some hair– although many were light shedders and some caused no reported problems with the allergy sufferers they were living with.

Canine experts believe that a first generation (F1) cross may benefit from 'hybrid vigour.' This is the belief that the first cross between two unrelated purebred lines is healthier and grows better than either parent line. The next generations are worked out by always **adding one number up from the lowest number parent**, and it is thought that hybrid vigour is lost with each successive generation. See **Chapter 4 Crossbreeds** for more information.

- ❖ An **F2** could be the offspring of two x F1 Labradoodles or the product of an F1 crossed with an F2, F3 or F4 dog.

- ❖ An **F3** is the offspring of one F2 parent where the other was F2 or higher, for example F2xF3 or F2xF4, etc.

- ❖ Then you can get an **F1B, F2B, F3B** and so on. The B stands for Backcross. This occurs when a litter has been produced as a result of a backcross to a purebred dog – normally a Poodle. This is usually done to improve consistency of appearance and coat type, often to increase the possibility of a low shedding coat. It is not common practice for breeders to backcross to a Labrador, so a typical F1B might be one quarter Labrador and three quarters Poodle.

A second generation backcross pup **(F2B)** is the result of an F1 bred to a backcross (F1B). Although three generations in the making, F2Bs are technically second generation dogs.

A **multigen** (or **multigeneration**) crossbreed is the result of successive breeding of crossbreed to crossbreed – such as Cockapoo to Cockapoo, Goldendoodle to

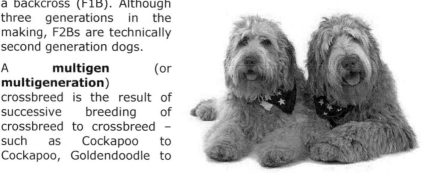

Goldendoodle or Labradoodle to Labradoodle (pictured right) - rather than mating a pedigree dog with another pedigree dog. While hybrid vigour may be lost, the advantage of multigeneration puppies is that good breeders can reproduce a more consistent size, appearance and coat type. So, although a multigen is not a purebred, where prospective owners have a pretty definite idea of what the adult dog will look like, they have a better idea than with an F1 puppy, which could take after the Poodle or the other breed.

By the way, all Australian Labradoodles are multigeneration, but not all multigenerations are Australian Labradoodles. Because multigens have become very popular - and expensive with prices sometimes rising to four or even five figures - there are people who advertise multigens and charge a high price for puppies which are either not technically multigeneration or are not the product of careful breeding. See **Chapter 6. Choosing a Good Breeder** for more information.

Poodles (like these Toy ones below) have a wool-type coat, so breeding from Poodles increases the likelihood of the offspring having a low-shed or non-shedding coat. It also introduces popular new colours such as red and parti (white and another colour).

There are so many new "designer" crossbreeds springing up all the time. Here is a list of popular ones below, with a star by the name if both parent breeds are regarded as hypoallergenic.

Affenpoo - Affenpinscher x Poodle

Airedoodle - Airedale Terrier x Poodle

Aki-Poo - Akita x Poodle

Australian Labradoodle – a multigeneration Labradoodle

Bassetoodle - Basset Hound x Poodle

Bichpoo * - Bichon Frise x Poodle

Bordoodle - Border Collie x Poodle

Cadoodle - Collie x Poodle

Cavapoo - Cavalier King Charles Spaniel x Poodle

Chipoo - Chihuahua x Poodle

Cockapoo (Cockerpoo) - Cocker Spaniel x Poodle

Doxiepoo -Dachshund x Poodle

English Boodle – Bulldog x Poodle

Foodle - Fox Terrier x Poodle

Goldador –Golden Retriever x Labrador

Goldendoodle – Golden Retriever x Poodle

Havapoo * – Havanese and Poodle

Irish Doodle - Irish Setter x Poodle

Lhasapoo * - Lhasa Apso x Poodle

Maltipoo * - Maltese x Poodle

Maltese Shih Tzu (Malshi) * - Maltese x Shih Tzu

Papipoo - Papillon x Poodle

Pekepoo (or Peekapoo) - Pekingese x Poodle

Pugapoo – Pug x Poodle

Puggle – Pug x Beagle

Shepadoodle – German Shepherd x Poodle

Shihpoo * – Shih Tzu x Poodle

Schnoodle * – one of the three Schnauzers x Poodle

Springerdoodle – English Springer Spaniel x Poodle

Yorkipoo * – Yorkshire Terrier x Poodle

Zuchon * –*Shih Tzu x Bichon* Frise

No breeder can guarantee that a specific crossbreed (or pedigree dog) will be 100% suitable for an individual allergy sufferer. However, when responsible breeders of crossbreeds select their dams and sires, coat is often an important factor. There is plenty of anecdotal evidence that many of these dogs shed little or no hair and do not trigger a reaction with some allergy sufferers. But each individual case is different; there are no guarantees.

For those people with consistent or severe allergies, another option is to consider a purebred hypoallergenic breed and then follow our guidance to select a breeder and then a puppy. Choosing a suitable dog is not completely straightforward and you do have to put in extra time to ensure you pick the right dog and maybe make a few adjustments at home as well. Remember:

- ❖ No breed or crossbreed is totally non-shedding
- ❖ No breed or crossbreed is totally hypoallergenic

6. Choosing the Right Breeder

Once you have decided what sort of dog you want, the next step is one of the most important decisions you will make: **choosing the right breeder**. This is especially important with pedigree and crossbreed puppies. And if you are buying a mixed breed pup, you should still ask lots of questions about the health and temperament of the dam and sire.

Like humans, your puppy - like these Labradoodles pictured - will be a product of his or her parents and will inherit many of their characteristics. His temperament and how healthy your puppy will be now and throughout his life will largely depend on the genes of his parents and ancestors.

It is essential that you select a good, responsible breeder. They check the temperament and health records of the parents and only breed from suitable stock. Some breeders have their own websites, particularly in the USA, and many are trustworthy and conscientious, but there are others for whom breeding puppies is their main source of income – and some of these are less scrupulous. This chapter will help you to spot the good ones and give the bad ones a wide berth.

With the cost of a pedigree puppy running into $2,000-$3,000 dollars or more - and often £1,000 and above in the UK - unscrupulous breeders with little knowledge have sprung up, tempted by the prospect of making easy cash. A healthy dog will be your companion for the next decade or more if you are lucky. You wouldn't choose a good friend without screening them and getting to know them first, so why buy an unseen puppy, or one from a pet shop or general advertisement?

Good breeders do not sell their dogs on general purpose websites or in pet shops. In fact they usually have a waiting list of prospective owners.

It is becoming increasingly common, especially in the USA, for unaccredited breeders (those not approved by the Kennel Clubs) to ask for a credit card or Paypal payment as a deposit for a puppy which you have only seen on a photograph. We strongly advise you NOT to buy a puppy like this. Visit the breeder, ask questions and spend time with the individual puppy before committing.

It is important to visit the breeder personally; another reason is so that you can see with your own eyes how the pups are kept. Are they inside or outside in a caged run? Are they socialised with other people and dogs? Are there lots of other types of dogs there? Do the dogs appear healthy and well fed?

Follow our **Top 10 Tips for Selecting a Good Breeder** to help make the right decision. Buying a poorly-bred puppy may save you a few hundred dollars or pounds in the short term, but could cost you thousands in extra veterinary bills in the long run, not to mention the terrible heartache of having a sickly dog.

Rescue groups know only too well the dangers of buying a poorly-bred dog. Many years of problems can arise, often these are health issues, but behaviour problems can also result from poor breeding, causing pain and distress for both dog and owner. All rescue groups strongly recommend taking the time to find a good breeder.

There's certainly the right breeder out there with the right puppy for you - but how do you find them? Everybody knows you should get your puppy from "a good breeder". But how can you tell the good guys from the bad guys?

The Kennel Club in your country is a great place to start as they have lists of approved breeders. In the USA, the American Kennel Club has an online Breeder Classifieds section for each breed at www.akc.org

The Kennel Club in the UK has an Assured Breeder scheme. Here is the link for the KC breeders, only the ones with the rosette symbol are "assured", which means they have been personally visited and approved by the KC: www.thekennelclub.org.uk

Most of the popular crossbreeds have breed clubs or societies which have a list of recommended breeders who agree to breed to a code of ethics. To find them, type the name of your crossbreed, e.g. Labradoodle, into Google followed by the words "breed society," "breed association" or "club." Breed and crossbreed clubs often strongly recommend that "all representations, promises, statements, warranties and guarantees made by either party be in  writing and signed by both parties." In other words, don't rely on a verbal promise, this is a big commitment, make sure the I's are dotted and the T's crossed in case there are any problems with the puppy when you get him or her home.

Many breeds and crossbreeds have online forums and pages on Facebook. You can ask questions here and ask other owners for breeder recommendations, but bear in mind that a lot of breeders use social marketing to sell their puppies.

You might have had a personal recommendation, or like the look of a friend's handsome pooch and want to have one which looks just the same. If that's the case, make sure you ask all the right questions of the breeder regarding how they select their breeding stock and ask to see the parents' health certificates, or at the very least what health screening the dam and sire have had.

Of course, there are no cast iron guarantees that your puppy will be healthy and have a good temperament, but choosing an approved breeder who conforms to a code of ethics is a very good place to start. On the AKC website you can search for breeders by geographical state. In the UK, some of the breed clubs recommend that you visit dog shows to chat to experienced breeders and get to know more about your chosen breed. Reputable breeders do not have to advertise, such is the demand for their puppies, so it's up to you to do your research to find a really good one.

If, for whatever reason, you're not able to buy a puppy from an accredited breeder and you've never bought a puppy before, how do you avoid a "backstreet breeder" or puppy mill? These are people who just breed puppies for profit and sell them to the first person with the cash. Unhappily, this can end in heartbreak for a family later when their puppy develops health or temperament problems due to poor breeding.

SIBERIAN HUSKIES

Remember, good breeders will only breed from dogs which have been carefully selected for health, temperament, physical shape and lineage. There are plenty out there, it's just a question of finding one and the good news is that there are plenty signs that can help the savvy buyer choose the right breeder.

Puppies usually leave the litter for their new homes when they are eight weeks or older. Some breeders prefer their pups to leave at seven weeks, and puppies from toy breeds may stay with the mother for up to 12 weeks. There is a good reason for these specific ages; the mothers continue teaching their pups correct manners and the do's and don'ts of life until they are around eight weeks old.

A responsible breeder will not let the pups go before seven or eight weeks, as they will be too immature and underdeveloped. Breeders who allow their pups to leave before this time may be more interested in a quick profit than a long-term puppy placement.

Due to top breeders often having waiting lists, it pays to plan ahead if you want a well-bred puppy. So, if you've definitely decided to take the plunge, here are some invaluable tips:

Top 12 Tips for Selecting a Good Breeder

1. Responsible breeders keep the dogs in the home as part of the family - not outside in kennel runs or in garages/outbuildings. Check that the area where the puppies are kept is clean and that the puppies themselves look clean.

2. Their pups appear happy and healthy. The dogs are alert, excited to meet new people and don't shy away from visitors. A litter of pups afraid of people may indicate that they have not been properly socialised or they have a reason to fear humans.

3. A good dog breeder will encourage you to spend time with the puppy's parents - or at least the pup's mother - when you visit. They want your entire family to meet the puppy and are happy for you to make more than one visit.

4. They breed only one - or maximum two - breeds such as Bulldogs and Pugs or French Bulldogs, or two types of Terrier, and they are very familiar with the breed standards.

5. Many breeds can have genetic weaknesses. Do your research, find out what health issues occur in the breed and ask the breeder about these. If necessary, the parents will have OFA (Orthopedic Foundation for Animals) or CERF (Canine Eye Registry Foundation) certificates in the USA, BVA certificates in the UK, to prove that both parents are free from genetic defects such as eye or heart issues, hip or elbow dysplasia.

6. Responsible breeders should provide you with a written contract and health guarantee and allow you plenty of time to read it. They will also show you records of the puppy's visits to the vet, vaccinations, worming medication, etc. and explain what other vaccinations your puppy will need.

7. They feed their adults and puppies high quality 'premium' dog food – a nutritious diet is especially important for growing pups. A good breeder will give you guidance on feeding and caring for your puppy and will be available for advice long after you take your puppy home.

8. They don't always have puppies available, but will keep a list of interested people for the next available litter.

9. Responsible breeders don't over-breed their females. A bitch should not have her first litter until two or three years old. Only a

SHIH TSU

minority of vets think that back-to-back breedings are acceptable (i.e. a litter every six-month heat cycle), but most good breeders only allow one litter every year or two years from a female, and they limit the number of litters in her lifetime. For some breeds, such as toy and some bull breeds, pregnancy and birth is very traumatic, and breeding dams may only have a maximum of three litters in their lifetime. Breeding a female too early or late in her life can have serious health consequences.

10. Good breeders want to know their beloved pups are going to good homes and **will ask YOU a lot of questions** about your suitability as owners. DON'T buy from a website or advert where a Paypal or credit card deposit secures you a pup without any questions. Puppies are not inanimate objects, they are warm-blooded, living creatures and you need to make sure the one you select will be suitable for you, your family and lifestyle.

11. Ask the breeder to provide references of other people who have bought their puppies - and make sure you contact at least one before you commit.

12. A good breeder will also agree to take a puppy back within a certain time frame if it does not work out for you, or if there is a health problem.

Healthy, happy puppies and adult dogs are what everybody wants. Taking the time beforehand to find a responsible and committed breeder with well-bred puppies is time well spent. It could save you a lot of time, money and heartache in the future and help to ensure that you and your chosen puppy are happy together for many, many years.

The Most Important Questions to Ask a Breeder

Some of these points have been mentioned in the previous section, but here's a checklist of the questions to ask:

1. Have the parents been health screened? Ask to see original copies of health certificates. If none are available, ask what guarantees the breeder is offering in terms of genetic illnesses, and how long these guarantees last – 12 weeks, a year, a lifetime?

It will vary from breeder to breeder, but good ones will definitely give you some form of guarantee – always ask for this in writing. They will also want to be informed of any hereditary health problems with your puppy, as they may choose not to breed from the dam or sire (mother or father) again. Some breeders keep a chart documenting the full family health history of the pup – ask if one exists and if you can see it.

2. Can you put me in touch with someone who already has one of your puppies?

3. Are you a member of one of the breed associations or clubs, and are you listed as a recommended/accredited breeder with the Kennel Club or the breed clubs? (If not, why not?)

4. How many years have you been breeding? You are looking for someone who has a track record with the breed.

5. How many litters has the mother had? Females should not have litters until they are two or three years old and then have not more than one litter a year. Many more and the breeder may be a "puppy mill", churning out cute – and expensive - pups for money.

6. Do you breed any other types of dog? Buy from a specialist.

7. What is so special about this litter? You are looking for a breeder who has used good breeding stock and his or her knowledge to produce **healthy, handsome dogs with good temperaments**, not just dogs which look good. All puppies are cute, don't buy the first one you see – be patient and pick the right one. If you don't get a satisfactory answer, look elsewhere.

8. What do you feed your adults and puppies? Many pups do not do well on cheap feed bulked up with corn. A reputable breeder will certainly feed a top quality dog food and advise that you do the same.

9. What special care do you recommend? Some breeds need regular eye, ear, tail or wrinkle cleaning, daily grooming or trips to the groomers, while others do well on a specialist diet. Find out as much as you can about any specialist care required and what type of diet the breeder recommends. A good breeder knows what his or her dogs thrive on.

10. How much exercise do the parents need? Generally, your pup's exercise requirements will be similar to his or her parents. Depending on your lifestyle, he or she will get used to a bit more or a bit less, but all dogs need a minimum level of exercise - even Chihuahuas. Working dogs will require considerably more exercise than other dogs. If you are considering a breed which was developed to hunt or retrieve, ask the breeder if the pups are bred from working lines or show (conformation) lines.

11. What is the average lifespan of your dogs? Pups bred from healthy stock generally have longer lives.

12. Why aren't you asking me any questions? A responsible breeder will be committed to making a good match between new owners and their puppies. If the breeder spends more time discussing money than the welfare of the puppy and how you will care for him, you can draw your own conclusions as to what his or her priorities are – and they probably don't include improving the breed.

Hallmarks of a Good Breeder

Good breeders aren't born, they learn their trade. They decide to breed dogs because of their love for the breed and a desire to improve that breed – not to make money.

The American Kennel Club has a blueprint which outlines the hallmarks of a good breeder and how to become one:

The AKC says: "Breeding involves art, science and total devotion. It will show you the best in the human-canine bond ... and the result of absolute commitment by responsible breeders.

A Responsible Breeder is Always a Student. Responsible breeders seek to improve their breeds with every litter. To reach this goal, they must devote hours to continually learning as much as they can about their breeds, including health and genetic concerns, temperament,

ROTTWEILER

appearance and type. They also need to know about general dog behavior, training and health care. In short, they become canine experts."

The AKC encourages new breeders to get involved with breed clubs, study the breed standard, read books, magazines and websites on every aspect of canines, and attend dog shows, obedience trials and performance events, which "provide the opportunity to observe purebreds in action. You can learn about different lines by viewing real dogs and studying the pedigrees of those you like.

A Responsible Breeder is Objective. Virtually every dog is the best in the world in the eyes of its owner. Responsible breeders have the ability to separate their love for their dog from an honest evaluation of its good and bad points.

Breeding is hard work. Every breeding is a carefully planned endeavor to produce a better dog. A good breeder recognizes a dog's flaws and finds a mate with characteristics that will help reduce or eliminate those flaws. Seek assistance from some of the best informational resources available - long-time breeders and the breeder of your dog. This person should have extensive knowledge of your dog's line and, like you, should want to see it continually improved.

An excellent way to develop an impartial eye is to test your dog against others. To see how well your dog conforms to the breed standard, get an assessment from an experienced breeder and dog fancier, and enter dog shows. Entering obedience and field tests and trials will allow you to measure your dog's intelligence and abilities. If your dog is a success in these events, you'll be more confident that breeding your dog will contribute to the betterment of its breed.

Responsible breeders are familiar with AKC rules and regulations concerning the sale and registration of AKC-registrable dogs. Before you breed your dog, you should contact the AKC to verify that you have all the correct paperwork, understand how to register a litter, and are able to provide proper documentation to your buyers.

A Responsible Breeder Conditions the Sire and Dam. Good puppies start long before their parents are bred. Both the sire and dam need constant care, or conditioning, to produce the best offspring. This means regular veterinary care, screening for genetic problems, pre-breeding health tests, regular exercise and good nutrition. It means consulting with a veterinarian or experienced breeder to ensure that you know how to meet the dam's (mother's) special nutritional needs while she is in whelp (pregnant).

"It also means maintaining your dog's mental health. Stressed animals can experience fertility problems. Many breeders swear by the belief that the dam's temperament affects the puppies - good puppies come from good mothers. Consequently, they avoid breeding shy or unstable dogs.

A Responsible Breeder Nurtures the Puppies. Preparing for puppies means building a proper nursery. A whelping box must be dry, very warm and draft-free. It should be big enough for the dam to be able to move about freely with sides that will safely contain the puppies.

"The dam normally takes care of the puppies' needs the first few weeks of their lives. Once the puppies are weaned, they become much more active and require lots more work. You will need to oversee feeding to ensure each puppy gets adequate food. You will need to keep the towels or shredded newspaper lining the whelping box clean. The puppies will need their first round of shots, they may need grooming and they will definitely need plenty of play time and opportunities for getting used to being around people. You may even want to start working with them on basic obedience commands to ease their transition to their new homes.

A Responsible Breeder Places Puppies Wisely. As you can probably imagine, once it's time for the puppies to go to new homes, you've invested a lot of yourself in them. A difficult and important aspect of breeding is making sure your puppies go to owners who will provide loving and permanent homes.

The complete picture is important to responsible breeders. They make sure new puppy owners know what to expect, both the pros and the cons, from the furry little bundles they're taking home. If their particular breed requires extensive grooming, drools profusely, or can be difficult to train, responsible breeders will point that out. They will also provide all the necessary paperwork for new owners to register their dogs with the AKC, which will allow them to participate in the sport of purebred dogs."

A responsible breeder will also ask YOU questions before placing a puppy with you. These are some questions to expect:

- ❖ Why do you or your family want a dog?

- ❖ Who will be primarily responsible for the dog's care?

- ❖ Are there any children? If so, how old are they?

- ❖ Does anyone in the household have allergies?

- ❖ What is the potential owner's attitude toward training and obedience?

- ❖ How often is someone at home?

❖ Will they have time to walk and play with the dog?

The AKC adds: "If feasible, it's not unreasonable for a breeder to make a house call after the puppy has had time to settle in with its new family. Some breeders require dog buyers to sign contracts indicating the specific conditions of care. Important qualities to look for in potential puppy owners are interest and inquisitiveness about you and the dogs you breed. A person or family truly committed to responsible dog ownership will want to learn about the breed and how to care for it.

"Responsible breeders are there for all situations - both good and bad. They know they were responsible for this puppy being born, so they are responsible for it until the day it dies. They are willing to provide guidance and answer as many questions as they are asked. They are always concerned about their puppies.

"One breeder once said the most satisfying phone call she received came 14 years after she bred her first litter. The caller said one of "her" (the breeder's) dogs had died of old age. At that moment the breeder knew she was responsible for bringing years of the same kind of love and joy she experienced from her dogs into someone else's home." ©
AKC

Is your chosen breeder up to the mark? Are they producing puppies for the betterment of the breed?

TOP TIPS: Take your puppy to a veterinarian to have a thorough check-up **within 48 hours** of purchase. Try to find one who is familiar with the breed, especially with toy and bull breeds which may be sensitive to anaesthetic. If your vet is not happy with the health of the dog, no matter how painful it may be, return the pup to the breeder. Keeping an unhealthy puppy will only cause more distress and expense in the long run.

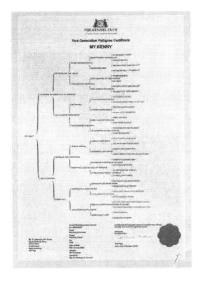

If you are buying a purebred (pedigree), the puppy will have official AKC or Kennel Club papers; make sure you are given original copies of these. If they are not available, then the puppy is not a true purebred/pedigree registered with the Kennel Clubs - no matter what the breeder says.

In the UK, an enhanced five generation pedigree registration certificate (pictured) is an impressive document. It is A3 size and includes an embossed Kennel Club seal with Champions printed in red text. The information provided includes Kennel Club registration number, breed, colour, sex, date of birth, breeder, owner and information on five generations of the pedigree dog's ancestry.

Some top show breeders may place restrictions on the purchase of your puppy. For example they may say that you cannot breed from the puppy, or you have to have her spayed or him neutered, or that if your pup is female and she has puppies, they have first pick of the litter.

In the UK, ask if the puppy is being sold with a Puppy Contract. These protect both buyer and seller by providing information on diet, worming, vaccination and veterinary visits from the birth of the puppy until he or she leaves the breeder.

Do your research before you go to see the litter, as once you are there the cute puppies will be completely irresistible, and you will buy with your heart rather than your head.

If you have any doubts at all about the breeder or the puppy, WALK AWAY.

7. Picking the Individual Puppy

So now you have chosen the breed or crossbreed and found a good breeder with puppies available, you're ready to pick the individual puppy.

At a few weeks old, many puppies within a litter look very similar. You may decide to go for a particular colour, or a female instead of a male, or vice versa. Maybe you like the look of the biggest pup, or the one with the cutest eyes, the puppy that makes you laugh the most, or the one which boldly skips forward and tugs at your trousers - and heartstrings - with her sharp little teeth.

But there is one attribute in all of these puppies which you should take into consideration – and that is **temperament**.

If you have gone this far and chosen your breeder wisely, all of these puppies should have been bred not only for how they look, but also for their health and temperament. Temperament is inherited; it is the general attitude a dog has towards life, and in particular people and other animals.

It is very important to consider it, as a dog's behaviour throughout his life and how he reacts to the world around him is a combination of his temperament and his environment, or how he is treated by you. Nature and nurture.

Choosing the Right Temperament

While different dogs of the same breed often share many characteristics and temperament traits, each puppy also has his or her own individual character, just like humans. You may share similar traits with your brother or sister, but you will also have differences - unless you are identical twins, in which case you're probably very similar in temperament. Otherwise, you might be naturally more strong willed than your brother or sister, or a bit more outgoing or introverted than him or her. It's the same with puppies.

Of course, there are differences between the breeds, some dogs bred to hunt or retrieve may be naturally more independent-minded than those

121

bred to be companion dogs. But when it comes to temperament, the differences WITHIN the breeds are great. Take the German Shepherd Dog as an example; you can have a timid, sedate dog or a bold, energetic one. However, the breed has a natural instinct to be protective. So whichever temperament you choose, you should spend time socialising him or her with other people and dogs so he develops into a well-rounded adult.

When it comes to choosing the specific puppy, take your time. Selecting a dog which will share your home and your life for the next decade is an important decision. Don't rush it. Visit the breeder more than once to see how your chosen pup interacts and get an idea of his or her character in comparison to the littermates.

Some puppies will run up to greet you, pull at your shoelaces and playfully bite your fingers. Others will be more content to stay in the basket sleeping. Watch their behaviour and energy levels. Which puppy will be most suitable? If you are rescuing or adopting an adult dog, spend time with the dog, especially at the beginning to get to understand him, and be prepared to cope with any health or behaviour problems – such as chewing – which may arise.

Useful Tips

A submissive dog will by nature be more passive, less energetic and quite probably easier to train. A dominant dog will often be more energetic and lively. He or she may also be more stubborn and need a firmer hand when training or socialising with other dogs.

There is no good or bad, it's a question of which type of character will best suit you and your lifestyle. Here are a couple of quick tests to try at the breeder's to see if your puppy has a submissive or dominant personality:

❖ Roll the puppy gently on to his or her back in the crook of your arm (or on the floor, as illustrated here with a Bernese Mountain Dog pup). Then rest a hand on the pup's chest and look into his eyes for a few seconds. If he immediately struggles to get free, he is considered to be **dominant**. A puppy that doesn't struggle, but is happy to stay on his or her back has a more **submissive** character.

❖ A similar test is the suspension test. Gently lift the puppy at arm's length under the armpits for a few seconds while allowing his hind legs to dangle free. A dominant pup will kick and

struggle to get free. A puppy that is happy to remain dangling is more submissive.

Here are some other useful signs to look out for:

❖ Watch how he or she interacts with other puppies in the litter. Does your chosen pup try and dominate them, does (s)he walk away from them or is (s)he happy to play with the littermates? This may give you an idea of how easy it will be to socialise him or her with other dogs.

❖ After contact, does the pup want to follow you or walk away from you? Not following may mean he or she has a more independent nature.

❖ If you throw something for the puppy is he or she happy to retrieve it for you or does (s)he ignore it? This may measure their willingness to work with humans.

❖ If you drop a bunch of keys behind the puppy, does (s)he act normally or does (s)he flinch and jump away? The latter may be an indication of a timid or nervous disposition. Not reacting could also be a sign of deafness.

Decide which temperament would fit in with you and your family and the rest is up to you. A puppy that has constant positive interactions with people and other animals during the first three to four months of life will be a happier, more stable dog. In contrast, a puppy plucked from its family and isolated at home alone for weeks on end will be less happy, less socialised and may well develop behaviour problems.

Puppies are like children. Being properly raised contributes to their confidence, sociability, stability and intellectual development. The bottom line is that a pup raised in a warm, loving environment and well exercised is likely to be more tolerant and accepting, and less likely to develop behaviour problems. (Our picture shows a Pug, left, and French Bulldog).

There are more detailed ways of evaluating the temperament of an individual puppy using a series of tests that measure traits including stability, confidence, shyness, friendliness, aggressiveness, protectiveness, prey instinct, play drive, self-defence instincts and the ability to distinguish between threatening and non-threatening situations.

For those of you who take a scientific approach to choosing the right puppy, we are including the full **Volhard Puppy Aptitude Test (PAT).**

This test has been developed by the highly respected Wendy and Jack Volhard who have built up an international reputation over the last 30 years for their invaluable contribution to dog training, health and nutrition. Their philosophy is: "We believe that one of life's great joys is living in harmony with your dog."

They have written several books and the Volhard PAT is regarded as the premier method for evaluating the nature of young puppies. Jack and Wendy have also written the excellent **Dog Training for Dummies** book. Visit their website at www.volhard.com for details of their upcoming dog training camps, as well as their training and nutrition groups.

The Volhard Puppy Aptitude Test

Here are the ground rules for performing the test:

- The testing is done in a location unfamiliar to the puppies. This does not mean they have to be taken away from home. A 10-foot square area is perfectly adequate, such as a room in the house where the puppies have not been.

- The puppies are tested one at a time.

- There are no other dogs or people, except the scorer and the tester, in the testing area.

- The puppies do not know the tester.

- The scorer is a disinterested third party and not the person interested in selling you a puppy.

- The scorer is unobtrusive and positions himself so he can observe the puppies' responses without having to move.

- The puppies are tested before they are fed.

- The puppies are tested when they are at their liveliest.

- Do not try to test a puppy that is not feeling well.

- Puppies should not be tested the day of or the day after being vaccinated.

Only the first response counts. ***Tip: During the test, watch the puppy's tail. It will make a difference in the scoring whether the tail is up or down.***

The tests are simple to perform and anyone with some common sense can do them. You can, however, elicit the help of someone who has tested puppies before and knows what they are doing.

Social attraction - the owner or caretaker of the puppies places it in the test area about four feet from the tester and then leaves the test area. The tester kneels down and coaxes the puppy to come to him or her by encouragingly and gently clapping hands and calling. The tester must coax the puppy in the opposite direction from where it entered the test area. Hint: Lean backward, sitting on your heels instead of leaning forward toward the puppy. Keep your hands close to your body encouraging the puppy to come to you instead of trying to reach for the puppy.

Following - the tester stands up and slowly walks away encouraging the puppy to follow. Hint: Make sure the puppy sees you walk away and get the puppy to focus on you by lightly clapping your hands and using verbal encouragement to get the puppy to follow you. Do not lean over the puppy.

Restraint - the tester crouches down and gently rolls the puppy on its back for 30 seconds. Hint: Hold the puppy down without applying too much pressure. The object is not to keep it on its back but to test its response to being placed in that position.

Social Dominance - let the puppy stand up or sit and gently stroke it from the head to the back while you crouch beside it. See if it will lick your face, an indication of a forgiving nature. Continue stroking until you see a behaviour you can score. Hint: When you crouch next to the puppy avoid leaning or hovering over it. Have the puppy at your side, both of you facing in the same direction.

Tip: During testing maintain a positive, upbeat and friendly attitude toward the puppies. Try to get each puppy to interact with you to bring out the best in him or her. Make the test a pleasant experience for the puppy.

Elevation Dominance - the tester cradles the puppy with both hands, supporting the puppy under its chest and gently lifts its two feet off the ground and holds it there for 30 seconds.

Retrieving - the tester

crouches beside the puppy and attracts its attention with a crumpled up piece of paper. When the puppy shows some interest, the tester throws the paper no more than four feet in front of the puppy encouraging it to retrieve the paper.

Touch Sensitivity - the tester locates the webbing of one of the puppy's front paws and presses it lightly between his index finger and thumb. The tester gradually increases pressure while counting to ten and stops when the puppy pulls away or shows signs of discomfort.

Sound Sensitivity - the puppy is placed in the centre of the testing area and an assistant stationed at the perimeter makes a sharp noise, such as banging a metal spoon on the bottom of a metal pan.

Sight Sensitivity - the puppy is placed in the centre of the testing area. The tester ties a string around a bath towel and jerks it across the floor, two feet away from the puppy.

Stability - an umbrella is opened about five feet from the puppy and gently placed on the ground. During the testing, make a note of the heart rate of the pup, this is an indication of how it deals with stress, as well as its energy level.

Puppies come with high, medium or low energy levels. You have to decide for yourself, which suits your lifestyle. Dogs with high energy levels need a great deal of exercise, and will get into mischief if this energy is not channelled into the right direction.

Finally, look at the overall structure of the puppy. You see what you get at 49 days of age (seven weeks). If the pup has strong and straight front and back legs, with all four feet pointing in the same direction, it will grow up that way, provided you give it the proper diet and environment. If you notice something out of the ordinary at this age, it will stay with puppy for the rest of its life. He will not grow out of it.

Scoring the Results

Following are the responses you will see and the score assigned to each particular response. You will see some variations and will have to make a judgment on what score to give them:

TEST	RESPONSE	SCORE
SOCIAL ATTRACTION	Came readily, tail up, jumped, bit at hands	1
	Came readily, tail up, pawed, licked at hands	2

	Came readily, tail up	3
	Came readily, tail down	4
	Came hesitantly, tail down	5
	Didn't come at all	6
FOLLOWING	Followed readily, tail up, got underfoot, bit at feet	1
	Followed readily, tail up, got underfoot	2
	Followed readily, tail up	3
	Followed readily, tail down	4
	Followed hesitantly, tail down	5
	Did not follow or went away	6
RESTRAINT	Struggled fiercely, flailed, bit	1
	Struggled fiercely, flailed	2
	Settled, struggled, settled with some eye contact	3
	Struggled, then settled	4
	No struggle	5
	No struggle, strained to avoid eye contact	6
SOCIAL DOMINANCE	Jumped, pawed, bit, growled	1
	Jumped, pawed	2
	Cuddled up to tester and tried to lick face	3
	Squirmed, licked at hands	4
	Rolled over, licked at hands	5
	Went away and stayed away	6
ELEVATION DOMINANCE	Struggled fiercely, tried to bite	1
	Struggled fiercely	2
	Struggled, settled, struggled, settled	3

	No struggle, relaxed	4
	No struggle, body stiff	5
	No struggle, froze	6
RETRIEVING	Chased object, picked it up and ran away	1
	Chased object, stood over it and did not return	2
	Chased object, picked it up and returned with it to tester	3
	Chased object and returned without it to tester	4
	Started to chase object, lost interest	5
	Does not chase object	6
TOUCH SENSITIVITY	8-10 count before response	1
	6-8 count before response	2
	5-6 count before response	3
	3-5 count before response	4
	2-3 count before response	5
	1-2 count before response	6
SOUND SENSITIVITY	Listened, located sound and ran toward it barking	1
	Listened, located sound and walked slowly toward it	2
	Listened, located sound & showed curiosity	3
	Listened and located sound	4
	Cringed, backed off and hid behind tester 5	5
	Ignored sound and showed no curiosity	6
SIGHT SENSITIVITY	Looked, attacked and bit object	1
	Looked and put feet on object and put	2

	mouth on it	
	Looked with curiosity and attempted to investigate, tail up	3
	Looked with curiosity, tail down	4
	Ran away or hid behind tester	5
	Hid behind tester	6
STABILITY	Looked and ran to the umbrella, mouthing or biting it	1
	Looked and walked to the umbrella, smelling it cautiously	2
	Looked and went to investigate	3
	Sat and looked, but did not move toward the umbrella	4
	Showed little or no interest	5
	Ran away from the umbrella	6

The scores are interpreted as follows:

Mostly 1s - Strong desire to be pack leader and is not shy about bucking for a promotion. Has a predisposition to be aggressive to people and other dogs and will bite. Should only be placed into a very experienced home where the dog will be trained and worked on a regular basis.

Tip: Stay away from the puppy with a lot of 1's or 2's. It has lots of leadership aspirations and may be difficult to manage. This puppy needs an experienced home. Not good with children.

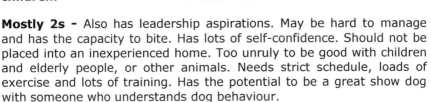

Mostly 2s - Also has leadership aspirations. May be hard to manage and has the capacity to bite. Has lots of self-confidence. Should not be placed into an inexperienced home. Too unruly to be good with children and elderly people, or other animals. Needs strict schedule, loads of exercise and lots of training. Has the potential to be a great show dog with someone who understands dog behaviour.

Mostly 3s - Can be a high-energy dog and may need lots of exercise. Good with people and other animals. Can be a bit of a handful to live with. Needs training, does very well at it and learns quickly. Great dog for second-time owner.

Mostly 4s - The kind of dog that makes the perfect pet. Best choice for the first time owner. Rarely will buck for a promotion in the family. Easy to train, and rather quiet. Good with elderly people, children, although may need protection from the children. Choose this pup, take it to obedience classes, and you'll be the star, without having to do too much work!

Tip: The puppy with mostly 3's and 4's can be quite a handful, but should be good with children and does well with training. Energy needs to be dispersed with plenty of exercise.

Mostly 5s - Fearful, shy and needs special handling. Will run away at the slightest stress in its life. Strange people, strange places, different floor or surfaces may upset it. Often afraid of loud noises and terrified of thunderstorms. When you greet it upon your return, may submissively urinate.

Needs a very special home where the environment doesn't change too much and where there are no children. Best for a quiet, elderly couple. If cornered and cannot get away, has a tendency to bite.

Mostly 6s – So independent that he doesn't need you or other people. Doesn't care if he is trained or not - he is his own person. Unlikely to bond to you, since he doesn't need you. A great guard dog for gas stations! Do not take this puppy and think you can change him into a lovable bundle - you can't, so leave well enough alone.

Tip: Avoid the puppy with several 6's. It is so independent it doesn't need you or anyone. He is his own person and unlikely to bond to you.

The Scores

Few puppies will test with all 2's or all 3's, there'll be a mixture of scores. For that first time, wonderfully easy to train, potential star, look for a puppy that scores with mostly 4's and 3's. Don't worry about the score on Touch Sensitivity - you can compensate for that with the right training equipment.

It's hard not to become emotional when picking a puppy - they are all so cute, soft and cuddly. Remind yourself that this dog is going to be with you for eight to 16 years. Don't hesitate to step back a little to contemplate your decision. Sleep on it and review it in the light of day.

Avoid the puppy with a score of 1 on the Restraint and Elevation tests. This puppy will be too much for the first-time owner.

It's a lot more fun to have a good dog, one that is easy to train, one you can live with and one you can be proud of, than one that is a constant struggle.

Don't overlook an animal shelter as a source for a good dog. Not all dogs wind up in a shelter because they are bad. After that cute puppy stage, when the dog grows up, it may become too much for its owner. Or, there has been a change in the owner's circumstances forcing him or her into having to give up the dog.

Most of the time, these dogs are housetrained and already have some training. If the dog has been properly socialized to people, it will be able to adapt to a new environment. Bonding may take a little longer, but once accomplished, results in a devoted companion.

Dog or a Bitch (Male or Female)?

One decision you will have to make is whether to get a male or female. Some people have already made up their minds that they prefer one gender over another. When my sister and I were children, my father always insisted on having male dogs, so that he would not be only male in the house! Unless you are intending to breed from your dog, there really is no superior gender; it's entirely your decision. The behaviour of a dog largely depends on temperament and how it has been raised by you.

The differences WITHIN the sexes are greater than the differences BETWEEN the sexes. In other words, you can get a dominant female and a submissive male, or vice versa. There are, however, some general traits which are more common with one gender or the other.

However, un-neutered males – referred to as 'dogs' – are more likely to display aggression if confronted by aggression from other male dogs. On walks, a male dog - whether entire or neutered – will mark his territory regularly. If you are walking him on a lead, this may mean every few paces. Some very dominant females also mark their territory, but this is unusual. Normally a female will urinate once towards the beginning of a walk and empty or nearly empty her bladder.

If you take a male Puppy for a walk, you can expect him to stop at every lamp-post, trash can and interesting blade of grass to leave his mark by urinating. A female will tend to urinate far less often on a walk.

Female dogs, or bitches, generally tend to be less aggressive towards other dogs, except when they are raising puppies. With some breeds, families consider a female if they have young children, as a bitch may be more tolerant towards young creatures. However, if you do have very young children the breed is more important than the gender of the dog. Choose one which is known to love children.

SIBERIAN HUSKIES

Females, especially large ones, can be messy when they come into heat every six months, due to the blood loss. If your female is not spayed, you will also have the nuisance of her becoming a magnet for all the free-wandering male dogs in your neighbourhood. During heat, which may last two to three weeks, she has to be kept indoors – preferably away from your expensive carpets – or on a lead when away from the home. She will also want to mate during this time, so you cannot let her wander.

If the size of the dog is a factor, bear in mind that a male will grow to be larger than a female dog from the same litter. Do you want a big or small version of the breed you have chosen? Teenage boys tend to mature later than girls, and it's the same with dogs, with females reaching maturity faster than males. This is an advantage when it comes to training. It does not mean that the female dog is more intelligent than the male dog, it just means that a female may be easier to train than a male dog of the same age because she is more mature.

Unless you bought your puppy specifically for breeding or showing under Kennel Club rules, it is recommended you have your dog neutered, or spayed if she is a female. If you plan to have two or more dogs living together, this is even more advisable. Bear in mind that when you select your puppy, you should also be looking out for the right temperament as well as the right sex.

Top 12 Tips for Choosing a Healthy Puppy

Before committing to a puppy, you should check him from head to tail to make sure he is in good physical shape.

1. The puppy's nose should be cool, damp and clean with no discharge. A pup which is sneezing or has a nasal discharge should be avoided. If you are selecting a brachycephalic breed, such as a Pug, Bulldog or Boxer, don't choose a puppy with very heavy skin folds/rolls around his nose; sometimes they will get proportionately smaller as the pup grows, but if they remain large they will need regular, even daily, cleaning as they become a breeding ground for bacteria.

2. The puppy should breathe normally. Watch him run around and then listen to his breathing – does it sound normal or laboured? With all puppies, but especially brachycephalic breeds, ensure that the nostrils are open, rather than slits, and that the puppy is not snuffling, snorting, coughing or wheezing – although this may appear cute, these are all signs of a pup struggling for breath.

3. A pup's eyes should be bright and clear with no discharge or tear stain. If you see tear stains on the muzzle, look for eyelids that roll in or out, extra eyelashes or conjunctivitis. The pupils should be dark and have no lines or white spots; these may be a sign of hereditary cataracts. You might be able to see the third eyelid (haw); this is fine as long as it is not red and inflames. Steer clear of a puppy which blinks a lot, this could also be a sign of an eye problem.

4. Ears should be clean with no sign of discharge, soreness or redness. They should also smell fine; a yeasty or unpleasant odour is a sign of infection.

5. Gums should be clean and a healthy pink colour. Pale gums might be a sign of anaemia, which could be caused by worms or other internal parasites.

6. Feel for a soft spot on the top of the skull. If one is present, it means that the fontanel (the soft spot between the bones) is open, which is not desirable. Although rare, in toy breeds it can be a sign that the puppy has hydrocephalus (water on the brain).

7. Check the puppy's bottom to make sure it is clean and there are no signs of diarrhoea.

8. A puppy's coat should be clean with no signs of ticks or fleas. Red or irritated skin or bald spots could be a sign of infestation or a skin condition. Also check between the toes of the paws for signs of redness or swelling, some breeds are prone to interdigital cysts.

9. Choose a pup that moves freely without any injury or lameness, check that the legs are straight and well-formed, not bowed.

10. When the puppy is distracted, clap or make a noise behind him - not too loud - to make sure he is not deaf.

11. What is the puppy's general appearance? Is he lively, healthy looking and alert? Does he seem interested in his surroundings? Lethargy and disinterest are often signs of something amiss.

12. Finally, ask to see veterinary records to confirm your puppy has been wormed and had his first injections. If you are unlucky enough to have a health problem with your pup within the first few months, a reputable breeder will allow you to return the pup. Also, if you get the puppy home and things don't work out for whatever reason, good breeders should also take the puppy back. Make sure this is the case before you commit.

Just a final note. If you are thinking of getting more than one dog, many experts believe that it is better to wait until-your first puppy is one-year old or older so that he or she can help to teach the new arrival some of the rules.

There is a school of thought that if you take two puppies from the same litter, they have known each other since birth and their first loyalty will be to each other and not to you, although owners do successfully raise siblings together. Bear in mind that puppies are incredibly hard work in terms of their demands on you and your time and it's even more difficult with two.

FRENCH
BULLDOGS

8. Bringing a Puppy Home

You've chosen the type of dog you want, found a good breeder, selected the individual puppy and now you're ready for the big day when you collect your little furry bundle of joy which, with any luck, will be a part of your life for the next decade or so, like the mixed breed puppy pictured. Before you do, there are a few things you'll need at home:

Puppy Checklist

✓ A dog bed or basket

✓ Bedding – old towels or a blanket which can easily be washed

✓ A small collar and leash

✓ An identification tag for the puppy's collar

✓ Food and water bowls, preferably stainless steel

✓ Newspapers for housetraining

✓ Poo(p) bags

✓ Puppy food – find out what the breeder is feeding

✓ Puppy treats

✓ Toys suitable for chewing puppies

✓ A puppy coat if you live in a cool climate

✓ A crate if you decide to use one

✓ Old towels for cleaning your puppy and partially covering the crate

✓ If possible, a towel or piece of cloth which has been rubbed on the puppy's mother to put in his bed

✓ PLENTY OF TIME!

Later on you'll also need a larger collar, a longer lead, a grooming brush, dog shampoo, flea and worming products and maybe other items such as a harness or a travel crate.

Puppy Proofing Your Home

Before your puppy arrives at his or her new home, you may have to make a few adjustments to make your home safe and suitable.

Young puppies are small bundles of instinct and energy (when they are awake), with little common sense and even less self control. They are like babies and it's up to you to set the boundaries – both physically and in terms of behaviour – but one step at a time.

It's a good idea to have an area where the puppy is allowed to go and then keep the rest of the house off-limits until housetraining is complete, and this can be anything from a few days to a few months in really stubborn cases. One of the biggest factors influencing the success and speed of housetraining is your commitment, which is another reason for taking a week or two off work when your puppy arrives home.

Like babies, most puppies are mini chewing machines and so remove anything breakable and/or chewable within the puppy's reach – including wooden furniture. Obviously you cannot remove your kitchen cupboards, doors, skirting boards and other fixtures and fittings, so don't leave him unattended for any length of time where he can chew something which is hard to replace.

A baby gate is a relatively inexpensive method of preventing a puppy from going upstairs and leaving an unwanted gift on your precious bedroom carpets. A puppy's bones are soft and recent studies have shown that if allowed to climb or descend stairs, young pups can develop joint problems later in life. You can also use a baby gate or wire panels available from pet shops to keep the puppy enclosed in one room – preferably one with a floor which is easy to wipe clean and not too far away from a door to the garden or yard for housetraining.

In any case, you may also want to remove your precious oriental rugs in other rooms until he or she is fully housetrained and has stopped chewing everything in sight. Make sure you have some toys suitable for

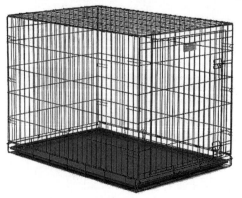

sharp little teeth – but don't give old shoes and slippers or they will think your footwear is fair game.

The puppy's designated area or room should be not too hot or cold, not damp and free from draughts. Some brachycephalic (flat faced) breeds are extremely sensitive to temperature fluctuations and cannot tolerate heat or cold. If you live in a hot climate and it's summer, your new puppy may need to be in an air conditioned room. Scientists have proved that the domestic dog is a direct descendant of the wolf and, like a wolf, a puppy needs a den.

This den is a haven where your puppy feels safe for the first few weeks after the traumatic experience of leaving his or her mother and littermates. Young puppies sleep for over 18 hours a day at the beginning, some may sleep for up to 22 hours a day; this is normal. If you have young children, you must restrict the time they spend with the puppy to a few short sessions a day. Plenty of sleep is **essential** for the normal development of the young dog. You wouldn't wake a baby up every hour or so to play and shouldn't do that with a puppy.

You have a couple of options with the den; you can get a dog bed or basket, or you can use a crate. Crates have long been popular in the USA and are becoming increasingly popular in the UK, particularly as it is often quicker to train a puppy using a crate.

The idea of keeping a dog in a cage like a rabbit or hamster is abhorrent to many animal-loving Brits. Using the crate as a prison to contain the dog hours on end certainly is cruel. But the crate has its place as a sanctuary for your dog, a place where he or she can go; it is their own space and they know no harm will come to them in there. See the section at the end of this chapter on **Crate Training**.

Most puppies' natural instinct is not to soil the area where they sleep. Put plenty of newspapers down in the area next to the den and your puppy should  choose to go to the toilet here if you are not quick enough to take him or her outside. Of course, they may also decide to trash their designated area by chewing their blankets and shredding the newspaper – patience is the key in this situation.

If you have a garden or yard that you intend letting your puppy roam in, make sure that every little gap has been plugged. You'd be amazed at the tiny holes they can escape through. Also, don't leave your puppy unattended as they can come to harm and dogs are increasingly being targeted by unscrupulous thieves, who are even stealing them from gardens.

In order for puppies to grow into well-adjusted dogs, they have to feel comfortable and relaxed in their new surroundings and they need a great deal of sleep. They are leaving the warmth and protection of their mother and littermates and so for the first few days at least, your puppy will feel very sad.

It is important to make the transition from the birth home to your home as easy as possible. His life is in your hands. How you react and interact with him in the first few days and weeks will shape your relationship and his character for the years ahead.

The First Few Days

Before you collect your puppy, let the breeder know what time you will be arriving and ask her not to feed the pup for three or four hours beforehand. He will be less likely to be car sick and should be hungry when he arrives in his new home. The same applies to an adult dog moving to a new home.

When you collect the puppy, ask her for an old towel which has been with the dam – you can leave one on an earlier visit to collect with the pup. Or take one with you and rub the mother with it to collect her scent and put this with the puppy for the first few days. It may help him to settle in.

Make sure you get copies of any health certificates relating to the parents. A good breeder will also have a contract of sale, which outlines your and the breeder's rights and responsibilities. It should also state that you can return the puppy if there are health issues within a certain time frame – although if you have picked your breeder carefully, it should hopefully not come to this. The breeder should also give you details of worming and any vaccinations.

It is **always** a good idea to have puppies checked out by a vet within a few days of picking them up. Keep the puppy away from other dogs in the waiting room as he or she will not be fully protected against canine diseases until the vaccination schedule is complete.

You should also find out exactly what the breeder is feeding and how much. You cannot suddenly switch a dog's diet; their digestive systems cannot cope with a sudden change, so you should stick to whatever the breeder is feeding initially.

When you pick up the puppy, you may have a crate or travel crate in  the car for the puppy, or you may choose to take someone along to hold him throughout the journey. If so, have an old towel between the person and the pup, as he may quite possible wee (the puppy, not the passenger!) If the pup is in a crate, he or she will probably cry; this is normal.

The first few days will be stressful for both you and the puppy. Your new arrival is feeling very sorry for himself and will probably whine a lot. Imagine a small child being taken away from his mother; that is how your pup will feel. One of the things your pup will desperately miss in the beginning is the physical closeness of his mother and littermates.

Our website receives many emails from worried new owners. Here are some of the most common concerns:

- ❖ My puppy sleeps all the time, is this normal?
- ❖ My puppy won't stop crying or whining
- ❖ My puppy is shivering
- ❖ My puppy won't eat
- ❖ My puppy is very timid
- ❖ My puppy follows me everywhere, she won't let me out of her sight

Most of the above are quite common. They are just a young pup's reaction to leaving his mother and littermates and entering into a strange new world. It is normal for puppies to sleep most of the time, just like babies. It is also normal for some puppies to whine a lot during the first few days. Make your new pup as comfortable as possible, ensuring he has a warm, quiet place which is his, where he is not pestered by children or other pets. Talk in a soft, reassuring voice to him and handle him gently, while giving him plenty of time to sleep. During the first few nights, your puppy will whine at night, buy yourselves some earplugs and try your best to ignore the pitiful cries.

Unless they are especially dominant, most puppies will be nervous and timid for the first few days. They will think of you as their new mother and may follow you around the house. This is also quite natural, but after a few days, start to leave your puppy for a few minutes at a time, gradually building up the time. If you are never parted, he may develop separation anxiety when you do have to leave him. See the section on **Separation Anxiety.**

If your routine means you are normally out of the house for a few hours during the day, try to get your puppy on a Friday or Saturday so he has at least a couple of days to adjust to his new surroundings. A far better idea is to book at least a week or two off work to help your puppy settle in. If you don't work, leave your diary free for the first couple of weeks. Helping a new pup to settle in properly is virtually a full-time job in the beginning.

It is normal for a new pup to sleep for most of the time at first. Make sure he gets plenty of rest and if you have children, don't let them constantly waken the pup, he needs his sleep. Don't invite friends round to see your new puppy for at least a day or two, preferably longer. However excited you are, he needs a few days bonding with you and your family.

This is a frightening time for your puppy. Talk softly and gently stroke him, he needs plenty of reassurance. Is your puppy shivering with cold or is it nerves? Make sure he is in a warm, safe, quiet place away. If your puppy won't eat, spend time gently coaxing him. If he leaves his food, take it away and try it later. Do not leave it down all of the time or he may get used to turning his nose up at food. Then the next time you put something down for him, he is more likely to be hungry.

If your puppy is crying, it is probably for one of the following reasons:

- ❖ He is lonely
- ❖ He is hungry
- ❖ He wants attention from you
- ❖ He needs to go to the toilet

If it is none of these, then check his body to make sure he hasn't picked up an injury. Try not to fuss over him. If he whimpers, just reassure him with a quiet word. If he cries loudly and tries to get out of his allotted area, he probably needs to go to the toilet. Even if it is the middle of the night, get up (yes, sorry, this is best) and take him outside. Praise him if he goes to the toilet.

The strongest bonding period for a puppy is between eight and 12 weeks of age. The most important factors in bonding with your puppy are TIME spent with him and PATIENCE, even when he or she makes a mess in the house or chews your furniture. Remember, they are just baby dogs and it takes time to learn not to do these things. Spend the time to love, exercise and train your pup and you will have a loyal friend for life who will always be there for you and never let you down.

Where Should the Puppy Sleep?

Dogs are pack animals and most puppies have a strong instinct to want to bond with humans. That emotional attachment between you and your puppy may even grow to become one of the most important aspects of your - and his - life.

Once your pup has been housetrained and can access other areas of the house, you have to think carefully where you want the dog to sleep. Some people will continue to keep them in the place where they started out, others will want the dog to sleep in the bedroom. But before you immediately choose the bedroom, bear in mind that most dogs scratch, wander about, snuffle, snore and fart!

Even if you decide to allow a young dog to sleep in the bedroom, it is not advisable to let him sleep on the bed. He may not be fully housetrained and he may grow into a very large or heavy adult. Dogs are hierarchical and a puppy needs to learn his place in the household – and it should be below you in the pecking order if you don't want him to rule your life. While it is not good to leave a dog alone all day, it is also not healthy to spend 24 hours a day with him. He becomes too reliant on you and will almost certainly develop separation anxiety when you do have to leave him. A puppy used to being on his own every night is less likely to develop attachment issues.

In a moment of weakness you might consider letting the puppy sleep in the bedroom for a couple of nights until he gets used to your home, but then it is even harder to turf him out later. Bite the bullet, get some earplugs and make his bed separate from yours. If you decide you definitely do want your pup to sleep in the bedroom from Day One, initially put him in a crate with a soft blanket covering part of the crate or in a high-sided cardboard box he can't climb out of. Put newspapers underneath as he will not be able to last the night without urinating.

Puppy Stages

Most puppies leave their mothers at eight weeks of age, some late developers and toy breeds may leave the litter as late as 12 weeks. To help your puppy grow into a confident and well-behaved adult who is a pleasure to take anywhere, it's important to understand a little about their world and how they develop. This knowledge will help you to be a good owner, as the first few months and weeks of a puppy's life will have an effect on his behaviour and temperament for the rest of his life.

What's really interesting is how your character and temperament will affect the personality of your dog. Treating a puppy with love and kindness will help that pup grow into a loving, well-adjusted adult dog. Smothering him with love and never leaving him alone may result in a possessive, snappy dog, especially with some toy breeds. Ignoring your dog, leaving him alone for long periods, hitting or scolding him frequently will result in the dog withdrawing from you or engaging in destructive or unwanted behaviour.

Puppies see the world differently from us – literally. Although not entirely colour blind, they have a limited colour spectrum and see everything in shades of grey, blue and yellow. On the other hand, they have an extremely acute sense of hearing and can hear things way beyond the human aural spectrum. Like babies, one of the ways they explore the world is by putting things into their mouth and chewing, and they have a sense of smell dozens of times more sensitive than our own.

We had a yellow Labrador, Harvey, which my father trained to find golf balls. Harvey could sniff out a ball buried several inches deep in dirt and leaf mould. Some of the balls had been lost for decades as inside they were made of elastic wound round a small paint ball. The dog found them entirely by scent – and knowing he would get a treat for each golf ball. Their record was 36 golf balls found on one walk around the golf links! This story highlights two points: the incredible canine sense of smell and the power of the treat when training.

Behaviourists now realise that there is a critical time for socialisation, when a dog should be exposed to as many new situations, people and other dogs (safely), noises and traffic as possible. That period is from the time he leaves the litter up to around 18 or 20 weeks of age. This is when he is interested in exploring the new world around him, dependent on, and eager to please, you. This Puppy Schedule will help you to understand the early stages:

Birth to seven weeks	**A puppy needs sleep, food and warmth. He needs his mother for security and discipline and littermates for learning and socialisation. The puppy learns to function within a pack and learns the pack order of dominance. He begins to become aware of his environment. During this period, puppies should be left with their mother.**
Eight to 12 wks	**A puppy should not leave his mother before eight weeks. At this age the brain is fully developed and he now needs socialising with the outside world, although he is still very dependent. He needs to change from being part of a canine pack to being part of a human pack. He wants to please and needs social and physical contact. This is a fear period for a puppy, avoid causing him fright and pain and introduce him to new things gently and safely.**
13 to 16 wks	**Training and game playing should be stepped up during this period when he is still very eager to please. He also needs further socialisation with other humans, places and situations. He becomes more aware of his environment and will begin to explore further, but is still dependent on his owner. This period will pass easily if you remember that this is a puppy's change to adolescence. Be firm and fair. He will chew, but**

	should be taught not to puppy bite. His flight instinct may be prominent. Avoid being too strict or too soft with him during this time and praise his good behaviour.
Four to eight months	Another fear period for a puppy is between seven to eight months of age. It passes quickly, but be cautious of fright or pain which may leave the puppy traumatised. The puppy reaches sexual maturity and dominant traits are established. Your dog should now understand basic commands such as 'sit', 'down', 'come' and 'stay'.

Vaccinations and Worming

When your new puppy arrives home, you need to make an appointment with your veterinarian to have your puppy checked over. He will also have to complete his vaccinations.

All puppies need these injections; very occasionally a puppy has a reaction, but this is very rare and the advantages of immunisation far outweigh the disadvantages.

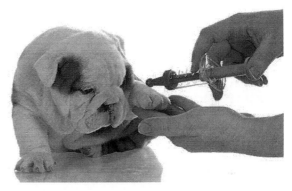

An unimmunised puppy is at risk every time he meets other dogs as he has no protection against potentially fatal diseases – and it is unlikely that a pet insurer will cover an unimmunised dog. It should be stressed that vaccinations are generally quite safe and side effects are uncommon. If your puppy is unlucky enough to be one of the very few that has an adverse reaction, here are the signs to look out for. A pup may exhibit one or more of these:

Mild Reaction - Sleepiness, irritability and not wanting to be touched. Sore or a small lump at the place where he was injected. Nasal discharge or sneezing. Puffy face and ears.

Severe Reaction - Anaphylactic shock. A sudden and quick reaction, usually before leaving the vet's, which causes breathing difficulties. Vomiting, diarrhoea, staggering and seizures.

A severe reaction is extremely rare. There is a far, far greater risk of your puppy being ill and spreading disease if he does not have the vaccinations.

The usual schedule is for the pup to have his first vaccination at six to eight weeks of age. This will protect him from a number of diseases in one shot. In the UK these are Distemper, Canine Parvovirus (Parvo), Infectious Canine Hepatitis (Adenovirus), Leptospirosis and Kennel Cough (Bordetella). In the USA, this is known as DHPP. Puppies in the US also need vaccinating separately against Rabies, and optional vaccinations for Coronavirus and, depending on where you live and if your dog is regularly exercised in woods or forests, Lyme Disease.

The puppy requires a second vaccination around four weeks later and then maybe a third to complete his immunity, which is often from 10 to 12 weeks of age. Seven days after that he is safe to mix with other dogs. Consult your vet to find out exactly what injections are needed.

Diseases such as Parvo and Kennel Cough are highly contagious and you should not let your puppy mix with other dogs - unless they are your own and have already been vaccinated - until a week after he has completed his vaccinations, otherwise he will not be fully immunised. Parvovirus can also be transmitted by fox faeces.

You shouldn't take your new puppy to places where unvaccinated dogs might have been, like the local park. This does not mean that your puppy should be isolated, far from it; this is an important time for socialisation. It is OK for the puppy to mix with another dog which you 100% know has been vaccinated and is up to date with its annual boosters. Perhaps invite a friend's dog round to play in your garden to begin the socialisation process.

Once your puppy is fully immunised, you have a window of a few weeks to introduce him to as many new experiences, dogs, people, noises, other animals, etc during that critical period when he is most receptive, before he gets to five months old. Socialisation should not stop at that age, but continue for the rest of the dog's life, and particularly when young.

Your dog will need a booster injection every year of his life. Your vet should give you a record card or send you a reminder, but it's a good idea to keep a note of the date in your diary.

All puppies need worming. The breeder should have given the puppies their first dose of worming medication at around two weeks old, then

again at five and eight weeks before they leave the litter. Get the details and inform your vet exactly what treatment, if any, your pup has already had. The main types of worms affecting puppies are roundworm and tapeworm.

Roundworm can also be transmitted from a puppy to humans – most often children and can in severe cases cause blindness, or miscarriage in women, so it's important to keep up to date with worming. Puppies can be quite susceptible to worms, most commonly picking them up through their mother's milk.

If you have children, get them into the habit of washing their hands after they have been in contact with the puppy – lack of hygiene is the reason why children are most susceptible. Most vets recommend worming a puppy once a month until he is six months old, and then around every two or three months.

Fleas can pass on tapeworms to dogs, but a puppy would not normally be treated unless it is known for certain he has fleas. And then only with caution. You need to know the weight of your pet and then speak to your vet about the safest treatment to rid your puppy of the parasites.

It is not usually worth buying a cheap worming or flea treatment from a supermarket, as they are often far less effective than more expensive vet-recommended preparations, such as Drontal. Many people living in the USA have contacted out website claiming the parasite treatment Trifexis has caused severe side effects and even death to their dogs. Although this evidence is only anecdotal, I would recommend that, to be on the safe side, you avoid Trifexis - even if your vet recommends it.

Crate Training

If you are unfamiliar with them, crates may seem like a cruel punishment for a puppy. They are, however, becoming increasingly popular to help with housetraining and to keep the dog safe while you are not there. Many dog trainers, behaviourists, breeders and people who show dogs recommend their use.

If you decide to use a crate, then remember that it is NOT a prison to restrain the dog. It should only be used in a humane manner and time should be spent to make the puppy feel like the crate is his own safe little haven. If the door is closed on the crate, your puppy must ALWAYS have access to water while inside. If used correctly and if time is spent getting the puppy used to the crate, it can be a valuable tool.

But crates are not for every puppy and they should never be used as a means of imprisonment because you are out of the house all day. Dogs are not like hamsters or pet mice which can adapt to life in a cage. They are pack animals and companion dogs which thrive on physically being close to their human owners. Being caged all day is a miserable existence for them.

Consider getting a wire crate where the air can pass easily through; dogs can overheat in plastic crates, particularly flat-faced breeds. Secondly, make doubly sure that the crate is not left in bright sunlight inside the house, but that it is shady throughout the day. The best place for it is in the corner of a room away from cold draughts or too much heat.

Dogs like to be near their pack - which is you and it is only natural for him to whine in the beginning. He is not crying because he is in a cage - he would cry if he had the freedom of the room and he was alone - he is crying because he is separated from you. However, with patience and the right training he will get used to it and come to regard his crate as a favourite place. Leave him where he can hear you. Some owners make the crate their dog's only bed, so he feels comfortable and safe in there.

Crates aren't for every owner or dog. But used correctly they:

- ❖ Are useful for housetraining; dogs don't like to soil their dens
- ❖ Limit access to the rest of the house while he learns the household rules
- ❖ Are a safe way to transport your dog in a car
- ❖ Create a canine den.

If you use a crate right from Day One, cover half of it with a blanket to help your puppy regard it as a den. He also needs bedding and it's a good idea to put a chew in as well. A large crate may allow your dog to eliminate at one end and sleep at the other, but this may slow down his housetraining. So, if you are buying a crate for a fully-grown dog, get adjustable crate dividers to block part of it off while he is small so that he feels safe and secure.

The crate should be large enough to allow your dog to stretch out flat on his side without being cramped, be able to turn round easily and to sit up without hitting his head on the top.

Once you've got your crate, you'll need to learn how to use it properly so that it becomes a safe, comfortable haven for your dog and not a prison. Here is a tried-and-tested method of getting your puppy firstly to accept it, and then to actually want to spend time in there. Initially a pup might not be too happy about going inside, but he will be a lot easier to crate train than an adult dog, which may have got used to having the run of your house. These are the first steps:

- ❖ Drop a few tasty puppy treats around and then inside the crate
- ❖ Put your puppy's favourite bedding in there
- ❖ Keep the door open
- ❖ Feed all of your puppy's meals inside the crate. Again, keep the door open.

Place a chew or treat INSIDE the crate and close the door while your puppy is OUTSIDE the crate. He will be desperate to get in there. Open the door, let him in and praise him for going in. Fasten a long-lasting chew inside the crate and leave the door open. Let your puppy go inside to spend some time eating the chew.

After a while, close the crate door and feed him some treats through the mesh while he is in there. At first just do it for a few seconds at a time, then gradually increase the time. If you do it too fast, he will become distressed. Slowly build up the amount of time he is in the crate. For the first few days, stay in the room, then gradually leave for a short time, first one minute, then three, then 10, 30 and so on.

Next Steps

❖ Put your dog in his crate at regular intervals during the day - maximum two hours

❖ Don't crate only when you are leaving the house. Place the dog in the crate while you are home as well. Use it as a "safe" zone

❖ By using the crate both when you are home and while you are gone, your dog becomes comfortable there and not worried that you won't come back, or that you are leaving him alone. This helps to prevent separation anxiety later in life

❖ Give him a chew and remove his collar, tags and anything else which could become caught in an opening or between the bars

❖ Make it very clear to any children that the crate is NOT a playhouse for them, but a "special room" for the dog

❖ Although the crate is your dog's haven and safe place, it must not be off-limits to humans. You should be able to reach inside at any time.

The next point is important if crate training is to succeed:

❖ Do not let your dog immediately out of the crate if he barks or whines, or he will think that this is the key to opening the door. Wait until the barking or whining has stopped for at least 10 seconds before letting him out

A puppy should not be left in a crate for long periods except at night time, and even then he has to get used to it first.

Whether or not you decide to use a crate, the important thing to remember is that those first few days and weeks are a critical time for your puppy. Try and make him feel as safe and comfortable as you can. Bond with him, while at the same time gently and gradually introducing him to the rules of the household, as well as new experiences and other animals and humans.

Top 10 Tips for Housetraining

The good news is that a puppy's instinct is not to soil his own den. From about the age of three weeks, a puppy will leave his sleeping area to go to the toilet. The bad news is that when you bring your little pup home, he doesn't realise that the whole house or apartment is his den. Therefore you need to teach him that it is unacceptable to make a mess anywhere inside the house.

How long this takes depends on how quickly your puppy learns and how persistent and patient you are. It could take from a few days to several months if neither of you are vigilant. Follow these tips to speed up the process:

1. **Constant supervision** for the first week or two is essential if you are to housetrain your puppy quickly. This is why it is important to book the week or so off work when you bring him home. Making sure you are there to take him outside regularly is very important. If nobody is there, he will learn to urinate or poo(p) inside the house.

2. **Take your pup outside at the following times:**
   - ❖ As soon as he wakes – every time
   - ❖ Shortly after each feed
   - ❖ After a drink
   - ❖ When he gets excited
   - ❖ After exercise or play
   - ❖ Last thing at night
   - ❖ Initially every hour – whether or not he looks like he wants to go

   You may think that the above list is an exaggeration, but it isn't. Housetraining a pup is almost a full-time job for the first few days. If you are serious about housetraining your puppy quickly, then clear your diary for a few days and keep your eyes firmly glued on your pup! Most puppies learn quickly once they know what is expected of them.

3. Take your puppy to **the same place** every time, you may need to use a leash in the beginning - or tempt him there with a treat if he is not yet leash-trained. Only pick him up and dump him there in an emergency, it is better if he learns to take himself to

the chosen toilet spot. Dogs naturally develop a preference for going in the same spot or on the same surface - often grass. Take him to the same patch every time so he learns this is his bathroom - preferably an area in a far corner of your yard or garden.

4. **No pressure – be patient.** You must allow your distracted little pup time to wander around and have a good sniff before performing his duties – but do not leave him, stay around a short distance away. Sadly, puppies are not known for their powers of concentration; it may take a while for them to select that perfect spot to wee on!

5. **Housetraining is reward-based.** Praise him or give him a treat immediately when he performs his duties in the chosen spot. Puppies love treats as well as pleasing their owners. Reward-based training is the most successful method and treats are particularly effective.

6. **Share the responsibility.** It doesn't have to be the same person that takes the dog outside all the time. In fact it's easier if there are a couple of you, as housetraining is a very time-consuming business. Just make sure you stick to the same routines and patch of ground.

7. **Stick to the same routine.** Dogs understand and like routine. Sticking to the same one for mealtimes, short exercise sessions, play time, sleeping and toilet breaks will help to not only housetrain him quicker, but help him settle into his new home.

8. **Use your voice if you catch him in the act indoors.** A short sharp negative sound is best - **NO! ACK! EH!** - it doesn't matter so long as it is loud enough to make him stop. Then start running enthusiastically towards your door, calling him into the garden and the chosen spot and patiently wait until he has finished what he started indoors.

9. **No punishment.** Accidents will happen at the beginning, do not punish your dog for them. He is a baby with a tiny bladder and bowels, and housetraining takes time - it is perfectly natural to have accidents early on. Remain calm and clean up the mess with a good strong-smelling cleaner to remove the odour, so he won't be tempted to use that spot again.

Dogs have a very strong sense of smell and to make 100% sure there is no trace of what they left behind, you can use a special spray from your vet or a hot solution of washing powder to completely eliminate the odour. Smacking or rubbing his nose in it can have the opposite effect: he will become afraid to do his business in your presence and may start going behind the couch or under the bed, rather than outside. Only shout if you catch him in the act, never afterwards.

10. **Look for the signs.** These may be sniffing the floor in a determined manner, circling looking for a place to go or walking uncomfortably, particularly at the rear end! Take him outside straight away. **Do not pick him up**, he has to learn to walk to the door himself when he needs to go outside.

Apartment Living

If you live on the 21st floor of an apartment in London or New York housetraining can be a little trickier, as you don't have easy access to the outdoors.

One suggestion is to indoor housetrain your puppy. Fortunately, most indoor dogs can be housetrained fairly easily - especially if you start early. Stick to the same principles already outlined, the only difference is that you will be placing your pet on training pads or newspaper instead of taking him outdoors.

Start by blocking off a section of the apartment for your pup, you can use a baby gate or make your own barrier - pick a chew-proof material! You will be able to keep a better eye on him than if he has free run of the whole place. It will also be easier to monitor his "accidents."

Select a corner away from his eating and sleeping area that will become his permanent bathroom area – a carpeted area is to be avoided if at all possible. At first, cover a larger area than is actually needed - about three to four square feet - with training pads. You can reduce the area as training progresses. Take your puppy there as indicated in the Housebreaking Tips on the pervious pages.

Praise him enthusiastically when he eliminates on the training pad or newspaper. If you catch him doing his business out of the toilet area pick him up and take him back there. Correct with a firm voice - never a hand. With positive reinforcement and a strict schedule, he will soon be walking to the area on his own.

Owners attempting indoor housetraining should be aware that it will generally take longer than outdoor training; some dogs will resist. Also, once a dog learns to go indoors, it can be difficult to train them to eliminate outdoors on their walks.

Any laziness on your part by not monitoring your puppy carefully enough - especially in the beginning – will make indoor housetraining a lot longer and more difficult process. The first week is crucial to your puppy learning what is expected of him.

GENERAL HOUSETRAINING TIP: You may also want to use a trigger to encourage your dog to perform his duties; this can be very effective. Some people use a clicker or a bell, we used a word, well two actually.

Within a few days we trained our Miniature Schnauzer to urinate on the command of "wee wee." Think carefully before choosing the word or phrase, as I often feel an idiot wandering around our garden last thing at night shouting "Max, wee wee!" in an encouraging manner (although I'm not sure that "Go potty" sounds much better!)

"How can you tell the dogs need to go out?"

9. Feeding and Health

If the number of emails to our website is anything to go by, feeding and health are without doubt the two issues which seem to concern owners most. They want to know what to feed their puppies and adult dogs, when and how often.

The first thing to realise is that a canine digestive system works differently from that of a human and you cannot suddenly change a dog's diet. While we can eat rare steak one day, a vegetable curry the next and a mound of fruit the following day, a dog's body needs more time to adapt to a change in diet. In addition, some everyday foods for humans are poisonous to dogs.

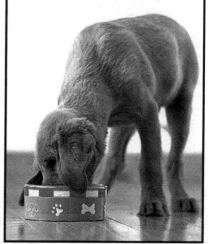

With a new puppy it is highly advisable to find out what the breeder has been feeding and to **stick to this for the first few weeks.** Your new arrival has enough to cope with, without a change of diet.

Puppies are little eating machines which can consume up to four times as much as an adult dog, pound for pound, and they grow at an incredible rate. Initially, a young puppy should be fed four times a day. This can be reduced to three times a day at three or four months old and then to twice a day when the dog reaches six months. Many owners prefer to stick to a twice-a-day feeding schedule for the rest of the dog's life - even owners of large breeds. Feeding large deep-chested dogs two smaller daily feeds helps to reduce the risk of bloat, a serious condition which can be caused by gulping food too quickly.

Do not feed your puppy in the corner of the room as this may encourage food-guarding. Feed him in an open space and, if you have more than one dog, make sure the new puppy is fed separately so he does not rush his food or become over-protective due to anxiety about his food being stolen. If your puppy is showing signs of food guarding, gradually put your hand near the bowl and remove it for a couple of seconds during his meal and then praise him when you return it. He should learn that you control the food.

Another point to remember is that once puppies have been weaned (meaning they are no longer taking their mother's milk), they do not need milk. Fresh water and a balanced diet are what's required. If your dog came from a good breeder, he is probably on a diet of premium or high quality dried food. There is also increasing interest in the raw diet – more on that later – and a minority of pups may already be eating raw. Whichever it is, continue with the breeder's diet when you bring your pup home.

Feeding time is also a perfect opportunity to start training. You can begin with simple commands such as Sit or Stay. Although your puppy will not initially understand them, be patient, keep encouraging him to sit and stay, moving him into the correct position before allowing access to the food. Eventually he will realise that when his bottom is touching the floor, this means Sit and he gets the food, or when he remains still, this is Stay, with the same result.

If you are thinking of changing your dog's diet after the first few weeks or months, this must be done gradually. It's OK to change flavours - for example to switch from turkey to fish flavour of the identical dried food brand - but to change the food completely or to switch to a raw diet takes time. Each day a little more of the new food replaces the old, starting with around 10% to 20% on the first day, until all the food is the new variety seven to 10 days later.

Feeding Puppies

Feeding your puppy the right diet is important to help his young body and bones grow strong and healthy. Puppyhood is a time of rapid growth and development, and puppies require different levels of nutrients to adult dogs. For the first few weeks, puppies need milk five to seven times a day, which they take from their mother. Generally they make a noise if they want to feed. The frequency is reduced when the pup reaches six to eight weeks old.

Puppies should stay with their littermates for at least eight weeks. During this time the mother is still teaching her offspring important rules about life. For some time after that, continue feeding the same puppy food and, if possible, at the same times as the breeder.

Puppies have little stomachs but large appetites, so feed them small amounts on a frequent basis. Smaller meals are easier to digest and energy levels don't peak and fall so much with frequent feeds; hungriness can lead to grumpiness. Establishing a regular feeding routine will also help with housetraining. Get him used to regular mealtimes and the moment he has finished take or let him outside to do his business. Puppies have fast metabolisms, so the results may be impressively quick!

Don't leave food out so the puppy can eat it whenever he wants. You should also be there at the same daily times for feeding as you want him and his body on a set schedule:

- ❖ Up to the age of three (or four) months, feed four times a day,
- ❖ Feed three times a day until the pup is six months old,
- ❖ Then twice a day for the rest of the dog's life.

After a few weeks if you wish you can slowly change his food based on information from the breeder and your vet. This should be done very gradually and if at any time your puppy starts being sick, has loose stools or is constipated, slow the rate at which you are switching. If he vomits or has diarrhoea for two days, seek veterinary advice as puppies can dehydrate very quickly with serious consequences.

Because of their special nutritional needs, you should only give your puppy a food that is approved either just for puppies or for all life stages. If a feed is recommended for adult dogs only, it won't have enough protein and the balance of calcium and other nutrients will not be right. Puppy food is very high in calories and nutritional supplements, so you want to switch to adult food once he begins to mature. This is usually around nine to 12 months old with small breeds and 12 to 18 months with large breeds, but can be earlier if a pup is developing too quickly. Initially you may have to moisten dry food with water or thin gravy from a stock cube to make it more palatable.

Feeding puppy food too long can result in obesity and orthopaedic problems – check with your vet on the right time to switch. Getting the correct amount and type of food is important. Feeding too much will cause him to put on excess pounds, and overweight puppies are more likely to grow into overweight adults.

DON'T:

- ❖ Feed scraps at the table. Your pup will get used to begging for food; not an attractive prospect when you end up with a not-so-cute drooling adult dog next to you every time you eat. It will also affect a carefully balanced diet.
- ❖ Feed food which may be off as puppies have sensitive stomachs.

DO:

- ❖ Regularly check the weight of your growing puppy to make sure he is within normal limits for his age.
- ❖ Remove his food after it has been down for 15 to 20 minutes. Food available 24/7 encourages fussy eaters.
- ❖ Take your puppy to the vet if he has diarrhoea or is vomiting for two days.

Large puppies

Over-feeding large pups or feeding too many carbohydrates, promotes too-rapid growth which puts stress on joints and can lead to problems such as hip dysplasia. Puppies grow many times faster than adult dogs and so require a special diet to aid their physical development. The average Golden Retriever, for example, grows from 14oz to over 65lb within one year – a 70-fold increase! Human beings take 18 years to do the same thing.

Most pet nutritionists recommend that big, fast growing puppies eat diets containing at least 30% protein and 9% fat (dry matter basis). The calcium content should be around 1.5% (or three grams per 1,000 kcal), check the labelling or ask your vet to recommend a feed - but be aware that they may well promote a particular, expensive food which they sell - such as Hill's or Science Plan (both of which are regarded as high quality foods). Do not feed a calcium supplement to a puppy; it may cause the bones to grow too big too fast, resulting in joint problems later in life.

Remember that treats add calories to the overall diet. Make sure the treats are small and do not contain added calcium – get used to giving fruit and vegetables as treats, these are healthier options. Most dogs like carrots and apples if fed from an early age.

Many manufacturers offer dried food formulated for large breed puppies. You should not over-feed any puppy, but protein, calcium and phosphorus levels may be more critical with larger breeds than with some smaller breeds. It's worth spending time to choose the right fuel to power your dog's healthy development. Think of it as a foundation stone towards future health.

Feeding Charts

Most puppies will eat until they burst, so it is up to you to control their intake. Manufacturers' guidelines are a starting point, although these can err on the side of over-feeding, rather than under-feeding. When you visit the vet for vaccinations, check that you are feeding the correct amount.

You should be able to feel but not see your pup's ribs and he should have a visible waist - this is true for puppies of any breed, big or small. You may want to do your own research, rather than rely on your vet's recommendation. Visit online forums dedicated to your particular breed

or crossbreed – what are other owners successfully feeding and which foods are causing problems? How does the breed, or crossbreed, do on a raw diet, how do owners prepare the food, where do they buy it from? There is a wealth of information on these forums.

A general rule of thumb is that a puppy should gain one to two grams per pound of predicted adult weight each day. So if a Labrador weighs 75 pounds as an adult, he should gain three to five ounces a day as a puppy. Ask your breeder for the pup's expected adult weight; this will vary according to breed, size within the breed and gender – males are generally larger than females.

We feed our dog a dried hypoallergenic dog food made by James Wellbeloved in England. Here are James Wellbeloved's recommended feeding amounts, listed in kilograms and grams (**28.3 grams=1 ounce. 1kg=2.2 pounds).** The number on the left is the dog's **expected adult weight** in kilograms.

The numbers on the right are the amount of daily food that an average dog with average energy levels requires, measured in grams (divide this by 28.3 to get the amount in ounces). For example, a three-month-old puppy which will grow into a 20kg adult would require around 305 grams of food per day (10.75 ounces).

Just like humans, each dog is an individual and the exact amount of food depends on a number of factors, including a puppy's energy levels. Some breeds are naturally more energetic than others and within each breed or crossbreed, some dogs will have higher energy levels than others.

NOTE: These are very general guidelines, your dog may need more or less food than this. Use the chart as a guideline only and if your dog appears to lose or gain weight, adjust his or her feeds accordingly.

PUPPY Size	Expected Adult Body Weight	Age of Puppy and daily Serving (grams)					
		2 mths	3 mths	4 mths	5 mths	6 mths	> 6 mths
Toy	2kg	50	60	60	60	60	change to
Small	5kg	95	115	120	115	115	adult
Medium	10kg	155	190	195	190	190	change to junior

PUPPY

Size	Expected Adult Body Weight	Age of Puppy and daily Serving (grams)					
		2 mths	3 mths	4 mths	5 mths	6 mths	> 6 mths
Medium/Large	20kg	240	305	325	320	315	change to junior /large breed jnr
Large	30kg	300	400	435	435	430	
Large/Giant	40kg	345	480	530	540	530	change to large breed junior
	50kg	390	550	615	630	630*	
Giant	60kg	430	610	690	720*	720*	
	70kg	460	675	765*	800*	810*	

JUNIOR

Size	expected adult body weight (kg)	Age of Puppy and daily Serving (g)						
		6 mths	7 mths	8 mths	10 mths	12 mths	14 mths	16 mths
Medium	10	200	195	185	175	change to adult		
Medium/Large*	20	330	325	310	290	300	change to adult/large breed adult	
	30	455	440	430	400	400		
Large*	40	565	555	540	520	485	495	change to large breed adult

ADULT Size	Body Weight (kg)	Daily Serving (g)
Toy	2-5	55-115
Small	5-10	115-190
Medium	10-20	190-320
Medium/Large	20-30	320-430
Large*	30*-40*	430*-520*
Large/Giant*	40*-50*	520*-620*
	50*-60*	620*-710*
Giant*	60*-70*	710*-790*
	70*-90*	790*-950*

Disclaimer: This chart is designed to give just a broad guideline on the amount of daily food based on size. Check your dog's ideal weight before embarking on a feeding regime and consult your vet if your dog loses or gains considerable weight.

Types of Dog Food

The correct diet is an essential part of keeping your dog fit and healthy. However, the topic of feeding the right diet is something of a minefield. Owners are bombarded with endless choices as well as countless adverts from dog food companies, all claiming that theirs is best.

There is not one food that will give every single dog the brightest eyes, the shiniest coat, the most energy, the best digestion, the longest life and stop him from scratching or having skin problems. Dogs are individuals just like people, which means that you could feed a premium food to a group of dogs and find that most of them do very well on it and some not so well, while a few may get an upset stomach or even an allergic reaction. The question is: "Which food is best for my dog?"

There are many different options. The most popular manufactured foods include dry complete diets, tinned food (with or without a biscuit mixer), and semi-moist. Some foods contain only natural ingredients. Then there is the option of feeding your dog a home-made diet; some owners swear by a raw diet, while others feed their dogs vegetarian food.

Within the manufactured options, there are many different qualities of food. Usually you get what you pay for, so a more expensive food is more likely to provide better nutrition in terms of minerals, nutrients and high quality meats rather than a cheap one, which will most likely contain a lot of grain. Dried foods, called kibble in the USA, tend to be less expensive than other foods. They have improved a lot over the last few years and some of the more expensive ones are now a good choice for a healthy, complete diet. Dry foods also contain the least fat and the most preservatives.

TIP: Beware of buying a food just because it is described as *'premium'*, many manufacturers blithely use this word, but there are no official guidelines as to what premium means. Always check the ingredients on any food sack, packet or tin to see which ingredients are listed first, and it should be meat or poultry, not corn or grain. If you are in the USA, look for a dog food which has been endorsed by AAFCO (Association of American Feed Control Officials).

In general, tinned foods are 60-70% water. Often semi-moist foods contain a lot of artificial substances and sugar, which is maybe why many dogs seem to love them!

Choosing the right food is important, it will certainly influence your dog's health, coat, temperament and even lifespan. There are also the three main stages of your dog's life to consider when feeding: puppy, adult and senior (also called veteran); four if you count junior food, formulated for adolescent dogs. Each of these caters for a different physical stage of a dog's life and you need to choose the right food to cope with his body during each particular phase. Also, a pregnant female will require a special diet to cope with the extra demands on her body.

Some owners feed two different meals to their dog each day to provide variety. One meal could be dried kibble, while the other might be home-made, with fresh meat, poultry and vegetables. If you do this, speak with your vet to make sure the two separate meals provide a balanced diet and that they are not too rich in protein.

This book will not recommend one brand of dog food over another, but will help to steer you towards what's best for your dog. There is also some advice for owners of dogs with food allergies or sensitivities.

Sufferers may itch, lick or chew their paws and/or legs, or rub their face, they may also get frequent ear infections as well as facial swelling and redness.

Switching to a grain-free diet can in some cases help to alleviate the symptoms, as the dog's digestive system does not have to work as hard. In the wild a dog or wolf's staple diet would be meat with some vegetable matter from the stomach and intestines of the herbivores (plant-eating animals) he devoured – but no grains. Dogs do not digest corn or wheat - which are often staples of cheap commercial dog food - very efficiently. Grain-free diets provide carbohydrates through fruits and vegetables, so your dog still gets all his nutrients.

Dry Dog Food

This is a popular and relatively inexpensive choice if bought in sacks, particularly for large dogs which get through a lot of food. It comes in different flavours and with differing ingredients to suit the various stages of a dog's life. It's worth paying for a high quality dried food as cheaper ones may contain a lot of grain. Cheap foods are often false economy, particularly if your dog does not tolerate grain/cereal very well. It may also mean that you have to feed larger quantities to ensure he gets sufficient nutrients.

Tinned Food

This is another popular choice with owners – and it's often very popular with dogs too! They love the taste, which generally comes in a variety of flavours. Canned food is often mixed with dry kibble, and a small amount may be added to a dog on a dry food diet if he has lost interest in food. This is not uncommon with older dogs.

Cans tend to be more expensive than dry food and many owners don't like the mess. A part-opened tin has to be refrigerated between meals and can have an unpleasant smell when you open the fridge door. As with dry food, read the label closely. Generally, you get what you pay for and the origins of cheap tins of dog food are often somewhat dubious. You may decide to feed canned food once daily and then kibble or another food for the second meal.

Semi-Moist

These are commercial dog foods shaped like pork chops, salamis, burgers or other meaty foods and they are the least nutritional of all dog foods. They are full of sugars, artificial flavourings and colourings to help make them visually appealing. Dogs don't care what their food looks like, they only care how it smells and tastes, the shapes are designed to appeal to us humans. While you may give your dog one as an occasional treat, they are not a diet in themselves and do not provide the nutrition that your dog needs. Steer clear of them for regular feeding.

Freeze-Dried

One of the newer options that is gaining in popularity is freeze-dried foods. These contain natural ingredients, such as meat or vegetables, and can provide all of the claimed health benefits of frozen raw foods without the mess and fuss of a frozen or refrigerated diet. Freeze-drying keeps the ingredients as close to fresh as possible and does not require chemical preservatives to allow it to be kept at room temperature for long periods. In most cases, freeze-dried foods are "just add water and serve."

This is made by frozen food manufacturers and keeps for six months to a year. It is a natural, convenient method of feeding, provided you can find a good supplier, and is also used by owners who take their dog on holiday. It says 'freeze-dried' on the packet and is highly palatable, but the freeze-drying process bumps up the cost.

Home-Cooked

Some dog owners want to be in complete control of their dog's diet, to know exactly what he is eating and to make absolutely sure that his nutritional needs are being met. Feeding your dog a home-cooked diet is time consuming and expensive, and the difficult thing – as with the raw diet - is sticking to it once you have started out with the best of intentions. But many owners think the extra effort is worth the peace of mind. If you decide to go ahead, you should spend the time to become proficient and learn about canine nutrition to ensure your dog gets all his vital nutrients.

Raw Food

There is a quiet revolution going on in the world of dog food. After years of feeding dry or tinned dog food, increasing numbers of owners are now feeding a raw diet to their beloved pets. There is much anecdotal evidence that many dogs thrive on a raw diet, although scientific proof is lagging behind. There are a number of claims made by proponents of the raw diet, including:

- ❖ Reduced symptoms of, or less likelihood of, allergies
- ❖ Better skin and coats
- ❖ Better weight management
- ❖ Improved digestion
- ❖ Less dog odour and fresher breath
- ❖ Helps fussy eaters
- ❖ Drier and less smelly stools, more like pellets
- ❖ Reduced risk of bloat
- ❖ Overall improvement in health and energy levels

If your dog is not doing well on a commercially-prepared dog food, you might consider a raw diet, which emulates the way dogs ate before the existence of commercial dog foods. After all, dry, canned and other styles of commercially prepared food were mainly created as a means of convenience. Unfortunately, this convenience sometimes can affect a dog's health. Some nutritionists believe that dogs fed raw whole foods tend to be healthier than those on other diets. They say there are inherent beneficial enzymes, vitamins, minerals and other qualities in meats, fruits, vegetables and grains in their natural forms that are denatured or destroyed when cooked. Many also believe dogs are less likely to have allergic reactions to the ingredients on this diet.

Unsurprisingly, the topic is not without controversy. Critics of a raw diet say that the risks of nutritional imbalance, intestinal problems and food-borne illnesses caused by handling and feeding raw meat outweigh any benefits. It is true that owners must pay strict attention to hygiene when preparing a raw diet and it may not be a suitable option if there are children in the household. The dog may also be more likely to ingest bacteria or parasites such as Salmonella, E.coli and Ecchinococcus.

Frozen food can be a valuable aid to the raw diet. The food is highly palatable, made from high quality ingredients and dogs usually love it. The downside is that not all pet food stores stock it and it is expensive. There are two main types of raw diet, one involves feeding raw, meaty

bones and the other is known as the BARF diet (*Biologically Appropriate Raw Food* or *Bones And Raw Food)*, created by Dr Ian Billinghurst. A typical BARF diet is made up of 60%-80% of raw meaty bones (bones with about 50% meat, such as chicken neck, back and wings) and 20-40% of fruit and vegetables, offal, meat, eggs or dairy foods.

Bones must not be cooked or they can splinter inside the dog. Another point to consider is that a raw diet is often not suitable for the jaws and teeth conditions of brachycephalic breeds (dogs with short, broad skulls, such as the Bulldog, Pekingese, Boston Terrier, etc).

You might also consider feeding two different daily meals to your dog - one dry kibble and one raw diet, for example. If you do, then read up around the subject, and consult your veterinarian to make sure that the two combined meals provide a balanced diet.

NOTE: Only start a raw diet if you have done your research and are sure you have the time and money to keep it going.

Reading Dog Food Labels

A NASA scientist would have a hard job understanding some dog food manufacturers' labels, so it's no easy task for us lowly dog owners. Here are some things to look out for on the manufacturers' labels:

> **Ingredients:** Chicken, Chicken By-Product Meal, Corn Meal, Ground Whole Grain Sorghum, Brewers Rice, Ground Whole Grain Barley, Dried Beet Pulp, Chicken Fat (preserved with mixed Tocopherols, a source of Vitamin E), Chicken Flavor, Dried Egg Product, Fish Oil (preserved with mixed Tocopherols, a source of Vitamin E), Potassium Chloride, Salt, Flax Meal, Sodium Hexametaphosphate, Fructooligosaccharides, Choline Chloride, Minerals (Ferrous Sulfate, Zinc Oxide, Manganese Sulfate, Copper Sulfate, Manganous Oxide, Potassium Iodide, Cobalt Carbonate), DL-Methionine, Vitamins (Ascorbic Acid, Vitamin A Acetate, Calcium Pantothenate, Biotin, Thiamine Mononitrate (source of vitamin B1), Vitamin B12 Supplement, Niacin, Riboflavin Supplement (source of vitamin B2), Inositol, Pyridoxine Hydrochloride (source of vitamin B6), Vitamin D3 Supplement, Folic Acid), Calcium Carbonate, Vitamin E Supplement, Brewers Dried Yeast, Beta-Carotene, Rosemary Extract.

❖ The ingredients are listed by weight and the top one should always be the main content, such as chicken or lamb. Don't pick one where grain is the first ingredient as this is a poor quality feed and some dogs can develop grain intolerances or allergies, often it is wheat they have a reaction to.

❖ High up the list should be meat or poultry by-products, these are clean parts of slaughtered animals, not including meat. They include organs, blood and bone, but not hair, horns, teeth or hooves.

❖ Guaranteed Analysis – This guarantees that your dog's food contains the labelled percentages of crude protein, fat, fibre and moisture. Keep in mind that wet and dry dog foods use different standards. (It does not list the digestibility of protein and fat and this can vary widely depending on their sources). While the guaranteed analysis is a start in understanding the food quality, be wary about relying on it too much. One pet food manufacturer made a mock product with a guaranteed analysis of 10% protein, 6.5% fat, 2.4% fibre, and 68% moisture (similar to what's on many canned pet food labels) – the only problem was that the ingredients were old leather boots, used motor oil, crushed coal and water!

❖ Chicken meal (dehydrated chicken) has more protein than fresh chicken, which is 80% water. The same goes for beef, fish and lamb. So, if any of these meals are number one on the ingredient list, the food should contain enough protein.

A certain amount of flavourings can make a food more appetising for your dog. Chose a food with a specific flavouring, like *'beef flavouring'* rather than a general *'meat flavouring'*, where the origins are not so clear.

❖ Find a food that fits your dog's age, breed and size. Talk to your vet or visit an online forum and ask other owners what they are feeding their dogs.

❖ If your dog has a food allergy or intolerance to wheat, check whether the food is gluten free. All wheat contains gluten.

❖ Natural is best. Food labelled *'natural'* means that the ingredients have not been chemically altered, according to the FDA in the USA. However, there are no such guidelines governing foods labelled 'holistic' – so check the ingredients and how it has been prepared.

❖ In the USA, dog food that meets minimum nutrition requirements has a label that confirms this. It states: **"[food name] is formulated to meet the nutritional levels established by the AAFCO Dog Food Nutrient Profiles for [life stage(s)]".** Even better, look for a food that meets the minimum nutritional requirements *'as fed'* to real pets in an AAFCO-defined feeding trial, then you know the food really delivers the nutrients that it is "formulated" to. AAFCO feeding trials on real dogs are the gold standard. Brands that do costly feeding trials (including Nestle and Hill's) indicate so on the package.

Crude Protein (min)	32.25%
Lysine (min)	0.43%
Methionine (min)	0.49%
Crude Fat (min)	10.67%
Crude Fiber (max)	7.3%
Calcium (min)	0.50%
Calcium (max)	1.00%
Phosphorus (min)	0.44%
Salt (min)	0.01%
Salt (max)	0.51%

❖ Dog food labelled *'supplemental'* isn't complete and balanced. Unless you have a specific, vet-approved need for it, it's not something you want to feed your dog for an extended period of time. Check with your vet if in doubt.

If it still all looks a bit baffling, you might find the following website useful: www.dogfoodadvisor.com run by Mike Sagman. He has a medical background and analyses and rates hundreds of brands of dog food based on the listed ingredients and meat content. You might be surprised at some of his findings. (I have no vested interest in this website, but include it as it is one of the best I have come across in giving unbiased advice on dog foods.)

To recap: no one food is right for every dog, you must decide on the best for your dog. Once you have decided on a food, monitor your puppy or adult. The best test of a food is how well your dog is doing on it. If your dog is happy and healthy, interested in life, has enough energy, is not too fat and not too thin, and has healthy-looking stools, then...**Congratulations,** you've got it right!

Top Feeding Tips

1. If you choose a manufactured food, **don't pick one where meat or poultry content is NOT the first item listed** on the bag. Foods with lots of cheap cereals or sugar are not the best choice for many dogs, particularly finely balanced ones.

2. As dogs develops, some dogs develop sensitive skin, 'hot spots' or allergies, usually when they are anything from six months to two or three years old, although they can develop later. A cheap dog food is likely to make the problem worse. If this is the case, bite the bullet and **choose a high quality – usually more expensive - food**. You'll probably save money in vets' bills in the long run and your dog will be happier. A food may be described as "hypoallergenic" on the sack; this means "less likely to cause allergies" and is a good place to start. You may also consider a raw diet, but bear in mind, this involves more time, effort and probably expense, on your part.

3. **Feed your adult dog twice a day**, rather than once. Two smaller feeds will reduce flatulence as well as the risk of gastric torsion, or bloat in larger dogs.

4. **Establish a feeding regime and stick to it.** Dogs like routine. If you are feeding twice a day, feed once in the morning and then again at tea-time. Stick to the same times of day. Do not give the last feed too late, or your dog's body will not have chance to process or burn off the food before sleeping. He will also need a walk or letting out in the garden or yard after his second feed. Feeding at the same times each day helps your dog establish a toilet regime.

5. **Take away any uneaten food between meals.** Most dogs love food, but they can become fussy eaters if it's available all day. Imagine if your dinner was left on the table for hours until you finished it. Returning to the table two or three hours later would not be such a tempting prospect, but coming back for a fresh meal would be far more appetising. Also when food is left

down all day, some dogs take it for granted and lose their appetite. Then they begin to leave the food and you are at your wits' end trying to find something they will eat. Put the food bowl down twice a day and then take it up after 20 minutes – even if he has left some. If he is healthy and hungry, he will look forward to his next meal and soon stop leaving food. If your dog is off his food for days, it could well be a sign that something is wrong and you should seek veterinary advice.

6. **Do not feed too many titbits or treats between meals.** Dogs are often greedy and obesity is a dangerous condition as it places extra strain on organs and joints, and has a detrimental effect on his health and even his lifespan. It also throws a balanced diet out of the window. Avoid feeding your dog from the table or your plate, as this encourages attention-seeking behaviour and drooling.

7. **NEVER feed the following items to your dog**: grapes, raisins, chocolate, onions, Macadamia nuts, any fruits with seeds or stones, tomatoes, avocadoes, rhubarb, tea, coffee or alcohol. ALL of these are poisonous to dogs.

8. **If you do feed leftovers, feed them INSTEAD of a balanced meal,** not as well as. High quality dog foods are already made up to provide all the nutrients, vitamins, minerals and calories that your dog needs. Feeding titbits or leftovers may be too rich in addition to a regular diet and cause your dog to scratch or have other problems, as well as get fat. You can feed your dog vegetables such as carrots as a healthy low-calorie treat, most dogs love 'em.

9. **Check your dog's faeces** (aka stools, poo or poop!) If his diet is suitable, the food should be easily digested and produce dark brown, firm stools. If your dog produces soft or light stools, or has diarrhoea, his diet may not suit him, so consult your vet or breeder for advice

10. **If you switch to a new food, do the transition gradually.** Unlike humans, dogs' digestive systems cannot handle sudden changes in diet. Begin by gradually mixing some of the new food in with the old and increase the proportion so that after

seven to 10 days, all the food is the new one. The following ratios are recommended by Doctors Foster & Smith Inc: Days 1-3 add 25% of the new food, Days 4-6 add 50%, Days 7-9 add 75%, Day 10 feed 100% of the new food. If you stick to the identical brand, you can change flavours in one go.

11. **Never give your dog cooked bones,** as these can splinter and cause him to choke or suffer intestinal problems. It's also a good idea to avoid rawhide, as some dogs have a tendency to briefly chew and quickly swallow rawhide, without first bothering to nibble it down into smaller pieces.

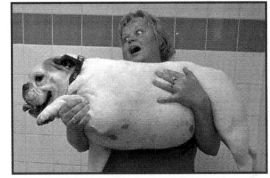

12. **Check your dog's weight regularly.** Obesity can lead to the development of some serious health issues, such as diabetes. Although the weight will vary from one dog to another, a good rule of thumb is that your dog's tummy should be higher than his rib cage. If his belly hangs down below it, he is overweight.

13. Feed your dog in stainless steel dishes. Plastic bowls don't last as long and, more importantly, a dog with sensitive skin can have a reaction to plastic. Ceramic bowls are best for keeping water cold.

14. **If you have more than one dog, feed them separately**. Feeding dogs together can lead to dog food aggression, either protecting his own food or trying to eat the food designated for another pet.

15. **Always make sure that your dog has access to clean, fresh water.** Change the water and clean the bowl (which gets slimy!) regularly.

16. **If a puppy has diarrhoea or vomits for two days, take him to the vet.**

Dogs are loyal creatures and the person who feeds the puppy will probably become the pack leader. In other words, this is the person to whom the dog will probably show most loyalty and affection. If your dog is not responding well to a particular family member, a useful tactic is to get that person to feed the dog every day. The way to a dog's heart is often through his stomach.

"You eat the dog food, I'll eat the steak."

If your mealtimes coincide with those of your puppy or adult dog, you should always eat something from your plate before feeding your dog. Dogs respect the pecking order, and in the wild the top dogs eat first. If you feed your puppy before you, he will think that he is higher up the pecking order than you. Feeding your dog after yourself and your family is an important part of training and discipline. Your dog will not love you any less because you are the boss -in fact, just the opposite.

If you are feeding your puppy correctly, he has access to water and his other needs are being met, he should be perfectly healthy. But how do you tell? You puppy can tell when your puppy is healthy by looking out for the following signs:

Top Ten Signs of a Healthy Puppy

1. **Eyes** - a healthy puppy's eyes are shiny and bright. The area around the eyeball (the conjunctiva) should be a healthy pink. Paleness could be a sign of underlying problems. There should be no thick, green or yellow discharge from the eyes. A cloudy eye may be a sign of cataracts.

2. **Coats** - these are easy-to-monitor indicators of a healthy dog. Puppies with smooth fur should have a sleek, shiny coat, while a fleecy or wiry coat should be springy and full of life. A dull, lifeless coat can be a sign that something is amiss.

3. **Skin** - This should be smooth without redness. Normal skin pigment can vary depending on the breed, and then within the breeds. It may be light coloured, pink, black, brown or even blue according to the colour of the dog. Open sores, scales, scabs or growths can be a sign of a problem. Signs of fleas, ticks and other external parasites should be treated immediately.

4. **Ears** – ear infections can be a particular problem for breeds with long, floppy ears under which little air circulates, making them a perfect breeding ground for bacteria. The warm place under the ear flap is an ideal breeding ground for mites and infections, The ears should smell normal and not be hot. A bad smell, a hot, swollen or red ear, or one full of brown wax is often a sign of infection, which needs prompt veterinary attention or it could ultimately lead to a burst eardrum or even deafness.

168

If your dog is a minimal shedder, you should check his ears regularly and hand-pluck hairs from inside the ear if necessary. This does not hurt and, once used to it, can become a normal part of regular grooming. Offer your dog a treat at the end of ear-plucking. You, like us, can also ask your groomer to pluck any excess ear hair each visit to stop the ears becoming clogged with hair.

5. **Mouth –** Gums should be pink or pigmented with black. Paleness can be a sign of anaemia. Red, inflamed gums can be a sign of gingivitis or other tooth disease. Again, your pup's breath should smell OK. Young dogs will have sparkling white teeth, whereas older dogs will have darker teeth, but they should not have any hard white, yellow, green or brown bits.

6. **Weight** – your puppy should be the correct weight and have a healthy appetite. The rib, back and hip bones should not show, but you should be able to feel them under the skin. Dogs may have weight problems due to factors such as diet, allergies, diabetes, thyroid or other problems. A general rule of thumb is that your dog's stomach should be in a line or above his rib cage when standing. If his stomach hangs below, he is overweight or he may have a pot belly which can be a sign that something is amiss, such as Cushing's Disease.

7. **Nose -** a dog's nose is an indicator of health symptoms. It could be black, pink or mottled. But whatever colour, it should be moist and cold to the touch in adult dogs. However, some puppies naturally have a warm, dry nose, The moistness should be free from clear, watery secretions. Any yellow, green or foul smelling discharge is not normal. In younger dogs this can be a sign of canine distemper.

8. **Temperature** - The normal temperature of a dog is 100.5-102.5°F. Excited or exercising dogs may run a slightly higher temperature. Anything above 103°F or below 100°F should be checked out. The exceptions are female dogs about to give birth which will often have a temperature of 99°F. It's not advisable to take a puppy's temperature as it is difficult for them to keep still. If you take your adult dog's temperature, make sure he is relaxed first and always use a purpose-made thermometer which will not snap off in his rectum.

9. **Attitude -** a generally positive attitude and personality is the sign of good health. Symptoms of illness may be lethargy, not eating food or a general lack of interest in surroundings. All puppies sleep a lot, they need more than 18 hours of sleep a day.

10. **Energy** – get to know your puppy's natural energy level. With most puppies, this is usually. He should have good energy levels with fluid and pain-free movements. Lethargy or lack of energy - if it is not the dog's normal character - could be a sign of an underlying problem.

So now you know some of the signs of a healthy dog – what are the signs of an unhealthy one? There are many different symptoms that can indicate your beloved canine companion isn't feeling great. If you don't know your dog, then we recommend you spend some time getting to do so.

What are his normal character and temperament? Lively or sedate, playful or serious, happy to be alone or loves to be with people, a keen appetite or a fussy eater? How often does he empty his bowels, does he ever vomit? (Dogs will often eat grass to make themselves sick, this is perfectly normal and a canine's natural way of cleansing their digestive system.)

You may think your dog can't talk, **but he can!** If you really know your dog, his character and habits, then he CAN tell you when he's not well. He does this by changing his patterns. Some symptoms are physical, some emotional and others are behavioural. It's important for you to be able to recognise these changes as soon as possible. Early treatment can be the key to keeping a simple problem from snowballing into a serious illness.

If you think your dog is unwell, it is useful to keep an accurate and detailed account of his symptoms to give to the vet. This will help him or her correctly diagnose and effectively treat your dog. Most canine illnesses are detected through a combination of signs and symptoms. Here are some signs that your dog may be unwell:

Four Vital Signs of Illness

1. **Temperature -** A newborn puppy will have a temperature of 94-97º F. This will reach the normal adult body temperature of 101ºF at about four weeks old. Anything between 100ºF and 102ºF is normal. A dog's temperature is normally taken via his rectum.

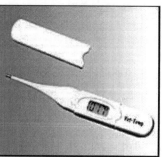

   Be very careful when doing this – it is not recommended with puppies, visit your vet instead.With adult dogs, get someone to hold the dog while inserting the thermometer, lubricated withy petroleum jelly, into the dog's anus and hold it there for around two minutes.

   Digital thermometers are a good choice, but **only use one specifically made for rectal use** as normal glass thermometers can easily break off in the rectum. Ear thermometers are now available, making the task much easier, although they can be expensive and don't suit all dogs' ears.

Remember - exercise or excitement can cause the temperature to rise by 2ºF - 3ºF when the dog is actually in good health. If your dog's temperature is above or below the norms, get him to the vet.

2. **Respiratory Rate** - You can check your dog's breathing by counting the number of breaths he takes per minute. Watch the movement of his chest, he should take 10-30 breaths a minute. If his breathing seems too slow or laboured, or if the rate is rapid while he's resting, consult your vet.

3. **Heart Rate** - Another symptom of canine illness is a change in breathing patterns. A puppy's heart rate should generally be between 80 and 140 beats per minute. Larger dogs tend to have slower heart rates than smaller dogs, and puppies and toy breeds may be at the high end of the scale.

You can check your puppy's heart rate in two ways. The first is to take his pulse on the inside upper thigh of a rear leg where the pulse is strongest. Place two fingers on the pulse and count the beats for one minute. If your puppy refuses to hold still that long, count for 15 seconds and multiply the beats by four. The beats should feel strong and regular. If his pulse is weak, erratic, too fast or slow, call your vet.

If you're having difficulty checking the thigh pulse, place your hand on the left side of your puppy's chest just behind the elbow and you'll feel the normal *bu-bum* of the heart's double beat. Count each double beat as one and count the beats for one minute.

4. **Behaviour Changes** - Classic symptoms of illness are any inexplicable behaviour changes. If there has NOT been a change in the household atmosphere, such as another new pet, a new baby, moving home or the absence of a family member, then the following symptoms may well be a sign that all is not well with your dog:

- ❖ Depression
- ❖ Anxiety
- ❖ Tiredness
- ❖ Trembling
- ❖ Falling or stumbling
- ❖ Loss of appetite
- ❖ Walking in circles

If your dog shows any of these signs, he needs to be kept under close watch for a few hours or even days. Quite often he will return to normal of his own accord. Like humans, dogs have off-days too.

If he is showing any of the above symptoms, then don't over-exercise him and try to avoid stressful situations. Make sure he has access to clean water. There are many other signals of ill health, but these are four of the most important.

Keep a record for your vet. If your dog does need professional medical attention, most vets will want to know:

- ❖ **WHEN** the symptoms first appeared

- ❖ **WHETHER** they are getting better or worse, and

- ❖ **HOW FREQUENT** the symptoms are. Are they intermittent, continuous or increasing in frequency?

Another excellent idea, particularly if your dog is acting strangely, is to video him with a camera or mobile phone. This will give the vet a real insight into his behaviour.

Disclaimer: The author is not a canine health expert. If you are worried about your puppy's health, always consult a veterinarian.

10. Early Training

Training a puppy is like bringing up a child. Put in the effort early on and you will be rewarded with a sociable individual who will be a joy to spend time with for years to come. Dogs make great companions for us humans, but let your pup do what he wants, allow him to think he's the boss and you may well finish up with a stubborn, attention-seeking adult.

Too many dogs end up in rescue shelters because they didn't turn out like their owners expected. This is more often than not the owner's fault, and lack of training often played a part in why the dog developed unwanted behaviour traits. If you want a perfect companion, rather than a pain in the you-know-what, spend time early on teaching him some good manners and your rules.

Training should always be positive, not punitive, and most puppies are highly motivated by treats - but don't overdo them. Daily feeding also provides a really good opportunity to start with basic commands, such as Sit and Stay.

Joining a local puppy class is highly recommended. This way the pup learns with his peers and is socialised with other dogs at the same time. You could also think about getting a dog training DVD - the beauty of this is that it brings training techniques right into your home – but it should not replace classes with other dogs.

When training, remember the golden rule: it should always be based on rewards and not punishment. It should be a positive learning experience for both, bawling at the top of your voice or smacking should play no part in training.

Dogs are pack animals and very hierarchical. They - and you – need to learn their place in the pack - and yours is as pack leader (alpha). This is not something forced on a dog through shouting and hitting, it is the establishment of the natural order of things by mutual consent and brought about by good training. If not made aware of their place in the household and the rules to abide by, puppies may end up ruling you and your family.

Dogs respect the pecking order and are happy when they know and are comfortable with their place in it. They may push the boundaries, especially when they are lively puppies and adolescents, but stick to your guns and establish yourself - or a family member - as pack leader and the household will run much smoother. Again, this is done with positive techniques, not threats.

It's your house, you set the rules and with proper training, your puppy will learn to follow them. Be firm, but **never** aggressive, you will either frighten him or teach him to be aggressive back.

Often your pup's concentration will lapse during training, so keep training short and fun - especially in the early days. If you have adopted an older dog, you can still train him, but it will take a little longer to get rid of bad habits and instil good manners. Patience and persistence are the keys here.

At what age can I start training my puppy?

As soon as he arrives home. Begin with a couple of minutes a day. Some puppy habits, such as jumping up and play biting, are not so cute with a fully grown dog.

How important is socialisation?

Extremely. It should begin as soon as your puppy is safe to go out after his vaccinations. Your puppy's breeder will begin this process for you with the litter and then it's up to you to keep it going when your new pup arrives home. A critical time for your puppy's learning is before he is four to five months old.

During this time, puppies are extremely receptive and can absorb a great deal of information, but they are also vulnerable to bad experiences. Don't leave your dog at home, take him out with you, get him used to new people and places and noises. Puppies that miss out on being socialised can later become aggressive, over-protective or jealous. A puppy class is a great place to help develop these socialisation skills.

Socialisation

Socialisation means learning to be part of society. When we talk about socialising puppies, it means helping them learn to be comfortable within a human society that includes many different types of people, environments, buildings, sights, noises, smells, animals and other dogs.

Most young animals, including dogs, are naturally able to get used to the everyday things they encounter in their environment—until they reach a certain age. When they reach that age, they naturally become much more suspicious of things they haven't yet experienced. Mother Nature is smart!

This age-specific natural development lets a young puppy get comfortable with the everyday sights, sounds, people and animals that will be a part of his life. It ensures that he doesn't spend his life jumping in fright at every blowing leaf or bird song. The suspicion they develop in later puppyhood also ensures that they do react with a healthy dose of caution to new things that could truly be dangerous.

Well-socialised puppies usually develop into safer, more relaxed and enjoyable adult dogs. This is because they're more comfortable in a wider variety of situations than poorly socialised canines. It also means they're less likely to behave fearfully or aggressively when faced with something new. Under-socialised dogs are much more likely to react with fear or aggression to unfamiliar people, dogs and experiences.

Dogs who are relaxed about other dogs, honking horns, cats, cyclists, veterinary examinations, crowds and long stairwells are easier and

safer to live with than dogs who find these situations threatening. Well socialised dogs also live much more relaxed, peaceful and happy lives than canines which are constantly stressed by their environment.

Socialisation isn't an "all or nothing" project. You can socialise a puppy a bit, a lot, or a whole lot. The wider the range of experiences you expose him to, the better his chances are of being comfortable in a wide variety of situations as an adult. Socialising from an early age is vitally important and then it should continue throughout your dog's life.

Don't over-face your pup in the beginning. Socialisation should never be forced, but approached systematically and in a manner that builds confidence and curious interaction. If your puppy finds a new experience frightening, take a step back, introduce him to the scary situation much more gradually, and make a big effort to do something he loves during the situation or right afterwards.

For example, if your puppy seems to be afraid of traffic at a busy intersection, take him further away from the action and offer him a treat each time a huge noisy lorry goes past. Another solution is to go to a much quieter road, use praise and treats to help convince him it's a great place to be, and then over days or even weeks, gradually approach the busy road again once he's started to get used to the sound of noisy traffic.

Meeting Other Dogs

When you take your gorgeous and vulnerable little pup out with other dogs for the first few times, you are bound to be a little nervous. To start with, introduce your puppy to just one other dog – one which you know to be friendly, rather than taking him straight to the park where there are lots of dogs of all sizes, which may frighten more timid dogs. Always make the initial introductions on neutral ground, so as not to trigger territorial behaviour. You want your pup to approach other dogs with confidence, not fear, which can turn to aggression.

From the first meeting, help both dogs experience "good things" when they're in each other's presence. Let them sniff each other briefly, which is normal canine greeting behaviour. As they do, talk to them in a happy, friendly tone of voice; never use a threatening tone. Don't allow them to investigate and sniff each other for too long, however, as this may escalate to an aggressive response. After a short time, get the attention of both dogs and give each a treat in return for obeying a simple command, such as "sit" or "stay." Continue with the "happy talk," food rewards, and simple commands.

So here are some signs of fear to look out for when your dog interacts with other canines.

- ❖ Running away
- ❖ Freezing on the spot
- ❖ Frantic/nervous behaviour, such as excessive sniffing, drinking or playing with a toy frenetically
- ❖ A lowered body stance or crouching
- ❖ Lying on his back with his paws in the air – this is a submissive gesture
- ❖ Lowering of the head, or turning the head away
- ❖ Ears flattened right back against the head
- ❖ Lips pulled back baring teeth and/or growling
- ❖ Hair raised on his back (hackles)

Some of these responses are normal. A puppy may well crouch on the ground or roll on to his back to show other dogs he is not a threat to them. Try not to be over-protective, your Pup has to learn how to interact with other dogs, but if the situation looks like escalating into something more aggressive, calmly distract the dogs or remove your puppy – don't shout or shriek. The dogs will pick up on your fear and this in itself could trigger an unpleasant situation.

Another sign to look out for is eyeballing - or staring at other dogs. In the canine world, staring a dog in the eyes is a challenge and may trigger an aggressive response in the other dog. This is more relevant to adult dogs, as a young pup will soon be put in his place by bigger or older dogs; it is how they learn.

Keep a close eye on your pup's reaction to whatever you expose him to so that you can tone things down if he seems at all frightened. Always follow up a socialisation experience with praise, petting, a fun game or a special treat.

A typical posture with some dogs when things are going well is a "play-bow" – when a dog will crouch with his front legs on the ground and his rear end in the air. This is an invitation to play, and a posture that usually gets a friendly response from the other dog.

Puppy Classes

One great way to help socialise a young dog is to attend puppy classes. In a typical class, off-lead play and play-fighting helps socialise puppies with each other, teaches them to be gentle with their mouthing and biting, and gets them used to being handled by a variety of people. Some classes even include exposure to odd sights and sounds using props, CDs of sounds, and theatrics with costumes. Puppy classes also teach some basic obedience skills, so as well as socialisation, you'll learn how to give your pup commands in the correct manner, enabling him to behave according to your expectations.

Socialisation is essential for helping your puppy develop into a happy, fun and safe companion. Most owners find it easier and more enjoyable to live with a dog which is relaxed with strangers, gets along well with other dogs and adapts easily to new experiences. Most puppies are very impressionable and can learn to take everything in stride, Socialisation gives him the greatest chance possible to develop into a dog that's comfortable in his environment and a joy to be with.

14 Tips for Training Your Puppy

1. **Start training and socialising early.** Like babies, puppies learn quickly and it's this learned behaviour which stays with them through adult life. Old dogs can be taught new tricks, but it's a lot harder to unlearn bad habits. It's best to start training with a clean slate. Puppy training should start with a few minutes a day from Day One, even if he's only a few weeks old.

2. **Your voice is your most important training tool.** Your dog has to learn to understand your language and you have to understand him. Your voice and the tone you employ are very

important. Commands should be issued in a calm, authoritative voice - not shouted. Praise should be given in a happy, encouraging voice, accompanied by stroking or patting. If your dog has done something wrong, use a firm, stern voice, not a harsh shriek. This applies even if your puppy is unresponsive at the beginning.

3. **Avoid giving your puppy commands you know you can't enforce.** Every time you give a command that you don't enforce, he learns that commands are optional.

4. **Train your puppy gently and humanely.** Puppies are sensitive and do not respond well to being shouted at or hit. Do not get into a battle of wills, instead teach him using friendly, motivational methods. Keep training sessions short and upbeat so the whole experience is enjoyable for you and him. If obedience training is a bit of a bore, pep things up a bit by "play training". Use constructive, non-adversarial games such as Go Find, Hide and Seek or Fetch.

5. **Begin your training around the house and garden or yard**. How well your puppy responds to you at home affects his behaviour away from the home as well. If he doesn't respond well at home, he certainly won't respond any better when he's out and about where there are 101 distractions, such as food scraps, other dogs, people, cats, interesting scents, etc.

6. **One command equals one response.** Give your puppy only one command - twice maximum - then gently enforce it. Repeating commands or nagging will make him tune out. They also teach him that the first few commands are a bluff. Shouting **"SIT, SIT, SIT, SIT!!"** is neither efficient nor effective. Give your dog a single "SIT" command, gently place him in the sitting position and then praise him.

7. **It's all about good communication**. It's NOT about getting even with the dog. If you're taking an "it's-me-against-the-dog, I'll soon whip him into shape" approach, you will build a relationship based on fear. It will undermine your relationship with him and you'll miss out on the fun that a positive training approach can offer.

8. **Use your puppy's name often and in a positive manner.** When you bring your pup home, start using his name often so

he gets used to the sound of it. He won't know what it means in the beginning, but it won't take him long to realise you're talking to him.

When training, DON'T use his name when you are reprimanding, warning or punishing him. He should trust that when he hears his name, good things happen. His name should always be a word he responds to with enthusiasm, never hesitancy or fear.

Use the words "NO" or "BAD BOY/GIRL" in a stern (not shouted) voice instead. Some people, especially those with children, prefer not to use the word "NO" with their dog, as it is a word they use often around the human kids and is likely to confuse the canine youngster! You can make a sound like "ACK!" instead. Say it sharply and the dog should stop whatever it is he is doing wrong – it works for us.

9. **Don't give your dog lots of attention (even negative attention) when he misbehaves.** Puppies love attention. If he gets lots of attention when he jumps up on you, his bad behaviour is being reinforced. If he jumps up, push him away, use the command "NO" or "DOWN" and then ignore him.

10. **Timing is critical to successful training.** When your puppy does something right, praise him immediately. Similarly, when he does something wrong, correct him straight away. If you don't praise or scold your puppy immediately for something he has done, you cannot do it at all, as he will have no idea what he has done right or wrong.

11. **Have a 'NO' sound.** When a puppy is corrected by his mother – for example if he bites her with his sharp baby teeth – she growls at him to warn him not to do it again. When your puppy makes a mistake, make a short sharp sound like **'ACK!'** to tell the puppy not to do that again. This works surprisingly well.

12. **Be patient.** Rome wasn't built in a day and a puppy won't be trained in a week either. But you'll reap the rewards of a few weeks of regular training sessions for the rest of the dog's life when you have a happy, well-behaved friend and loving companion for life.

13. **Give your puppy attention when YOU want to** – not when he wants it. Dogs are pack animals and sociable creatures, they

love being with you and around the family. When you are training, give your puppy lots of positive attention when he is good. But if he starts jumping up, nudging you constantly or barking to demand your attention, ignore him.

If you give in to his every demand, he will start to think he is the boss and become more demanding. Wait a while and pat him when you want and when he has stopped demanding your attention.

14. **Start as you mean to go on.** In other words, set down the rules you want your little puppy to live with as a fully grown dog. If you don't want him to take over your couch or jump up at people when he is big, don't allow him to do it when he is small. You can't have one set of rules for a pup and one set for an adult dog, he won't understand.

And remember: treats not threats.

Starting Off on the Right Foot

Despite what you may think, training a dog can be a pleasure of toil. Properly done it is a rewarding experience, a learning curve and a lot of fun - for both you and your dog. No matter how placid or laid back your puppy is, obedience training is an absolute must. As he grows and gets more confident in his new surroundings, he may try to push the boundaries and jump up at people, ignore your call or sit in your favourite chair - if you'll let him.

These things may happen around adolescence - between a few months and two years old. If you decide to allow your puppy onto the sofa or bed, that is your decision. But what you can't do is allow him up there as a puppy and then tell him it's out of bounds when he's bigger, older, noisier and gassier! If you allow your dog to get away with bad habits, the poor behaviour will soon become ingrained – dogs soon figure out what they can and can't get away with. If you don't want yours to become a pest, start your training early and stick with it.

Dogs love to be with their humans at the centre of family life, many are attention seekers. Praise for a job well done or a treat have a powerful effect during training. Negative reinforcement only increases stress and anxiety.

Without discipline and guidelines, stubbornness can become a problem. Some dogs, just like children, will act up in order to get attention – or treats. However hard it might be, ignore your dog and even leave him alone in the room, deprived of your company, if he is behaving badly and refuses to stop. Don't shout, or he will soon realise that shouting means he gets attention, which makes his behaviour even worse. Or he will become frightened.

Most puppies have short attention spans. When training they may be tempted to wander off to sniff or follow something more interesting than you, or simply switch off and ignore you. The key to successful training is **variety**, keep training interesting, short and fun. Try and do a little bit every day, starting with a few minutes, and once your dog has learned good behaviour, reinforce it every now and again, rewarding him with an occasional treat. Training doesn't stop because a puppy grows up, he continues to learn throughout his life. Like humans, canines can develop bad habits as they get older and more set in their ways!

If you start your training early and then take a few minutes in your normal daily routine to reinforce what your dog has learned, you'll end up with a wonderful companion that is a pleasure to be with and take anywhere.

Teaching Basic Commands

Sit

Teaching the Sit command is relatively easy. Teaching a young puppy to sit still is a bit more difficult! In the beginning you may want to put your protégé on a lead to hold his attention.

1. Stand facing each other and hold a treat between your thumb and fingers just an inch or so above his head. Don't let your fingers and the treat get any farther away or you might have trouble getting him to move his body into a sitting position. In fact, if

your dog jumps up when you try to guide him into the Sit, you're probably holding your hand too far away from his nose. If your dog backs up, you can practice with a wall behind him. NOTE: It's rather pointless paying for a high quality, possibly hypoallergenic dog food and then filling him with trashy treats. Buy premium treats with natural ingredients which won't cause allergies, or use natural meat, fish or poultry titbits.

2. As he reaches up to sniff it, move the treat upwards and back over the dog towards his tail at the same time as saying "Sit". Most dogs will track the treat with their eyes and follow it with their noses, causing their snouts to point straight up.

3. As his head moves up toward the treat, his rear end should automatically go down towards the floor. TaDa! (drum roll!)

4. As soon as he sits, say "Yes!" give him the treat and tell your dog (s)he's a good boy/girl. Stroke and praise him for as long as he stays in the sitting position. If he jumps up on his back legs and paws you while you are moving the treat, be patient and start all over again. Another method is to put one hand on his chest and with your other hand, gently push down on his rear end until he is sitting, while saying "Sit". Give him a treat and praise, even though you have made him do it, he will eventually associate the position with the word 'sit'.

5. Once your dog catches on, leave the treat in your pocket (or have it in your other hand). Repeat the sequence, but this time your dog will just follow your empty hand. Say "Sit" and bring your empty hand in front of your dog's nose, holding your fingers as if you had a treat. Move your hand exactly as you did when you held the treat.

6. When your dog sits, say "Yes!" and then give him a treat from your other hand or your pocket.

7. Gradually lessen the amount of movement with your hand. First, say "Sit" then hold your hand eight to 10 inches above your dog's face and wait a moment. Most likely, he will sit. If he doesn't, help him by moving your hand back over his head, like you did before, but make a smaller movement this time. Then try again. Your goal is to eventually just say "Sit" without having to move or extend your hand at all.

Once your puppy reliably sits on cue, you can ask him to sit whenever you meet and talk to people. The key to this is anticipation. Give him the cue before he gets too excited to hear you and before he starts jumping up on the person just arrived. Generously give a reward the instant he sits. Say "Yes" and give him treats every few seconds while he holds the Sit. Whenever possible, ask the person you're greeting to help you out by walking away if your dog gets up from the sit and lunges or jumps towards him or her. With many consistent repetitions of this exercise, your puppy will learn that lunging or jumping makes people go away, and polite sitting makes them stay and give him attention.

'Sit' is a useful command and can be used in a number of different situations. For example when you are putting his lead on, while you are preparing his meal, when he returned the ball you have just thrown, when he is demanding attention or getting over-excited.

Come

This is another basic command which you can teach right from the beginning. Teaching your dog to come to you when you call (also known as the recall) is the most important lesson. A dog who responds quickly and consistently can enjoy freedoms that other dogs cannot. Although you might spend more time teaching this command to your puppy than any other, the benefits make it well worth the investment.

No matter how much effort you put into training, no dog is ever going to be 100% reliable at coming when called. Dogs are not machines. They're like people in that they have their good days and their bad days. Sometimes they don't hear you call, sometimes they're paying attention to something else or they misunderstand what you want, and sometimes they simply decide they would rather do something else.

Whether you're teaching a young puppy or an older dog, the first step is always to establish that coming to you is the best thing he can do. Any time your dog comes to you whether you've called him or not, acknowledge that you appreciate it. You can do this with smiles, praise, affection, play or treats. This consistent reinforcement ensures that your dog will continue to "check in" with you frequently.

1. Say your puppy's name followed by the command **'Come!'** in an enthusiastic voice. You'll usually be more successful if you walk or run away from him while you call. Pups find it hard to resist chasing after a running person, especially their pet parent.

2. He should run towards you. NOTE: Dogs tend to tune us out if we talk to them all the time. Whether you're training or out for an off-lead walk, refrain from constantly chattering to your dog. If you're quiet much of the time, he is more likely to pay attention when you call him.

3. When he does, praise him and give him a treat.

183

4. Often, especially outdoors, a puppy will start off running towards you, but then get distracted and head off in another direction. Pre-empt this situation by praising and cheering him on when he starts to come to you and before he has a chance to get distracted. Your praise will keep him focused so that he'll be more likely to come all the way to you. If he stops or turns away, you can give him feedback by saying 'Hey!' in a different tone of voice (displeased or unpleasantly surprised). When he looks at you again, smile, call and praise him as he approaches.

Progress your puppy's training in baby steps. If he's learned to come when called in your kitchen, you can't expect him to be able to do it straight away at the park when he's surrounded by lots of distractions. When you try this outdoors, make sure there's no one around to distract your puppy when you first test his recall. It's a good idea to consider using a long training lead - or to do the training within a safe, fenced area. Only when your dog has mastered the recall in a number of locations and in the face of numerous distractions can you expect that he'll come to you.

At home, you can repeat the Come! command before you go for a walk, to train him to come to you for the collar and lead. You can also call him for mealtimes, when his bowl of food is the reward.

Down

There are a number of different ways to teach this command. It is one which does not come naturally to a young pup, so it may take a little while for him to master. Don't make it a battle of wills and, although you may gently push him down, don't physically force him down against his will. This will be seen as you asserting dominance in an aggressive manner and your dog will not respond well.

1. Give the Sit command.

2. When your dog sits, don't give him the treat immediately, but keep it in your closed hand. Slowly move your hand straight down toward the floor, between his front legs. As your dog's nose follows the treat, just like a magnet, his head will bend all the way down to the floor.

3. When the treat is on the floor between your dog's paws, start to move it away from him, like you're drawing a line along the floor. (The entire luring motion forms an L-shape).

4. At the same time say 'Down!' in a firm manner.

5. To continue to follow the treat, your dog will probably ease himself into the Down position. The instant his elbows touch the floor, say "Yes!" and immediately let him eat the treat. If your dog doesn't automatically stand up after eating the treat, just move a step or two away to encourage him to move out of the Down position. Then repeat the sequence above several times. Aim for two short sessions of five to 10 minutes per day.

If it doesn't work, try using a different treat. And if your dog's back end pops up when you try to lure him into a Down, quickly snatch the treat away. Then immediately ask your dog to sit and try again. It may help to let him nibble on the treat as you move it toward the floor. If you've tried to lure him into a Down but he still seems confused or reluctant, try this trick:

❖ Sit down on the floor with your legs straight out in front of you. Your dog should be at your side. Keeping your legs together and your feet on the floor, bend your knees to make a "tent" shape.
❖ Hold a treat right in front of your dog's nose. As he licks and sniffs the treat, slowly move it down to the floor and then underneath your legs. Continue to lure him until he has to crouch down to keep following the treat.
❖ The instant his belly touches the floor, say "Yes!" and let him eat the treat. If your dog seems nervous about following the treat under your legs, make a trail of treats for him to eat along the way.

Some dogs find it easier to follow a treat into the Down while standing.

❖ Hold the treat right in front of your dog's nose, and then slowly move it straight down to the floor, right between his front paws. His nose will follow the treat.
❖ If you let him lick the treat as you continue to hold it still on the floor, your dog will probably plop into the Down position.
❖ The moment he does, say "Yes!" and let him eat the treat.

(Many dogs are reluctant to lie on a cold floor. It may be easier to teach yours to lie down on a carpet.) The next step is to introduce a hand signal. You'll still reward him with treats, though, so keep them nearby or hidden behind your back.

❖ Start with your dog in a Sit.
❖ Say "Down!"

- ❖ Without a treat in your fingers, use the same hand motion you did before.
- ❖ As soon as your dog's elbows touch the floor, say "Yes!" and immediately get a treat to give him. Important: Even though you're not using a treat to lure your dog into position, you must still give him a reward when he lies down. You want your dog to learn that he doesn't have to see a treat to get one!

Clap your hands or take a few steps away to encourage him to stand up. Then repeat the sequence from the beginning several times for a week or two. When your dog readily lies down as soon as you say the cue and then use your new hand signal, you're ready for the next step. You probably don't want to keep bending all the way down to the floor to make your dog lie down. To make things more convenient, you can gradually shrink the signal so that it becomes a smaller movement. To make sure your pup continues to understand what you want him to do, you'll need to progress slowly.

Repeat the hand signal, but instead of guiding your dog into the Down by moving your hand all the way to the floor, move it almost all the way down. Stop moving your hand when it's an inch or two above the floor. Practice the Down exercise for a day or two, using this slightly smaller hand signal. Then you can make your movement an inch or two smaller, stopping your hand three or four inches above the floor. After practising for another couple of days, you can shrink the signal again. As you continue to gradually stop your hand signal farther and farther away from the floor, you'll bend over less and less. Eventually, you won't have to bend over at all. You'll be able to stand up straight, say "Down," and then just point to the floor.

Your next job is to practice your dog's new skill in many different situations and locations so that he can lie down whenever and wherever you ask him to. Slowly increase the level of distraction, for example, first practice in calm places like different rooms in your house or in your backyard when there's no one else around. Then increase the distractions, practice at home when family members are moving around, on walks and then at friends' houses, too.

Stay

This is a very useful command, but it's not so easy to teach a lively young pup to stay still for any length of time. Here is a simple method to get your dog to stay, but if you are training a young dog, don't ask him to stay for more than a few seconds at the beginning.

1. As this requires some concentration from your dog, pick a time when he's relaxed and well exercised, especially if training a youngster.

2. Start with your dog in the position you want him to hold, either the Sit or the Down position.

3. Command him to sit or lie down, but instead of giving a treat as soon as he hits the floor, hold off for one second. Then say "Yes!" in an enthusiastic voice and give him a treat. If your dog tends to bounce up again instantly, have two treats ready. Feed one right away, before he has time to move; then say "Yes!" and feed the second treat.

4. You need a release word or phrase. It might be "Free!" or "Here!" or a word which you only use to release your dog from this command. Once you've given the treat, immediately give your release cue and encourage your dog to get up. Then repeat the exercise, perhaps up to a dozen times in one training session, gradually wait a tiny bit longer before releasing the treat. (You can delay the first treat for a moment if your dog bounces up.)

5. A common mistake is to hold the treat high up and then give the reward slowly. As your dog doesn't know the command yet, he sees the treat coming and gets up to meet the food. Solve this problem by bringing the treat toward your dog quickly - the best place to deliver it is right between his front paws. If you're working on a Sit-Stay, give the treat at chest height.

6. When your dog can stay for several seconds, start to add a little distance. At first, you'll walk backwards, because he is more likely to get up to follow you if you turn away from him. Take one single step away, then step back towards your dog and say "Yes!" and give the treat. Give him the signal to get up immediately, even if five seconds haven't passed.

   The stay gets harder for your dog depending on how long it is, how far away you are, and what else is going on around him. Trainer shorthand is "distance, duration, distraction." For best success in teaching a stay, work on one factor at a time. Whenever you make one factor more difficult, such as distance, ease up on the others at first, then build them back up. That's why, when you take that first step back from your dog, adding **distance,** you should cut the **duration** of the stay.

7. Now your dog has mastered the Stay with you alone, move the training on so that he learns to do the same with distractions. Have someone walk into the room, or squeak a toy or bounce a ball once. A rock-solid stay is mostly a matter of working slowly and patiently to start with. Don't go too fast, the ideal scenario is that he never breaks out of the Stay position until you release him. If he does get up, take a breather and then give him a

short refresher, starting at a point easier than whatever you were working on when he cracked. If you think he's tired or had enough, leave it for the day and come back later – just finish off on a positive note by giving one very easy command you know he will obey, followed by a treat reward.

Don't use the "Stay" command in situations where it is unpleasant for your Dog. For instance, avoid telling him to stay as you close the door behind you on your way to work. Finally, don't use Stay to keep a dog in a scary situation.

Clicker Training

Clicker training is a method of animal training that uses a sound (a click) to tell an animal when he does something right. The clicker is a tiny plastic box held in the palm of your hand, with a metal tongue that you push quickly to make the sound.

The clicker creates an efficient language between a human trainer and a trainee. First, a trainer teaches a dog that every time he hears the clicking sound, he gets a treat. Once the dog understands that clicks are always followed by treats, the click becomes a powerful reward.

When this happens, the trainer can use the click to mark the instant the animal performs the right behaviour. For example, if a trainer wants to teach a dog to sit, she'll click the instant his rump hits the floor and then deliver a tasty treat. With repetition, the dog learns that sitting earns rewards.

So the 'click' takes on huge meaning. To the animal it means: "What I was doing the moment my trainer clicked, **that's** what she wants me to do!" The clicker in animal training is like the winning buzzer on a game show that tells a contestant she's just won the money! Through the clicker, the trainer communicates precisely with the dog, and that speeds up training.

Although the clicker is ideal because it makes a unique, consistent sound, you do need a spare hand to hold it. For that reason, some trainers prefer to keep both hands free and instead use a one-syllable word like "Yes!" or "Good!" to mark the desired behaviour. In the steps below, you can substitute the word in place of the click to teach your pet what the sound means.

It's easy to introduce the clicker to your puppy. Spend half and hour or so teaching him that the sound of the click means "Treat!" Here's how:

1. Sit and watch TV or read a book with your dog in the room. Have a container of treats within reach.

2. Place one treat in your hand and the clicker in the other. (If your dog smells the treat and tries to get it by pawing, sniffing, mouthing or barking at you, just close your hand around the treat and wait until he gives up and leaves you alone.)

3. Click once and immediately open your hand to give your dog the treat. Put another treat in your closed hand and resume watching TV or reading. Ignore your dog.

4. Several minutes later, click again and offer another treat.

5. Continue to repeat the click-and-treat combination at varying intervals, sometimes after one minute, sometimes after five minutes. Make sure you vary the time so that your dog doesn't know exactly when the next click is coming. Eventually, he'll start to turn towards you and look expectantly when he hears the click—so he understands that the sound of the clicker means a treat is coming his way.

If your dog runs away when he hears the click, you can make the sound softer by putting it in your pocket or wrapping a towel around your hand that's holding the clicker. You can also try using a different sound, like the click of a retractable pen or the word "Yes."

Once your dog seems to understand the connection between the click and the treat, you're ready to get started:

1. Click just once, right when your pet does what you want him to do. Think of it like pressing the shutter of a camera to take a picture of the behaviour.

2. Remember to follow every click with a treat. After you click, deliver the treat to your pet's mouth **as quickly as possible.**

3. It's fine to switch between practicing two or three behaviours within a session, but work on one behaviour at a time. For example, say you're teaching an older dog to sit, lie down and raise his paw. You can do 10 repetitions of sit and take a quick play break. Then do 10 repetitions of down, and take another quick break. Then do 10 repetitions of stay, and so on. Keep training sessions short and stop before you or your pet gets tired of the game.

4. End training sessions on a good note, when your dog has succeeded with what you're working on. If necessary, ask him to do something you know he can do well at the end of a session.

Collar and Lead Training

Your Dog has to be trained to get used to a collar and lead – and then he has to be taught to walk nicely on the lead. Teaching manners to large breeds can be challenging because large dogs tend to be strong and they don't necessarily want to walk at the same pace as you.

Firstly, you have to get him used to the collar and lead – some puppies don't mind them and others will resist. You need to be patient and calm and proceed at a pace comfortable to your dog, don't fight him and force the collar on.

1. The secret to getting a collar is to buy one that fits your puppy now (not one he is going to grow into), so choose a small lightweight one that he will hardly notice. A big collar will be too heavy and frightening for him. You can buy one with clips to start with, just put it on and clip it  together, rather than fiddling with buckles, which can be scary when he's wearing a collar for the first time.

   Stick to the principle of positive reward-based training (treats not threats) and give him a treat once the collar is on. Give the treat while the collar is on, not after you have taken it off. Then gradually increase the length of time you leave the collar on.

   IMPORTANT: If you leave your puppy in a crate or alone in the house, take off the collar. He is not used to it and it may get caught on something, causing panic or injury.

   So put the collar on when there are other things that will occupy him, like when he is going outside to be with you, or in the home when you are interacting with him. Or put it on at mealtimes or when you are doing some basic training. Don't put the collar on too tight, you want him to forget it's there. If he scratches the collar, get his attention by encouraging him to follow you or play with a toy, so he forgets the irritation.

2. Once your puppy is happy wearing the collar, introduce the lead. An extending or retractable one is not really suitable for a large dog, they are not strong enough and also no good for training him to walk close. Buy a fixed-length, strong lead. Start

190

off in the house, don't try to go out and about straight away. Think of the lead as a safety device to stop him running off, not something to drag him around with. You want a Dog that doesn't pull on the lead, so don't start by pulling him around. You definitely don't want to get into a tug of war contest.

3. Attach the lead to the collar and give him a treat while you put it on. The minute the lead is attached, use the treats (instead of pulling) to lure him beside you, so that he gets used to walking with the collar and lead. As well as using treats you can also make good use of toys to do exactly the same thing - especially if your puppy has a favourite. Walk around the house with the lead on and lure him forwards with the toy.

It might feel a bit odd but it's a good way for your pup to develop a positive relationship with the collar and lead with the minimum of fuss. Act as though it's the most natural thing in the world for you to walk around the house or apartment with your dog on a lead – and just hope that the neighbours aren't watching!

Some dogs react the moment you attach the lead and he feels some tension on it – a bit like when a horse is being broken in for the first time. Drop the lead and allow him to run round the house or yard, dragging it after him, but be careful he doesn't get tangled and hurt himself. Try to make him forget about the lead by playing with him or starting a short fun training routine with treats. Treats are a huge distraction for most Dogs! While he is concentrating on the new task, occasionally pick up the lead and call him to you. Do it gently and in an encouraging tone.

4. The most important thing is to never pull on the lead. If it is gets tight, just lure him back beside you with a treat or a toy while walking. All you're doing is getting him to move around beside you with the lead and collar on. Remember to keep your hand down (the one holding the treat or toy) so your dog doesn't get the habit of jumping up at you. If you feel he is getting stressed when walking outside on a lead, try putting treats along the route you'll be taking to turn this into a rewarding game: good times are ahead! That way he learns to focus on what's ahead of him with curiosity and not fear.

Take collar and lead training slowly, give your puppy time to process all this new information about what the lead is and does. Let him gain confidence in you, and then in the lead and himself. Some dogs can sit and decide not to move. If this happens, walk a few steps away, go down on one knee and encourage him to come to you using a treat, then walk off again.

For some pups, the collar and lead can be restricting and they will react with resistance. Some dogs are perfectly happy to walk alongside you off-lead, but behave differently on the lead. Patience and repetition are the keys. Proceed in tiny steps if that is what your puppy is happy with, don't over face him, but stick at it if you are met with resistance. Your puppy will learn to walk nicely on a lead, it is just a question of time.

Walking on a Lead

Firstly, you have to get your puppy used to the whole idea of a collar and lead and, as already stated, some take to it much quicker than others. Some dogs hate the idea of being constrained, so progress at a pace your dog is happy with. When you are both ready, pick up the lead, but don't try and get him to walk to heel straight away – it's one step at a time, literally!

There are different methods, but we have found the following one to be successful for quick results. Initially the lead should be kept fairly loose. Have a treat in your hand as you walk, it will encourage your dog to sniff the treat as he walks alongside. He will not pull ahead, as he will want to remain near the treat. Give him the command **'Walk'** or **'Heel'** and then proceed with the treat in your hand, keep giving him a treat every few steps initially, then gradually extend the time between treats. Eventually, you should be able to walk with your hand comfortably at your side, periodically (every minute or so) reaching into your pocket to grab a treat to reward your dog.

We have found that a training collar is very useful in getting a dog to walk to heel in a short space of time. The training collar is half chain, half leather or nylon, so that when you pull the lead sharply, it tightens around the dog's neck, but only to a point. It is much less severe than a choke collar.

If your dog starts pulling ahead, first give him a warning, by saying **'No,'** **'Easy'** or a similar command. If he slows down, give him a treat. But if he continues to pull ahead so that your arm becomes fully extended, give the lead a quick jerk backwards and upwards. You need to move your arm forward a few inches to give yourself the slack on the lead to pull back. (Make sure your action is a sharp jab and not a slower pull.) You may need to do this a couple of times before the dog slows down.

Your dog will not like the sensation of the tightened training collar, but soon realises that this is what happens when he pulls ahead. How much pressure you apply depends on the individual dog. If your dog is sensitive, you will need only slight force, if he's a bit more single minded or stubborn, he'll need a sharper jab. Be sure to quickly reward him with treats and praise any time he doesn't pull and walks with you with the lead slack. If you have a lively young puppy who is dashing all over the place on the lead, try starting training when he is already tired - after playing or running round.

Many owners have a body harness instead of a collar, but these are not suitable for training, as they actually encourage the dog to pull in the beginning. Before you progress to a body harness, train with a collar and lead. Similarly, extendable leads are not suitable for training a dog to walk to heel.

Puppy Biting

All puppies spend a great deal of time chewing, playing and investigating objects. All of these normal activities involve them using their mouths and their needle-sharp teeth. When puppies play with people they often bite, chew and mouth on people's hands, limbs and clothing. Play biting is normal for puppies, they do it all the time with their littermates. They bite moving targets with their sharp teeth; it's a great game. But when they arrive in your home, they have to be taught that human skin is sensitive and body parts are not suitable material for biting.

Try not to encourage play-biting. As a puppy grows and feels more confident in his surroundings, he may become slightly more aggressive and his bites may hurt someone – especially if you have children or elderly people at home. Make sure every time you have a play session, you have a soft toy nearby and when he starts to chew your hand or feet, clench your fingers (or toes!) to make it more difficult and distract him with a soft toy in your other hand.

Keep the game interesting by moving the toy around or rolling it around in front of him. (He may be too young to fetch it back if you throw it.) He may continue to chew you, but will eventually realise that the toy is far more interesting and lively than your boring hand.

If he becomes over-excited and too aggressive with the toy, if he growls a lot, stop playing with him and **walk away**. Although it might be quite cute and funny now, you don't want your dog doing this as an adult with powerful jaws. Remember, if not checked, any unwanted behaviour traits will continue into adulthood, when you certainly don't want him to bite your children's hands – even accidentally.

When you walk away, don't say anything or make eye or physical contact with your puppy. Simply ignore him, this is extremely effective and often works within a few days. If your pup is more persistent and tries to bite your legs as you walk away, thinking this is another fantastic game, stand still and ignore him. If he still persists, tell him **'No!'** in a very stern voice, then praise him when he lets go. If you have to physically remove him from your trouser leg or shoe, leave him alone in the room for a while and ignore his demands for attention if he starts barking.

Many puppies are sensitive and another method which can be very successful is to make a sharp cry of **'Ouch!'** when your pup bites your hand – even when it doesn't hurt. This worked very well for us. Your dog may well jump back in amazement, surprised that he has hurt you.

Divert your attention from your puppy to your hand. He will probably try to get your attention or lick you as a way of saying sorry. Praise him for stopping biting and continue with the game. If he bites you again, repeat the process. A sensitive Dog will soon stop biting you. You may also think about keeping the toys you use to play with your puppy separate from other toys he may have. That way he will associate certain toys with having fun with you and will work harder to please you.

Biting and chewing can be a big issue with puppies. Train your dog only to chew the things you give him – so don't give him your footwear, an old piece of carpet nor any object that resembles anything you don't want him to chew. Instead get purpose-made long-lasting chew toys suitable for puppies. You will also need patience, as it may take much repetition of a command (in short doses) before your pup obeys naturally.

CREDIT: With thanks to the American Society for the Prevention of Cruelty to Animals for assistance with parts of this chapter. The ASPCA has lots of good advice and training tips on its website at: http://www.aspca.org/pet-care/virtual-pet-behaviourist/dog-behaviour/training-your-dog

11. Spaying and Neutering

Judging by the number of questions our website receives, there is a lot of confusion about the canine facts of life out there. Many owners want to know at what age they should have their dog spayed (females) or neutered (males) and what, if any, are the risks involved.

Owners of females often ask when she will come on heat, how long this will last and how often it will occur. Sometimes they want to know how you can tell if a female is pregnant or how long a pregnancy lasts. Others want to know if they should breed from their dogs. So here, in a nutshell, is a short chapter on the birds and bees as they relate to dogs.

By the way, spaying and neutering are also referred to as gonadectomy or surgical sterilisation, and whether you get a male or a female puppy, it is worth reading the sections on both spaying and neutering for crossover information.

Spaying

Spaying is the term used to describe the removal of the ovaries and uterus (womb) to prevent a female dog, known as a bitch (this is the correct term, it is not derogatory) from becoming pregnant. Although this is a routine operation, it is major abdominal surgery and she has to be anaesthetised.

A popular myth is that a female dog must have her first heat cycle before she is spayed, but this is not necessarily the case. In fact, it is now known that spaying a bitch before her first heat prevents the development of mammary gland tumours later in life.

The British Veterinary Association (BVA) says: "The BVA believes that there is no current scientific evidence to support the view that the spaying of bitches should take place after the first season."

There is as much debate among veterinarians as there is among owners about what is the optimum age to spay a female or neuter a male dog. Most veterinarians recommend that the best age is between six and nine months. However, this is not an exact science as some breeds, like Bulldogs, mature later than others and some toy breeds are so tiny that it wiser to wait until the female has grown into an adult. It is certainly not a good idea to have a puppy spayed if she weighs less than two pounds.

Some vets even spay female puppies from as early eight weeks old. But the whole subject of early spaying and neutering is a hot potato, and much research has been bandied about by both camps. Some vets believe that it is OK to spay and neuter at any age, while others claim that sterilising a very young puppy may lead to problems later in life, such as stunted growth, obesity, urinary problems, diabetes and even behavioural problems.

They believe that a puppy needs his or her hormones as part of the normal growing process, so spaying – or neutering - should be carried out when the dog is slightly older.

The BVA is hedging its bets: "At the current time there is insufficient scientific data available to form a position on the early neutering of dogs and bitches."

The AMVA (American Veterinary Medical Association) has this to say on the spaying and neutering of young puppies less than six months old: "The AVMA supports the concept of pediatric spay/neuter in dogs and cats in an effort to reduce the number of unwanted animals of these species.

"Just as for other veterinary medical and surgical procedures, veterinarians should use their best medical judgment in deciding at what age spay/neuter should be performed on individual animals."

Many breeds of dog reach puberty at around six months old, which is why this time is often considered the optimum time for the sterilising procedure. However, before you have your dog spayed, you should speak with your vet about the best time for her; all breeds are different and all dogs are individuals.

Some vets claim that the risk of mammary cancer in unspayed female dogs can be as high as one in four. Some females may put weight on easier after spaying and will require slightly less food afterwards. Spaying is a much more serious operation for a female than neutering is for a male. This is because it involves an internal abdominal operation, whereas the neutering procedure is carried out on the male's testicles, which are outside his abdomen.

If you do decide to have your dog spayed, you cannot have it done while she is on heat or pregnant; it is best to wait two to three months after all the visible signs of heat have disappeared. As with any major procedure, there are pros and cons.

Advantages

❖ Spaying prevents infections, cancer and other diseases of the uterus and ovaries. If spayed before her first heat cycle, your dog will have an almost zero risk of mammary cancer (the equivalent of breast cancer in women). Even after her first heat, spaying reduces the risk of this cancer by 92%. The risk increases with each successive season.

❖ Spaying eliminates the risk of the potentially fatal disease pyometra (womb infection), which affects unspayed middle-aged females. Spaying a healthy young female does not involve the risks of spaying an older one with toxaemia (blood poisoning) caused by pyometra.

❖ Spayed females do not have false pregnancies, which are common and can occur after each season. It can be distressing for the dog and stressful for the owner.

❖ Spayed females have no oestrus cycle, in other words they will not come into heat or season ever again. Normally this happens about every six months and during this time owners have to guard their female, keeping her away from male dogs who all want to mate with her. A female on heat also produces a vaginal discharge.

❖ Spaying can reduce behaviour problems, such as roaming, aggression with other dogs, anxiety or fear.

❖ It reduces hormonal changes which can interfere with the treatment of diseases like diabetes or epilepsy.

❖ A spayed female does not contribute to the pet overpopulation problem.

Disadvantages

❖ Spaying is a major surgical procedure and not all breeds do well under anaesthetic. Complications can occur, including an abnormal reaction to the anaesthetic, bleeding, stitches breaking and infections. None of these are common. The brachycephalic breeds, such as Pug, Bulldog, French Bulldog, Boxer, Pekingese, Cavvies, etc may be particularly sensitive to anaesthetic. Choose a vet familiar with these breeds and discuss any anaesthetics beforehand.

❖ Occasionally, spaying can have long-term effects connected to hormonal changes. These may include weight gain or reduced stamina and these problems can occur years after a female has been spayed.

❖ Older females may suffer some urinary incontinence, but it only affects a very few spayed females. Discuss this with your vet.

❖ Spaying can affect the growth and texture of your dog's coat, although supplements help.

❖ Cost. This can range from £100 to around £250 in the UK ($160 - $400 in the USA), more if there are complications.

If you decide to have your female spayed or male neutered, you will typically drop her or him off at the veterinary surgery early in the morning. They are not allowed any food for at least 12 hours before the operation. A dog will not be accepted for surgery if it is coughing, sneezing, has diarrhoea or otherwise appears unwell.

Normally, your dog will be ready to be picked up at the end of the day. She will be groggy from the anaesthetic and needs to be kept quiet for the next few days. If you have small children or other animals, keep them away from her for 48 hours. Your dog will be feeling sore and sleepy, and he or she might even be a little bit short-tempered for a couple of days until they get back to feeling normal again.

After spaying, your female may need to wear an E-collar to stop her licking the wound (like the Havanese pictured here). She might have a small lump at the surgery site, but this should disappear after a few days. Check the wound a couple of times a day; after the first day or so any swelling, redness or weeping should disappear.

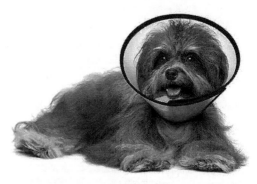

Although your dog may seem fine after a couple of days, she should not have any strenuous exercise, swimming or jumping for a week, or she may tear the stitches. She must also not be bathed until the stitches have been removed by the vet, usually around a week to 10 days after the operation.

If you are at all worried, contact your vet - and do not give any medication except that which has been prescribed by your vet.

As with the field of human medicine, great advancements have been made in animal medicine and it is worth mentioning that some vets perform an operation known as an ovariectomy or a laparoscopic ovariectomy, commonly known as keyhole surgery. Ask your vet if he or she carries out this less-invasive procedure or if you're in the UK, visit www.veterinarylaparoscopy.com for a list of vets who perform keyhole surgery.

Overall, spaying is a routine procedure and it is unusual for complications to occur. If you talk to a vet or a volunteer at a rescue shelter, they will say that the advantages of spaying far outweigh any disadvantages.

Neutering

Neutering male dogs involves castration; the removal of the testicles. This can be a difficult decision for some owners, as it causes a drop in the pet's testosterone levels which some humans (men in particular!) feel affects the quality of their dog's life.

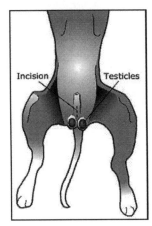

Fortunately, dogs do not think like people and male dogs do not miss their testicles or the loss of sex. We believe that our male dogs have been much more content after neutering. We decided to have our Miniature Schnauzer neutered after he went missing three times on walks – he ran off on the scent of a female on heat. Fortunately, he is micro-chipped and has our phone number on a tag on his collar and we were lucky that he was returned to us on all three occasions.

Unless you specifically want to breed from or show your dog, or he has a special job, neutering is recommended by animal rescue organisations and vets. Guide Dogs for the Blind, Hearing Dogs for Deaf People, and Dogs for the Disabled are routinely neutered and this does not impair their ability to perform their duties.

There are countless unwanted puppies, especially in the USA, many of which are destroyed. Unbelievably, three to four million dogs and cats are euthanized every year in the US. There is also the problem of a lack of knowledge from the owners of some breeding dogs, resulting in the production of puppies with congenital health or temperament problems.

As with spaying, neutering is often performed around puberty, i.e. about six months old. The operation is a relatively straightforward procedure, being much less of a major operation than spaying is for a female. Complications are less common and less severe than with spaying. Although he will feel tender afterwards, your dog should return to his normal self within a couple of days. However, as with females, keeping the dog quiet and avoiding strenuous exercise and jumping are important aspects of after care.

Dogs neutered before puberty tend to grow a bit bigger than dogs done later in life. This is because testosterone is involved in the process which stops growth, so the bones grow for longer without testosterone.

When he comes out of surgery, your dog's scrotum (the sacs which held the testicles) will be swollen and it may look like nothing has been done. But it is normal for these to slowly shrink in the days following surgery. Here are the main pros and cons of neutering:

Advantages

❖ Behaviour problems such as roaming and aggression are usually reduced.

❖ Unwanted sexual behaviour, such as mounting people or objects, is usually reduced or eliminated.

❖ Testicular problems such as infections, cancer and torsion (painful rotation of the testicle) are eradicated.

❖ Prostate disease, common in older male dogs, is less likely to occur.

❖ A submissive entire (uncastrated) male dog may be targeted by other dogs. After he has been neutered, he will no longer produce testosterone and so will not be regarded as much of a threat by the other males, so he is less likely to be bullied.

❖ A neutered dog is not fathering unwanted puppies.

Disadvantages

❖ As with any surgery, there can be bleeding afterwards; you should keep an eye on your dog for any blood loss after the operation. Infections can also occur, generally caused by the dog licking the wound, so try and prevent him doing this. If he persists, use an E-collar. In the **vast majority** of cases, these problems do not occur.

❖ Some dogs' coats may be affected; supplementing their diet with fish oil can often compensate for this.

❖ Cost. This starts at around £80 in the UK ($130 in the USA).

❖ Some breeds and small dogs are sensitive to anaesthesia – select a vet who is familiar with your type of dog.

Spaying and neutering are definitely worth considering if you have more than one dog in the household. With two healthy dogs, it is not possible for an unspayed female and an unneutered male to live together without the female becoming pregnant.

Myths

Here are some common myths about neutering and spaying:

Neutering or spaying will spoil the dog's character - There is no evidence that any of the positive characteristics of your dog will be altered. He or she will be just as loving, playful and loyal. Neutering may reduce aggression or roaming, especially in male dogs because they are no longer competing to mate with a female.

A female needs to have at least one litter - There is no proven physical or mental benefit to a female having a litter. Pregnancy and whelping (giving birth to puppies) can be stressful and can have complications. In a false pregnancy, a female is simply responding to the hormones in her body.

Mating is natural and necessary - Dogs are not humans, they do not think emotionally about sex or having and raising a family. Because puppies generally like the company of humans so much, we tend to ascribe human emotions to them. Unlike humans, their desire to mate or breed is entirely physical, triggered by the chemicals called hormones within their body. Without these hormones – i.e. after neutering or spaying – the desire disappears or is greatly reduced.

Male dogs will behave better if they can mate - This is simply not true; sex does not make a dog behave better. In fact it can have the opposite effect. Having mated once, a male may show an increased interest in females. He may also consider his status elevated, which may make him harder to control or call back.

Should I Breed From My Dog?

Contrary to what you might think, breeding dogs is a complex issue – if you want a healthy mother and pups, that is. The pedigree breed societies discourage regular dog owners from breeding from their pets, as doing so properly requires a great deal of knowledge and experience. Today's responsible breeders are continually looking at ways of improving the health and temperament of their puppies through selective breeding.

You can put a male and a female together, let them get on with it and then sit back and wait for a cute litter of pups to arrive two months later. But without expert knowledge and experience, there is no guarantee that these puppies will be healthy and have good temperaments.

Responsible breeding is backed up by genetic information and screening as well as a thorough knowledge of the desired traits of the breed or crossbreed. It is definitely not an occupation for the amateur hobbyist. Breeding is not just about the look of the dogs; health and temperament are important factors too. Many dog lovers do not realise that the single most important factor governing health and certain temperament traits is genetics.

These Standard Schnauzers pictured are not only handsome, they are the product of responsible breeding. They have no inbred temperament flaws and their parents and grandparents have been screened for genetic illnesses.

Top breeders have years of experience in selecting the right pair for mating after they have considered the lineage (ancestry), health, temperament, size and physical characteristics of the two dogs involved. They may travel hundreds of miles to find the right breeding partner for their dog.

Anyone breeding from their dog must first consider these questions:

- ❖ Are you 100% sure that your dog has no health or temperament problems which may be inherited by his or her puppies?

- ❖ Have you researched your dog's lineage to make sure there are no problems lurking in the background? Puppies inherit traits from their grandparents and great-grandparents as well as from the dam (female) and sire (male).

- ❖ Are you positive that the same can be said for the dog you are planning on breeding yours with?

- ❖ Have your dog, the mate and their parents all been screened for health issues which can be inherited? Has your dog got OFA (Orthopedic Foundation for Animals) or BVA (British Veterinary Association) certificates for inheritable diseases?

- ❖ Do you have expert knowledge of the breed or crossbreed's genetics and health, as well as the know-how and finances to successfully deal with keeping the mother healthy through pregnancy and whelping and caring for the puppies and mother after birth?

Having said that, experts are not born, they learn their trade over many years. Anyone who is seriously considering getting into the specialised art of breeding should first spend time researching the breed and its genetics. Make sure you are going into breeding for the right reasons and not just to make money - **ask yourself how you intend to improve the breed.**

Visit dog shows and make contact with established breeders. If at all possible, find yourself a mentor, somebody who is already very familiar with the breed and make sure you have a vet who is also familiar with the breed. Committed breeders aren't in it for the money. They use their skills and knowledge to produce healthy pups with good temperaments which conform to breed standards and ultimately improve the breed.

Our advice is: unless you have the time to devote to learning all about the breed and it specific genetics and genuinely intend to improve the breed, leave it to the experts.

Females and Heat

Just like all other animal and human females, a bitch has a menstrual cycle - or to be more accurate, an oestrus cycle. This is the period when she is ready (and willing!) for mating and is more commonly called **heat** or being **on heat**, **in heat** or **in season**.

A female puppy has her first cycle from about six to nine months old. However, some breeds and bloodlines have longer spans between heat cycles and these females may not have their first heat until they are anywhere from 10 months to 15 months old. Typically, small breeds have their first heat at six months old and larger breeds tend to be later.

A female will then generally come on heat every six to eight months, though the timescale becomes more erratic with old age and can also be irregular with young dogs when cycles first begin.

On average heat lasts from 12 to 21 days, although it can be anything from just a few days up to four weeks. Within that time there will be several days which will be the optimum time for her to get pregnant. This middle phase of the cycle is called the *oestrus.*

The third phase, called *diestrus*, then begins. During this time, her body will produce hormones whether or not she is pregnant. Her body thinks and acts like she is pregnant. All the hormones are present; only the puppies are missing. This can sometimes lead to what is known as a false pregnancy. Breeders normally wait until a female has been in heat two or three times before breeding from her.

While a female dog is on heat, she produces hormones which attract male dogs. Because dogs have a sense of smell hundreds of times stronger than ours, your girl on heat is a magnet for all the males in the neighbourhood. They may congregate around your house or follow you around the park, waiting for their chance to prove their manhood – or mutthood in their case.

Don't expect your precious princess (like this Tibetan Terrier) to be fussy. Her hormones are raging when she is on heat and during her most fertile days, she is ready, able and … very willing! As she approaches the optimum time for mating, you may notice her tail bending slightly to one side. She will also start to urinate more frequently. This is her signal to all those virile male dogs out there that she is ready for mating.

The first visual sign you may notice is a swollen rear end – or vulva to be more precise, which she will lick. She will then bleed, this is sometimes called spotting. It will be a light red or brown at the beginning of the heat cycle; some breeds can bleed quite heavily and others hardly at all. But if you have any concerns about your dog's bleeding, contact your vet.

Breeding good puppies requires a lot of specialised knowledge on the part of the owner, but this does not stop a female on heat from being extremely interested in attention from any old scruffy male. Canine hormones have been engineered so that when a female is on heat, her greatest desire is to mate. To avoid an unwanted pregnancy, you must keep a close eye on your female and not allow her to freely wander where she may come into contact with other dogs while she is on heat.

Unlike women, female dogs do not go through the menopause and can have puppies even when they are quite old. However, a first litter for an elderly female can also result in complications.

Pregnancy

A canine pregnancy will normally last for 61 to 65 days - typically 63 days – regardless of the size or breed of the dog. Sometimes pregnancy is referred to as the **gestation period.**

There is now a blood test available which measures levels of a hormone called **relaxin**. This is produced by the developing placenta, and pregnancy can be detected as early as 22 to 27 days after mating. The level of relaxin remains high throughout pregnancy and declines rapidly following whelping (giving birth). After 45 days, X-rays can confirm the pregnancy. X-rays also give the breeder an idea of the number of puppies. Here are some of the signs of pregnancy:

- After mating, many females become more affectionate. (However, some will become uncharacteristically irritable and maybe even a little aggressive).

- A female may produce a slight clear discharge from her vagina about one month after mating.

- Her appetite will increase in the second month of pregnancy.

- She may seem slightly depressed and/or show a drop in appetite. These signs can also mean there are other problems, so you should consult your vet if in doubt.

- Her teats (nipples) will become more prominent, pink and erect 25 to 30 days into the pregnancy. Later on you may notice a fluid coming from them.

- After about 35 days, or seven weeks, her body weight will noticeably increase.

- Her abdomen will become noticeably larger from around Day 40, although first-time mothers and females carrying few puppies may not show as much.

- Many pregnant females' appetite will increase in the second half of pregnancy.

- Her nesting instincts will kick in as the delivery date approaches. She may seem restless or scratch her bed or the floor

- During the last week of pregnancy, females often start to look for a safe place for whelping. Some seem to become confused, wanting to be with their owners and at the same time wanting to prepare their nest.

False Pregnancies

A As many as 50% or more of intact (unspayed) female dogs may display signs of a false pregnancy.

In the wild it was common for female dogs to have false pregnancies and to lactate (produce milk). This female would then nourish puppies if their own mother died.

False pregnancies occur 60 to 80 days after the female was in heat - about the time she would have given birth – and are generally nothing to worry about for an owner. The exact cause is unknown. However, hormonal imbalances are thought to play an important role. Some dogs have shown symptoms within three to four days of spaying.

Typical symptoms include:

 ❖ Mothering or adopting toys and other objects
 ❖ Making a nest
 ❖ Producing milk (lactating)
 ❖ Appetite fluctuations
 ❖ Barking or whining a lot
 ❖ Restlessness, depression or anxiety
 ❖ Swollen abdomen
 ❖ She might even appear to go into labour

Try not to touch your dog's nipples, as touch will stimulate further milk production. If she is licking herself repeatedly, she may need an E-collar to minimise stimulation.

Under no circumstances should you restrict your dog's water supply to try and prevent her from producing milk. This is dangerous as she can become dehydrated.

Some unspayed bitches may have a false pregnancy with each heat cycle. Spaying during a false pregnancy may actually prolong the condition, so better to wait until the false pregnancy is over and then have her spayed to prevent it happening again.

False pregnancy is not a disease, but an exaggerated response to normal hormonal changes. Owners should be reassured that even if left untreated, the condition almost always resolves itself.

However, if your dog appears physically ill or the behavioural changes are severe enough to worry you, visit your vet. He or she may prescribe tranquilisers to relieve anxiety, or diuretics to reduce milk production and relieve fluid retention. In rare cases, hormone treatment may be necessary. Generally, dogs experiencing false pregnancies do not have serious long-term problems as the behaviour disappears when the hormones return to their normal levels - usually in two to three weeks.

One exception is pyometra, a disease mainly affecting unspayed middle-aged females, caused by a hormonal abnormality. Pyometra follows a heat cycle in which fertilisation did not occur and the dog typically starts showing symptoms within two to four months. These are excessive drinking and urination, with the female trying to lick a white discharge from her vagina, and she may also have a slight temperature. If the condition becomes severe, her back legs will become weak, possibly to the point where she can no longer get up without help.

Pyometra is serious if bacteria take a hold and in extreme cases it can be fatal. It is also relatively common and needs to be dealt with promptly by a vet, who will give the dog intravenous fluids and antibiotics for several days. In most cases this is followed by spaying.

12. Getting a Rescue Puppy

Are you thinking of adopting a puppy or young dog from a rescue organisation? What could be kinder and more rewarding than giving a poor, abandoned dog a happy and loving home for the rest of his life?

Not much really, adoption saves lives. The problem of homeless dogs is truly depressing, particularly in the USA. The sheer numbers in kill shelters there is hard to comprehend. Randy Grim states in "Don't Dump The Dog" that 1,000 dogs are being put to sleep every hour in the US.

Taking on a rescue dog is a big commitment for all involved. It is not a cheap way of getting a dog and shouldn't be viewed as such, as it could cost you as much as a few hundred pounds or dollars. You'll have adoption fees to pay and often vaccination and veterinary bills as well as worm and flea medication and spaying or neutering.

Many rescue dogs have had difficult lives, particularly older ones, so you need to devote plenty of time to help them rehabilitate. Some may have initial problems with housebreaking, others may need socialisation with people as well as other dogs.

According to the International Doodle Owners Group (IDOG), which rescues Labradoodles and Goldendoodles, the reason so many dogs end up in rescue can be summed up in two words: **unrealistic expectations.**

IDOG's Jo Cousins says: "In many situations, dog ownership was something that the family went into without fully understanding the time, money and commitment to exercise and training that it takes to raise a dog. While they may have spent hours on the internet pouring over cute puppy photos, they probably didn't read any puppy training books or look into actual costs of regular vet care, training and boarding.

"With Doodles, many are going to homes that have never had a dog before because of allergies. The marketing of doodles as "hypo-allergenic" and/or non-shedding has caused a general misconception that *all doodles* are non-shedding, or will not cause allergies to flare up."

The most common reasons for re-homing are that the dog:

- ❖ Has too much energy and is knocking children over and jumping on people

- ❖ Is growling and/or nipping at the kids

- ❖ Chews or eats things it shouldn't

- ❖ Needs way more time and effort than the owner is able to or prepared to give

The Dog's Point of View...

If you are serious about adopting a dog, then you should do so with the right motives and with your eyes wide open. If you're expecting a perfect puppy, you could be in for a shock. Rescue dogs can and do become wonderful companions, but much of it depends on you.

Many dogs in rescue centres are traumatised. They don't understand why they have been abandoned and in the beginning may arrive with problems of their own until they adjust to being part of a loving family home again. Ask yourself a few questions before you take the plunge:

- ❖ Are you prepared to accept and deal with any problems - such as bad behaviour, shyness, aggression or making a mess in the house - which the dog may display when he initially arrives in your home?

- ❖ How much time are you willing to spend with your new pet to help him integrate back into normal family life?

- ❖ Can you take time off work to be at home and help the dog settle in at the beginning?

- ❖ Are you prepared to take on a new addition to your family that may live for another 10 years or so?

Of course, if you get a young puppy, then he will not be so set in his ways, he will have had less time to get bored or destructive or learn bad habits and may well arrive without much emotional baggage. But think about the implications before taking on a rescue dog - try and look at it from the dog's point of view. What could be worse for the unlucky animal than to be abandoned again if things don't work out between you?

Screening the Humans

IDOG Rescue has some excellent advice for anyone considering starting out on the adoption process:

"Seeing a dog in a photo is a great start to finding the right dog for your family, but please remember that our rescue coordinators have the very best understanding about what type of family and home environment will be most suitable for each individual dog.

"Very specific preferences will limit your chances: Sometimes people get distracted with what a dog looks like and often forget that there is a personality under all that fur. The perfect dog for you may be the opposite sex of the one you imagined. The right dog for your family might be black, or have a scruffy coat, or be a different age than you imagined.

"If you overlook some dogs because of sex, color or looks, you might just miss out on some great dogs. We urge you to consider all the dogs in our program based on their listing descriptions, and not on their photos. Please understand that our focus is on *rescuing* nice dogs and finding them good homes, not helping people find the picture-perfect dog that they can tell people they "rescued" because it is more socially acceptable.

"If your family really wants a puppy, or must have a blonde or female, or if your family has allergy issues to consider, our best recommendation is that you work with a responsible breeder to get exactly what you want. There is no shame in getting a pup from a responsible breeder.

"Please do not apply for a dog unless you are able and willing to travel to the foster's location to meet the dog. We rarely ship dogs and will do so only if we feel that it is the best option for the dog. Please realize that first-time dog owners comprise the majority of people who surrender dogs to shelters. For that reason, we are very hesitant to place a dog in a first time situation. Most rescue dogs need experienced owners."

IDOG Rescue does not place dogs in homes that use an electric fence or shock training collars, as they claim that this can spell disaster for rescue dogs. The website is at **www.idogrescue.com**.

If you do decide to adopt a rescue dog, be prepared to answer lots of questions. The last thing rescue organisations want is for a dog to be placed with an unsuitable home and for the poor animal to be returned. For this reason, prospective owners are also screened to try and match up a dog with a new owner's expectations and lifestyle – and you might be surprised how detailed and personal some of the questions are. Here are some things a rescue centre may ask before you are considered suitable to adopt:

- ❖ Why do you want to adopt a dog?

- ❖ Have you got young children? Some shelters will not let their dogs go to homes where there are very young children.

- ❖ Do you have a garden?

- ❖ Do you own or rent your home? If you rent, they may not be willing to allow you to adopt unless you can prove it is a very secure tenure and you have the landlord's permission to keep a dog.

- ❖ Does everyone in your home want a dog?

- ❖ Do you have cats or other small pets?

- ❖ Does anyone in your home have allergies and are you prepared to accept a dog which sheds hair?

- ❖ How many hours a day would the dog be left alone? Shelters will not let a dog go to a home where he will be on his or her own for more than four or five hours at a stretch, so if you are out at work all day, they would not let you adopt one of their dogs.

- ❖ How much time have you got to exercise a dog? How long and how often will you exercise him or her?

- ❖ Is this your first dog? If so, you may not be considered suitable.

- ❖ Who will look after the dog when you are on holiday?

- ❖ Which veterinarian will you use and are your current animals (if you have any) up to date with their vaccinations, flea and worm medications?

- ❖ Are you prepared to train a dog?

- ❖ What type of dog do you want – size, colour, age, male or female, etc. Are you prepared to accept a dog with a manageable medical condition?

You might also have to supply references! With all these questions, it's a wonder anybody ever adopts a dog – but they do, thank goodness. Every year many thousands of people in North America, the UK and countries all around the world adopt a rescue dog and, when all these checks have been made, many thousands of dogs are given the chance of starting a happy new life.

Fostering

If you are serious about adopting, you may have to wait a while until a suitable dog comes up – particularly if you are looking for a puppy or young dog, which are often more popular. One way of finding out if you, your family and home are suitable is to volunteer to become a foster home for one of the rescue centres. Fosters offer temporary homes until a forever home becomes available. It's a shorter term arrangement, but still requires commitment and patience.

This is what USA-based Doodle Rescue Collective Inc (DRC) has to say about fostering - and most of the questions apply equally to anyone thinking of permanent adoption of whatever type of dog (with thanks to Jacquie Yorke):

DRC: "Fostering - like adoption - requires a tremendous amount of time, commitment, patience, flexibility and tolerance among other things. Fostering is not always easy. We hope that if you decide to foster for DRC that you will be willing to work with the dogs in your care and not only help them find their way to their new forever homes, but help them to also become wonderful family members.

"There are many reasons why a doodle ends up needing a new home. Some were purchased on a whim by people that didn't understand the temperament and needs of the breed. Sometimes lifestyle changes such as job loss or divorce are a factor in a dogs re-homing. Other doodles lose their homes when their owners become too sick or elderly to provide them with the necessary care. Sometimes owners are forced to enter an

assisted-living facility or they pass away.

"Others are surrendered by people who just no longer want them. Regardless of the reasons why a doodle finds its way into rescue, the care that the dog will require while in a transitional foster home can at times involve more than just the provision of basic food, water and shelter.

"We are always looking for special loving foster homes and families that will provide not only the basics, but the extra care and attention that are sometimes necessary to insure that the doodles in our program become better companions and ultimately find their way to new forever homes.

Fostering Puppy Mill Survivors

"In the case of mill dogs, they have never had an actual home and are usually completely unfamiliar with human contact and life outside of their small cramped cages. Many have never felt the ground or grass beneath their feet. Many suffer from muscle atrophy and have never used their legs to do anything but stand within the confines of their cages. Many have never walked at all and need to learn how.

"Mill dogs are unfamiliar with human interaction, love, kindness, play, house manners etc. Many of these dogs were starved, physically abused, neglected and have had little or no veterinary care. They tend to be frightened, unsocialized, easily stressed and have difficulties with the concept of house training.

"Because of the lack of food available to them, many mill dogs have grown accustomed to eating their own feces and other non-edible substances. In most cases as a foster you will be providing these dogs with their very first experiences of life as a normal dog. Whatever the reasons, some doodles do come into rescue with "baggage." A foster home should be prepared for anything and have a basic understanding of the techniques used to help dogs in transition adjust.

What Will Be Expected of Me If I Decide to Foster?

"Fostering can involve house-training and/or crate training as well as introducing some basic obedience. Some will require special care, such as medical attention and you may be asked to take the foster dog to scheduled veterinary appointments. It could require giving them medication at certain times of the day or perhaps bathing them periodically. They may need to increase their weight and/or strength.

"Do you have a safe place to keep the rescue separate from the other animals in your home if necessary? The dog may need an area where it can be quarantined from other pets for approx. a week in case it has any types of infections etc that may be passed to your own animals. All of your own animals should be up to date on vaccinations (rabies, DHPP, bordatella), have monthly flea treatments, and get along well with other animals.

Do You Agree with Crate Training?

"You should be open to using a crate when you are not home or during the period of work on house-training as dogs often will find the crate a secure spot. You need to be familiar with how to properly use a crate.

Do You Have a Nice White Carpet?

"Be aware that the many of the dogs will not be house-trained and will require work in that area. They may soil your carpets and other flooring so be prepared to clean up messes.

Do You Have Children? Are Your Children Respectful Around Pets?

"Some dogs can easily be hurt by children who don't know how to treat them, while other dogs can be "over-enthusiastic" around small children, and are capable of knocking kids over while attempting to play. For the safety of both the dog and the children, we are quite cautious about placing dogs with families that have children under 12 years of age and generally will not place foster dogs in homes with very young children.

Are You Willing to Accept a Dog With Some Behavioral Issues?

"Some dogs have experienced emotional or physical trauma, while others have never received adequate socialization or training. Others have absolutely no issues. It depends on the dog and the circumstances.

Are You Willing to Surrender a Dog to its New Forever Home Even After You Have Created a Strong Bond With That Dog?

"This is one of the most difficult aspects of being a foster caretaker, but it is inevitable. For many foster parents, the single biggest concern about fostering is falling in love. It takes a very special person to open their hearts to one of these dogs, to love and nurture them for a period of time, and then give them up when their new permanent home is found.

"We won't lie to you. There are usually some tears when your foster pet leaves, but there is also an immense feeling of satisfaction. It is especially rewarding to get an update from the new home and hear them brag about the most wonderful dog in the whole world, and know that it was your love and care that helped to make them such a special pet. Keep in mind, that if you choose to adopt a doodle that you're fostering, you may be at your limit of household pets and consequently you may not be able to continue to foster other doodles in need.

"When you foster a DRC doodle, you have the full support of the entire organization. We are always available to assist you and answer your questions and address your concerns at any time of the day or night. We in turn will rely on your experience and opinions when the time comes to select your foster doodle's new forever home. After all you know the dog, his or her issues, habits and personality best and we will always take your recommendations into consideration. DRC adopters and fosters alike become part of our BIG family so you will be able to stay in contact with your foster doodle's adoptive family and see that dog's progress.

"Please remember, it takes two weeks to a month for a dog to adjust to a new environment and it may not always be practical or possible to move a dog to another foster home at a moment's notice so you must be flexible. Still ready to foster? We hope so! We may not be able to save every doodle in the world, but we do mean the world to the ones we do manage to save."

With thanks to the Doodle Rescue Collective - **http://doodlerescue.org**

However you decide to get involved, Good Luck!

Saving one dog will not change the world
But it will change the world for one dog

Puppy Quiz

Questions

1. **What is generally the optimum age for puppies to leave the litter?**

   A) Three or four weeks old

   B) Five weeks old

   C) Six weeks old

   D) Seven or eight weeks old

   E) Nine weeks or older

2. **What is the world's most popular name for a male puppy in English-speaking countries?**

   A) Max

   B) Charlie

   C) Buster

   D) Buddy

   E) Dog

3. **Which of these breeds has webbed feet?**

   A) Newfoundland

   B) Bulldog

   C) German Shepherd Dog

   D) Duckhound

   E) Chihuahua

4. **Humans have about 9,000 taste buds. How many do puppies have?**

   A) 1,700

   B) 7,700

C) 770,700

D) 700,000

E) 7 million

5. What is the gestation period for dogs? In other words, how long does a canine pregnancy last?

A) One month

B) Two months

C) Three months

D) Four months

E) Five months

6. What is a parti puppy?

A) One which loves to go wild and drink cocktails with other puppies, especially at night

B) A puppy which has a Poodle as one of its parents

C) A mixed breed or mongrel dog

D) A puppy which has a similar temperament to his or her mother

E) A coloured puppy, usually with some white in the coat

7. Audrey Hepburn had a Yorkshire Terrier. What was his name?

A) Mr Stinky

B) Mr Mischief

C) Mr Yorkie

D) Mr Famous

E) Mr Mini

8. Which of these foods is poisonous to dogs?

A) Grapes

B) Chocolate

C) Onions

D) Macadamia nuts

E) Alcohol

9. Some breeds of dog are hypoallergenic. What does this mean?

A) They are more likely to have lots of allergies

B) They have low blood sugars

C) They are less likely to cause an allergic reaction

D) They are allergic to hypodermic needles & syringes

E) They are super alert watchdogs.

10. What is the best age to start training a puppy?

A) As soon as you bring him or her home

B) Three months old

C) Six months old

D) Nine months old

E) One year old

11. Some brachycephalic (flat-faced) breeds are prone to hyperthermia. What does this mean?

A) They cannot tolerate cold

B) They overheat easily

C) They love to sunbathe

D) They are overactive

E) They love to exaggerate

11. If allowed to get away with things, some small breed puppies can develop 'Little Emperor' or 'Small Dog' Syndrome. What does this mean?

A) They start ordering other puppies around

B) They like dressing up in fancy clothes

C) They will only eat very expensive food

D) They take over other pups' beds and toys

E) They become cocksure and behave badly

13. According to the Humane Society, how many dogs were there in the USA in 2012?

A) 3 million

B) 23 million

C) 53 million

D) 83 million

E) 103 million

14. How many dogs and cats are put to sleep (euthanized) in the USA every year?

A) 250,000

B) 500,000

C) 1 million

D) 2 to 2.5 million

E) 3 to 4 million

15. The primary role of the Kennel Club and AKC is to..?

A) House unwanted dogs

B) Register pedigree dogs and maintain breed standards

C) Run dog shows

D) Help dog breeders find homes for their puppies

E) Breed championship dogs

16. Which is the world's tallest dog breed?

A) Irish Wolfhound

B) Great Dane

C) Saint Bernard

D) Mastiff

E) Giant Chihuahua

17. How much exercise per day is a good guideline for a young puppy?

A) Two minutes per month old

B) Five minutes per month old

C) Ten minutes per month old

D) Twenty minutes per month old

E) Thirty minutes per month old

18. Dogs have a limited colour spectrum. Which colours CAN'T they see?

A) Yellows

B) Blues

C) Reds and greens

D) Greys

E) Blacks

19. How much sleep does an eight-week to 12-week-old puppy need?

A) Eight hours a day

B) Ten hours a day

C) Twelve hours a day

D) Sixteen hours a day

E) More than 18 hours a day

20. When puppies are born they have no teeth and they cannot see or hear. True or False?

Answers

1. D – Seven or eight weeks - and E with toy breeds. All dogs learn the rules of the pack from their mothers, and most mothers continue teaching their pups the correct manners and do's and don'ts until they are around eight weeks old, at which point they are ready to go into the world and learn new things. Toy breeds may stay with the mother for up to 12 weeks.

2. B – Charlie. This has just overtaken Max as the most popular name. Buddy is number three, followed by Rocky, Bailey and Jack. Bella is the top name for a female, followed by Molly, Daisy and Lucy.

3. A – Newfoundland. Hunters bred dogs with webbed feet to swim and retrieve ducks and other waterfowl. Other webbed feet breeds include the Akita, Chesapeake Bay Retriever, Chinook, Field Spaniel, Irish Water Spaniel, Labrador Retriever, Nova Scotia Duck Tolling Retriever, Otterhound, Portuguese Water Dog, Spanish Water Dog and Weimaraner. There is no such dog as a Duckhound and some breeds cannot swim at all.

4. A - 1,700. Cats only have about 470. However, dogs have taste buds for water - something humans do not have - so your puppy might prefer the flavour of water from muddy puddles instead of a metal bowl.

5. B - Two months or 61 to 65 days. It is the same for all breeds of dog, from the Chihuahua to the Irish Wolfhound and everything in between.

6. E - A coloured puppy. These days partis come in a range of different colours, but one of them is generally white. The word 'parti' comes from the French word for *divided* and means two (or more) colours.

7. D – Mr Famous.

8. All of them.

9. C - They are less likely to cause an allergic reaction in others. However, no individual dog or breed is guaranteed 100% NOT to cause a reaction, as allergies vary greatly from one person to the next.

10. A – As soon as you bring him or her home. Once a puppy leaves the litter, he or she stops learning from the mother and is ready to learn from you.

11. B – They overheat easily. Some flat faced breeds love to sunbathe but can become overheated before they realise it, so owners need to monitor them outdoors. **Hypo**thermia means having a dangerously low body temperature.

12. E - They become cocksure and behave badly. As a result of being pampered or spoilt, they think that they rule the roost and begin to behave badly. When this happens, a firm hand is needed along with some training sessions.

13. D – 83 million. Cats are more popular, Americans own 96 million cats.

14. E – 3 to 4 million.

15. B - To register pedigree dogs and maintain breed standards. The Kennel Club also has a number of other functions. It runs the Petlog database, the UK's biggest reunification service for micro-chipped animals, as well as the Good Citizen Dog Training Scheme, the UK's largest dog training programme. And since 1891 the Kennel Club has run Crufts, the world's largest dog show.

16. A – Irish Wolfhound is generally considered to be the world's tallest breed, averaging 31 to 34 inches at the withers (shoulders). In 2012 an English Mastiff from the UK called Zorba, which measured almost 8ft from nose to tail, claimed the record for the world's heaviest dog at 343lbs, or 155.6kg

17. B- Five minutes per month of age. So if your puppy is three months old, he should be getting a total of 15 minutes of exercise a day. All pups need daily exercise, but over-exercising young puppies can lead to joint problems later in life.

18. C – Reds and greens. A dog's vision consists of blues, yellows and shades of grey.

19. E – More than 18 hours a day. Young dogs need 18 to 20 hours of sleep per day to rest their developing brains.

20. True – Puppies are born without teeth and unable to hear or see. Initially a pup depends on his or her mother for guidance during his first couple of weeks. A puppy arrives in the world with fully developed senses of touch, smell and taste and once its hearing develops, it is far superior to that of a human.

The End – how many did you get right?

Copyright

Disclaimer

This book has been written to provide helpful information on dogs and puppies. It is not meant to be, nor should it be, used to diagnose or treat any medical condition. For diagnosis or treatment of any animal medical problem, consult a qualified veterinarian. The author is not responsible for any specific health or allergy conditions that may require medical supervision and is not liable for any damages or negative consequences from any treatment, action, application or preparation, to any person reading or following the information in this book. References are provided for informational purposes only and do not constitute endorsement of any websites or other sources.

Help Save a Dog

Leave a review of **How to Pick the Perfect Puppy** on Amazon, send an email with the link to your review to thehandbooks@btinternet.com and we promise to donate US$3, £2 or equivalent to canine rescue.

Made in the USA
Middletown, DE
10 June 2021